The Medieval Prison

The Medieval Prison

A SOCIAL HISTORY

G. Geltner

PRINCETON UNIVERSITY PRESS

PRINCETON AND OXFORD

Copyright © 2008 by Princeton University Press

Published by Princeton University Press, 41 William Street, Princeton, New Jersey 08540

In the United Kingdom: Princeton University Press, 6 Oxford Street, Woodstock,
Oxfordshire OX20 1TW

Library of Congress Cataloging-in-Publication Data

Geltner, Guy, 1974–

The medieval prison : a social history / G. Geltner.

p.   cm.

Includes bibliographical references and index.

ISBN 978-0-691-13533-5 (alk. paper)

1. Prisons—Italy—History.   2. Social history—Medieval, 500–1500.
3. Imprisonment—Italy—History.   4. Criminal justice, Administration of—Italy—
History.   I. Title.

HV8532.I8G45 2008

365'.9450902—dc22   2007028662

British Library Cataloging-in-Publication Data is available

This book has been composed in Palatino

Printed on acid-free paper. ∞

press.princeton.edu

Printed in the United States of America

1   3   5   7   9   10   8   6   4   2

לְסַבָּא
To Grandpa

———————————

CONTENTS

ILLUSTRATIONS

FIGURES

TABLE

ACKNOWLEDGMENTS

CREDIT AND ESPECIALLY debit are central themes of the present work. If I were a fourteenth-century debtor, mere gratitude—however sincere—would do little to keep me away from prison. Luckily, in the economy of modern academe, genuine thanks are still worth more than their weight in gold.

It is a true pleasure therefore to thank William Chester Jordan, Peter Brown, Edward Peters, and Anthony Grafton, who in their gentle guidance, sage advice, and consistent encouragement helped hammer a fledgling historian's random thoughts into coherent shape. Andrea Zorzi, Chris Wickham, Trevor Dean, Simone Marchesi, Amanda Wilkins, and Jeff Schwegman scrutinized earlier drafts of the text at different times; Abu Farouk and Rotem Ravé were instrumental in manipulating the statistical data; Yuval Samuelov and Andrea Magnaghi toiled for many hours over the rather bizarre task of reconstructing a medieval prison; and two anonymous readers for Princeton University Press, along with Brigitta van Rheinberg and the Press's obliging staff, helped transform the original manuscript into its present shape. Armando Antonelli, Sarah Blanshei, Paola Foschi, Massimo Giansante, Giorgio Marcon, and Giuseppe Del Torre have been perfect guides in the Bolognese and Venetian archives. In Florence, Francesco Martelli and Salvatore Favuzza kindly enabled me to study the sparse and now semidestroyed financial registers of Le Stinche. Last, Giandomenico Romanelli, director of the Musei Civici di Venezia, gave me easy access to the Doge's Palace, including the unique pleasure of a solitary visit to the Pozzi. I am deeply grateful to them all, as well as to my teachers, peers, and colleagues in Jerusalem, Madison, Princeton, Oxford, and elsewhere.

Princeton University's History Department and the Graduate School, the Social Science Research Council's International Dissertation Research Fellowship (funded by the Andrew W. Mellon Foundation), the Porter Ogden Jacobus Fellowship, the Yad Hanadiv Foundation, and Lincoln College, Oxford, through the Hardie Fellowship and the Michael Zilkha Trust, have provided me with generous support during the past several years. The assistance I received at various local archives, libraries, and museums across Italy, France, the United States, and the United Kingdom has been constant and courteous—for which their directors and staffs deserve kind and warm thanks.

On a different but no less genuine note, I would also like to thank my friends and family, especially my mother, whose patience, love, and attention over the years have been inexhaustible; the *famiglia* Gazzini in Rome, who have made their home mine; and of course Claudia. I dedicate this work to my grandfather, Isaac Ellman, whose enthusiasm for his grandchildren's education continues to know no boundaries.

This book draws some comparisons between medieval and modern prisons. While these are not intended to be facile, ideally they should serve as bridges to be dropped upon arrival: present-day prisons have very little indeed to do with their medieval predecessors, for reasons I hope will become clear in the following pages.

A NOTE ON DATES AND MONEY

During the period under discussion the new calendar year commenced in Bologna on 25 December (Christmas),[1] in Florence and Siena on 25 March (Annunciation), and in Venice on 1 March. In order to impose uniformity, all dates have been modernized both in the body of the text and in the notes. The form *Day Month Year* has been adopted to avoid confusion among various modern dating systems. Thus, for example, the death of Pope John XXII occurred on 4 December 1334.

Italian city-states often minted their own currency, whose basic division was into lire (l.), soldi (s.), and denari (d.). Twelve denari constituted one soldo; twenty soldi comprised one lira. Thus:

$$1l. = 20s. = 240d.$$

This basic agreement in division did not entail any necessary parallel in value among local currencies. Moreover, various polities used different currencies at different times for calculation, especially when dealing with large sums for commercial purposes; and the conversion rates between the lira and account currencies such as the Florentine *fiorino* or the Venetian *ducato* were in constant flux. As a rule, all sums are expressed in their contemporary, local lira value.[2]

PROLOGUE

IT LASTED FOUR DAYS AND FOUR NIGHTS. Heaven's gates opened over Tuscany on 1 November 1333, drenching cities and villages, sweeping mills and bridges off their foundations, drowning fields and wildlife. By the third day of incessant rain the Arno overflowed its shallow banks, undermining Florence's walls and carrying with it the bridges of the Carraia, Santa Trinita, and even the formidable Ponte Vecchio. The sight must have been incredible; as one contemporary admitted, "Few would have believed it, had they not seen it themselves."[1]

The first building to buckle under the water's rising pressure that day was the Franciscan dormitory at Santa Croce. As the water advanced from there into the city, residents leapt from one rooftop to the next, seeking shelter in whatever higher ground they could reach.[2] The cries filling the air were so loud that, according to Giovanni Villani, the city's acclaimed chronicler, "one could barely hear the thunder." This was not the first flood to assail Florence—nor would it be the last[3]—yet Villani insisted that the deluge of 1333 was the greatest disaster the city had known since its defeat by Attila, *flagellum Dei*.[4]

The perennial solution for men besieged by a flood—climbing upward—was not available to the inmates of Le Stinche, Florence's main prison, located a stone's throw northwest of Santa Croce. Even if they had been allowed to move freely, the prisoners had limited options: with one exception, all the wards were low, single-story structures.[5] As the water and crying from without continued to penetrate the compound's tall walls, it became apparent that hundreds of lives were at risk:[6] mostly unfettered, but locked in their wards, debtors, prostitutes, criminals of all types, even unruly slaves and children, not to mention the residents and amputees at the little infirmary—all faced collective drowning.

Aware of or alerted to the impending disaster, the Priors of the Guilds and the Gonfaloniere di Giustizia, essentially the city's top executives, sent word to the four prison wardens: without delay, they were to withdraw those inmates who were kept on or below ground. By that point, the water at Santa Croce had climbed to six *braccia*, or nearly twelve feet, probably submerging all but the upper *malevato* ward.[7] Although wary of the consequences, the wardens obeyed the sealed decree, which was formally delivered by two messengers. Aided by the prison guards, the wardens proceeded to evacuate the prisoners "so they would avoid the death that the said flood and assault of water would have certainly brought upon them, unless they were immediately released."[8] Hundreds

Fig. P.1. Le Stinche (*center, left*) in the Florentine landscape. Detail from a fifteenth-century manuscript of Ptolmey's *Tabulae Geographicae* (Biblioteca Apostolica Vaticana, MS Vat. Lat. 5569, fol. 126v). (By kind permission of the Biblioteca Apostolica Vaticana.)

of lives were saved, yet in the event, and as the wardens feared, eleven prisoners escaped by scaling the prison walls. Apparently, they jumped from the rooftop, the higher ground made available to them.[9]

The unfolding drama at Le Stinche went unmentioned in contemporary and later chronicles. And were it not for the escape of those eleven prisoners, no direct trace would have remained of this aspect of the famous flood of 1333. Villani estimated the total casualties of the disaster at three hundred; without the magistrates' intervention and the wardens' action, this number could have easily been doubled, probably securing a tragic mention for Le Stinche in the Florentine annals.[10]

Prison inmates today live at the far edge of society, and are, ironically, more vulnerable than is usually realized. Two recent environmental disasters—the tsunami of 2004 and Hurricane Katrina in 2005—offer sharp reminders of this fact. Rescue teams that reached Aceh, Indonesia, more than a week after the devastating wave had struck, found the entire prison community drowned within the bolted compound;[11] and well into the second day of flooding in New Orleans, state officials were still "putting together a plan to evacuate some 5,000 prisoners."[12] In 1333 Florence, where the scale and logistics of a rescue were simpler, attempts were still four days in coming. Nonetheless, they came. And they did so in due time.

What had motivated the rescue? It is reasonable to attribute the magistrates' actions to a genuine concern for the inmates, given how many lives were at stake and the prison's proximity to the water's breaking path. Moreover, whatever their vices, most of Le Stinche's residents were Florentine citizens—men, women, and children from all walks of

life and social strata, natives of the city, its protectorates, and its hinterland—and as such they were wont to receive fair treatment, at least by
contemporary standards: mass drowning or death under the collapsing
structure would have been seen as undisguised neglect. That and more,
the prison's economy and location and the social constitution of the
inmate community, ensured that the latter were not forgotten. For they
were mostly citizens, technically in debt, sequestered within earshot of
their families, friends, and associates.[13] To be sure, among the prisoners there were homicides, rapists, heretics, as well as thieves, brigands,
sodomites, prostitutes, and counterfeiters; and it is likely that some
of their victims or critics were oblivious to their chances of survival.
Nevertheless, in 1333, prisoners were mostly propertied citizens, the
woof of the fabric of Florentine society.

Other considerations may have goaded the magistrates into action.
Even at the flood's climax it was yet unclear how much the city stood
to lose from the damages (a staggering 150,000 florins, according to
Villani). What was certain, however, was that, for the most part, the
prisoners' death would translate into an irrevocable loss of the fines
or debts they owed and for which, formally, they were imprisoned. A
mass drowning at Le Stinche would have cost the commune an estimated five hundred lire, and private creditors would have collectively
lost anywhere between six hundred and twelve hundred lire, by no
means a negligible sum.[14] Saving the inmates, then, had an important
financial incentive as well.

But there were other possible motivations for the rescue. Notwithstanding the magistrates' timely intervention, there must have been
other people that night who were aware of the inmates' plight. Not
least among these would have been the prisoners' own families and
friends and the neighboring residents of San Simone, whose parish
church oversaw the inmates' spiritual welfare. Furthermore, it was a
time-honored tradition to hold prisoners (especially poor prisoners) as
worthy objects of charity. Their socioreligious status—as with most lay
recipients of charitable aid: lepers, widows, the elderly and sick—was
ambiguous; on the one hand, they were untouchable for their predicaments; on the other, they were precious vessels for spiritual growth.
Either way, allowing them all to die, helpless and enclosed, would have
been perceived as malicious, individual enmities notwithstanding.

For Le Stinche's inmates were not anonymous faces in Florence. Just
as the prison compound featured prominently in the urban landscape,
so its residents participated in the city's daily life. Prisoners' comings
and goings for commercial and legal affairs, their festive releases on
Christmas, Easter, and the Feast of St. John the Baptist (Florence's patron
saint), the daily alms they gathered (or those that were collected on

their behalf), and the routine visits they received from family, friends, and various officials, brought them into frequent contact with a wide segment of the city's residents. Unlike present-day inmates, medieval prisoners were hard to ignore.

Although our records do not disclose who originally called for the inmates' rescue, many could have drawn attention to the impeding danger. Yet, as later observers would comment, altruism was not always a popular choice among Florentines in crisis: at the onset of the Black Death in 1348, fear was so great "that one citizen avoided another, almost no one cared for his neighbor, and relatives rarely or hardly ever visited one another."[15] Such alienation was absent, evidently, from local responses to the flood of 1333. How to account for the difference? Did the plague seem more threatening than convicts at large? Had violence, so characteristic of the fourteenth century, engendered an increasing apathy?[16] Whatever the answer, it seems that preventing the collective drowning of Le Stinche's inmates was a commendable, if complex, contingency.

By November 1333, merely three decades after its foundation, Le Stinche, along with its inmates, personnel, and auxiliary staff, was tightly woven into Florence's social, political, administrative, religious, and financial fabric. In a moment of crisis the compound emerged as a point of convergence for the imperatives of local individuals, groups, and institutions. More than simply a place of detention, coercion, and punishment, an abandoned island surrounded by four tall walls,[17] the communal prison of Florence was a central site for the negotiation of civic identity, secular jurisdiction, and popular charity. At the same time, the human world that the prison walls enclosed was as much a part of surrounding society as it was a living, breathing testimony to a new solution for social deviants. For by the early fourteenth century, in Florence and elsewhere, the prison was effectively born.

The Medieval Prison

INTRODUCTION

On 17 February 1327, a group of appellants at the Sienese General Council decried the state of local prisons. Reminding those assembled that "not two years have passed since over sixty men died there [in prison] on account of the terrible conditions and neglect" (*propter pessimam condictionem et corruptionem*), the petitioners reiterated the need for a facility "in which there would be distinct places for holding perpetrators of major offenses, for those of minor offenses, and for those held for debt."[1] The plea was summarily adopted, and soon the commune purchased the properties occupying the site of the future compound.[2] A master mason was at work on the project by December,[3] and within three years Siena's new prison stood complete as the lateral extension of the Palazzo Pubblico on the side of via di Malcucinato.[4] On 28 July 1330, the prisoners left their old cells at the Palazzo Cerretani (Alessi), and entered the new facility.[5]

Constructing a new prison was a sound move. First, it ended the migration of local custodial spaces among several aristocratic *torri* rented by the commune since the 1240s.[6] Next, the new compound was planned to enable the magistrates to distinguish among categories of prisoners, provide for the inmates' efficient processing, and improve their living conditions. All these purposes were deemed imperative since by that point prisoners were more numerous and the duration of their incarceration lasted longer than ever before. Last but not least, the act corresponded nicely with the reorganization of Sienese civic space under the Nine (1287–1355) in two interrelated ways. The new prison flanked—in fact, it completed—the communal palace, the most concrete expression of the city's transition from a polycentric oligarchy to a centralized communal regime, a process commonly dubbed "from tower to palazzo."[7]

At the same time, erecting a prison at the city center reflected a broad shift in contemporary attitudes toward social marginals, namely from expulsion to containment. This strategy is evident across western Europe, especially in urbanized regions such as central and northern Italy, the Rhine Valley, the Lowlands, and directly north and south of the Pyrenees. Here local governments developed mechanisms for maintaining social order in a new key.[8] Rather than physically annihilate or otherwise eliminate the presence of social and religious deviants,

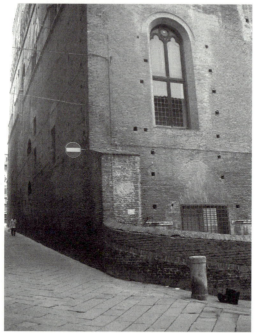

Fig. I.1. The Palazzo Pubblico of Siena and its former prison wing.

various regimes created or annexed "marginalizing" institutions such as leper-houses, brothels, hospitals, and Jewish quarters.[9] The central, municipally run prison was a later but equally ubiquitous expression of such attitudes to social control.

For Siena's was not an isolated case. By the early fourteenth century, responding to similar needs and under analogous circumstances, prisons already dotted the landscape of western Europe. This moment in the history of the prison marked the end of a process that commenced sometime around 1250, when scores of city-states, capitals, and rural strongholds began founding such facilities and employing them as punitive institutions for sentenced culprits alongside their traditional role as places of custody (e.g., pretrial arrest) and coercion (e.g., torture chambers and debtors prisons). In its geographical scope and quantitative scale such recourse to incarceration in *any* of its modes was virtually unprecedented prior to the mid–thirteenth century. And although five centuries would go by before imprisonment became the cornerstone of European penology, both the measure and its physical counterpart—the prison—were widely integrated into judicial administrations by the close of the fourteenth century. This trajectory, from foundation to routinization, established the chronological boundaries of the present study.

Although ubiquitous, the process is nowhere clearer than among the Italian city-states, whose prisons are the best-documented institutions of their kind. Yet there are few detailed modern studies of these facilities' medieval phase.[10] Over time, tangential works such as urban surveys and histories of charity have helped chart the creation of local prisons, and topical investigations have remarked the medieval origins of these institutions as preludes to their modern successors.[11] What remains untold is the story of the many and varied local facilities—a necessary step toward a well-grounded regional portrait, which is the major object of this book.

The specific contribution of this study is threefold: first, in filling the Italian lacuna; second, in augmenting the traditional historiography of the prison with anthropological, urbanistic, and sociological perspectives; third, in grounding arguments about the history of the prison in documents of practice rather than by recourse to prescriptive texts, as has been the norm so far. I posit that the birth of the prison was more than a legal development, "a sign of advancing civilisation."[12] Rather, it was a complex and contingent creation in which politics engaged architecture, religious imagination fused with penal practices, and an ancient legal tradition that abhorred punitive incarceration yielded to the reorganization of urban space according to new attitudes toward social marginals. In the process, prisons emerged as constituents of the urban landscape and proud symbols of a hard-won independence: their foundation dovetailed with the communes' desire to impose security in the city, efficiency in the courts, and expediency in business; and it responded to changing attitudes toward the "other," namely, a shift from ejecting to containing deviants. In fine, this study seeks to understand the advent of prisons in general and of punitive incarceration in particular by taking surrounding society and culture into account.[13]

Two partially overlapping goals guide this book. The first is to delineate the variety of processes by which medieval society developed practices of punitive imprisonment, mostly against the grain of contemporary jurisprudence. To this end, I trace a range of alternative structures underwriting the proliferation of prisons particularly in urban environments, and relate the ways in which these facilities became engrained in contemporaries' political thinking, embedded in their concepts of justice, sovereignty, and citizenship, and integrated as a sine qua non of their social and physical environment. To those who consider the prison as axiomatic to Western penology, this study underscores both the contingency of institutional development and the diversity of its functions.

The second is to offer a living image of medieval imprisonment by focusing on the various persons comprising the human fabric of these institutions and the relations among them. These men, women, and children, however, are not limited to debtors, prostitutes, criminals, heretics, or vagabonds. This is due in part to the legal and administrative roles of communal prisons, in part to their physical centrality in late-medieval cities. For instance, a main factor in alleviating the inmates' conditions was the constant human traffic passing through the prison gates (and occasionally over its walls and through its windows). Prisoners, moreover, were visible: they roamed the city as licensed beggars, as debtors in search of settlement, and as criminals en route to court. And inmates' visibility increased during civic events such as routine festive releases, triumphal amnesties, and occasional riotous break-ins accompanying political turmoil. At the same time, there were many incomers to the prison: servicemen, lawyers, and physicians; guards and prison administrators; local priests, lay and religious friars, confraternity members, and court magistrates; families traveling far and near to supply their imprisoned kin with food and cash; prostitutes on nocturnal calls; and of course the daily flow of new and recidivist offenders. Prisons' location and accessibility meant that their inmates were not fully cast out of late-medieval urban life: the deprivation of these men's freedom failed to turn them into liminal people, altogether stripped of their social identity and ties. Rather, prisons developed as semi-exclusive—and ipso facto semi-inclusive—institutions, places of punishment and detention whose walls operated as breathing membranes, not hermetic seals.

As in modern, "total" institutions, the realities of medieval incarceration often departed from their intended political and theoretical aims.[14] The effective factors on daily life in this nascent institution were many and diverse, and jointly lend themselves to an interpretation of local power relations and social norms. It is not the case, for instance, that prison routines—insofar as they existed—were entirely dictated by local governments, nor were they always fashioned in response to inmates' behavior and concerns. While such pressures were certainly operative, many other elements shaped life in and around the prison, from altruistic or egotistic interventions to broader and changing contemporary outlooks on social deviancy, civic identity, and lay piety. Accordingly, the urban prison not only marked a new stage in the history of punishment, but also epitomized an increasingly complicated attitude that developed toward indexing social "in" and "out."

Beyond shedding light on an obscure aspect of medieval urban life and legal history, the study of medieval prisons illuminates the so-called persecuting mentality of late-medieval society from a fresh perspective. For the creation of these institutions and especially their physical and administrative organization reveals an impulse not simply to eradicate, but rather to *contain* and *maintain* deviancy. If prisons played an important role in what Alfred Soman defined as "a process of sensitization and desensitization to crime,"[15] they also testify to an increasingly nuanced understanding of social control in the late thirteenth and fourteenth centuries.

The Medieval Prison is based on archival research conducted in Siena, Venice, Florence, and Bologna. The prison profiles of the latter three cities are related in chapter 1, while information drawing on Sienese documents is interspersed throughout the book. (The division is not a commentary on Siena's inherent significance or lack of pertinent documentation; my intention was to obviate burdening the reader with yet another profile.) Chapter 2 examines how each city tackled common problems connected with the creation and running of its prisons, under the general headings of urban development, administration, finance, and law. This chapter also adopts a comparative view toward similar facilities and problems in England and France. Jointly, the first two chapters serve as a frame of reference for chapter 3, which advances through stations in prison life, from arrest to the end of incarceration. As such it offers a sense of the variety of medieval prison regimes and experiences, occasionally juxtaposing them with major observations by and debates among students of modern prison life. How contemporaries perceived and interpreted local prison spaces and the purpose of incarceration itself is the subject of chapter 4. The conclusion situates the creation of urban prisons at the intersection of local power and social marginality by examining this process vis-à-vis the development of other facilities that ostensibly defined social marginals. This comparison proved to be particularly useful, for while much has been said recently about medieval leprosaria, brothels, hospitals, and Jewish quarters, situating the prison among them deepens our understanding of the social functions of deviancy in general and of "marginalizing" institutions in particular.

Numerous studies inform the time frame, geographical focus, and methodology of the present investigation. In general, earlier works on medieval prisons jointly point to the years 1250–1400 as a period of concentrated activity in and around these facilities; and despite premonitions to the contrary, scholars have left the prisons of Italy's urbanized center and north as a lamentable lacuna. In any case, the variety of approaches pursued by previous scholars, be they religious, institutional, legal, literary, or social historians, enabled the multiplicity of perspectives that this study adopts.

Although few and far between, scholars have been tracing the early history of the prison for over three hundred years, ever since Giovanni Battista Scanaroli's *De visitatione carceratorum libri tres* (1655). Scanaroli, archbishop of Modena, sought to document the impact of ecclesiastical ethics on civil penal practices. His work was a Catholic apology, yet it also betrays clerical anxieties over the rise of Absolutism, since identifying the role of Christian piety under a new political order was one of its main concerns. A later attempt to underscore the church's role in the development of modern penology was F.A.K. Krauss's edifying *Im Kerker vor und nach Christus*, published in 1895. After delineating the use of prisons in several ancient cultures, the work links the impetus of contemporary prison reforms to the imperatives of early Christianity, whose advent Krauss construes as *the* watershed in penal history. Despite their antiquarianism and strong pious bent, both Scanaroli and Krauss convinced later scholars of the church's seminal role in fostering imprisonment as a penalty against clerics, monks, and, later, heretics. They also implicitly argue that the imaginary of the prison was mostly developed among monastic and clerical milieus, which shaped their contemporaries' horizons of expectations regarding the roles and functions of incarceration. While their historical claims are basically correct, they are nonetheless overstated and, insofar as they ignore nonecclesiastical agents of change, they are misleading and partial.

Precious information on the origins of European penology was also recovered by early prison reformers such as John Howard (1726–90) and Martino Beltrani-Scalia (1829–1909).[16] These learned state officials drafted platforms for overhauling the penal systems of England and Italy, respectively. Fortunately, they were also historically minded, and their reports are replete with data about the institutions they visited, some of which can be dated to the late Middle Ages. Beltrani-Scalia had even perused several local archives, culling on occasion information that would otherwise be lost today. On the whole, however, they conducted no systematic inquiries into the history of any specific prison, took its existence more or less for granted, and assumed, at least implicitly, that earlier facilities were at least as problematic as those they sought to reform. This telescopic view is one that the present study seeks to correct.

Around the turn of the twentieth century, already in the age of professional historiography, and responding to the growing prestige of modern prisons, there appeared several studies that focused on the legal and institutional origins of prisons in France and Italy.[17] Among their many contributions, these efforts were the first carefully to sketch the profiles of premodern facilities and to document the employment of punitive incarceration in the Middle Ages. Jointly they coalesced into a compelling revision of European penal and institutional history, and built up a confidence that underwrites the greatest achievement of prison history in that period, Gotthold Bohne's two-volume *Die Freiheitsstrafe in den italienischen Stadtrechten des 12.–16. Jahrhunderts* (1922–25). To this day, Bohne's tomes remain a point of departure for any study of medieval incarceration.

As its title suggests, *Die Freiheitsstrafe* is not limited to imprisonment, but also encompasses deprivations of freedom such as slavery and forced labor. Yet its significance lies especially in the attempt to understand the cultural origins of a new form of punishment— incarceration—and the mobilization of resources for its employment. In particular, it is a somewhat long-winded study of dozens of Italian city-statutes available in print at the time, from among whose rubrics Bohne amassed prescriptions that dealt with incarceration, prison administration, inmates' welfare, and their terms of release.[18] This was also the first major work systematically (albeit perhaps too rigidly) to distinguish among coercive, custodial, and punitive incarceration (respectively, *Zwangshaft*, *Sicherungshaft*, and *Strafhaft*), and to assert that all three modes are already attested in late-medieval Italy.

Bohne sought to relate the development of penal incarceration in the early Renaissance to Jacob Burckhardt's influential ruminations about the roots of modernity, as developed in *The Civilization of the Renaissance in Italy* (1860). According to Bohne, the so-called rise of individualism enabled, and in a profound way accomplished, the introduction of imprisonment as a routine penalty. He argued that, prior to the emergence of freedom as the desirable state of the individual, limitations on personal liberty would not have been effective, and, to an extent, even conceivable, as a viable punishment. Conversely, the notion of personal liberty allowed incarceration to be perceived as an independent measure, distinct from the variety of corporal punishments with which it was associated, and possessing a rehabilitative element.[19]

Die Freiheitsstrafe was adamantly revisionist. Its geographical and chronological focus sought to undermine the prevailing view, originally expressed by Robert von Hippel in 1907, that the modern prison stems from the Amsterdam prison-workhouse, the Tuchtuis, inaugurated in 1596.[20] Thus, the publication of Bohne's first volume in 1922 sparked a heated exchange between the author and notable legal scholars such as Eberhard Schmidt and Georg Dahm, who were followers of von Hippel with a Weberian bent. Bohne's opponents reiterated that, prior to the late sixteenth century, imprisonment was essentially a corporal punishment and that the origins of rehabilitative deprivations of freedom could only be a manifestation of the social values embodied by the Protestant Reformation (as construed by Max Weber) and perpetuated under the aegis of the modern, rational state, with its monopoly over legitimate violence. Schmidt in particular was so appalled by Bohne's thesis, that he suggested forgoing the publication of the planned second volume.[21]

Thankfully, Bohne stayed his course, but throughout the twentieth century his opponents have had the upper hand, at least outside of medieval studies: the foundation of the Amsterdam workhouse and Elizabethan bridewells, the first institutions explicitly designed for rehabilitative confinement, continue to be seen as seminal moments in informed discussions on the birth of modern penology.[22] That the explicit association among incarceration, labor, and rehabilitation is an early modern one is not an argument that the present study refutes, especially since both the "total" and rehabilitative attributes of modern prisons were absent from even the most highly regulated medieval facility. Nor does it seek to resurrect Bohne's Burckhardtian idealism and uncritical reliance on prescriptive texts in order to prove the widespread employment of punitive incarceration. However, it is possible to distinguish between the "birth" of the prison per se and that of modern penology. It is in this sense that Bohne's chronology resurfaces as coherent, correct, and applicable well beyond late-medieval Italy.

Interest in the early history of prisons continued to increase throughout the turbulent twentieth century, now underwritten by legal and institutional enquiries that privileged documents of practice over prescriptive texts and jurisprudential literature. Ironically, this development passed over the Italian city-states, despite Beltrani-Scalia's learned survey, Bohne's massive study, and the relative abundance of peninsular records. Instead, legal and institutional historians such as Roger Grand, Annik Porteau-Bitker, Margery Bassett, and Ralph Pugh focused their attention on medieval French and English institutions.[23] And in fact it was Pugh who produced, in 1968, the first monograph on English medieval incarceration, thoroughly based on local archival records. Forty years after its publication, *Imprisonment in Medieval England* remains the only regional study of its kind, a testimony to the fine state of English and Welsh records and a tribute to Pugh's capacity as an institutional historian.[24] As such, it not only informed the methodology of the present study, but also enabled a responsible transregional comparison.

For many years, Marxism presented a special obstacle to the study of medieval imprisonment, quite apart from the contentions of Bohne's Weberian antagonists. According to this strand of historiography, punitive incarceration developed out of a new stage in labor relations in which imprisonment could be identified with one's loss of control over productive time. Since this phase is usually associated with the rise of capitalist ideology in the early modern era, the deprivation of freedom would have been an unworkable penalty in earlier times.[25] The claim is largely erroneous, as nearly a century of scholarship has by now established, and notwithstanding the recognized protocapitalistic tendencies among the Italian city-states.[26] However, neo-Marxist historiography did succeed in promoting fruitful methodologies for studying punishment in terms of its social functions and the cultural values that it engenders. Such an approach informs much of the scholarship on modern penology and other "total" institutions, a category seminally framed by Erving Goffman.[27] Yet, with one exception to be discussed below, it has yet to be applied to the study of medieval prisons.

As already noted, the early development of ecclesiastical (episcopal, monastic, and inquisitorial) prisons has long been acknowledged as an important, albeit indirect, contribution to the reception of penal incarceration among secular jurisdictions. Although the imprisonment of religious deviants is mostly peripheral to the present investigation, it must be recognized that it was the medieval papal inquisition, particularly in Languedoc, northern Spain, and northern Italy, that first brought this erstwhile clerical punishment into the urban public sphere through the wide-scale immuring of laymen. As Yves Dossat, James Given, and others have shown, the majority of penalties imposed by thirteenth- and fourteenth-century inquisitors involved or were limited to incarceration.[28] Local inquisition campaigns, moreover, foreshadowed legal developments underlying the proliferation of secular prisons in another way, namely through the introduction of the inquisitorial method into

criminal jurisprudence and its gradual encroachment on accusatorial forms of litigation.[29] Relinquishing accusatorial procedures meant
longer detainment of defendants for questioning (and torture) by the
state, so that the overall impact of this process on the history of the
prison was to increase the number of imprisoned defendants and prolong their stay. One response to these developments was the creation
of new custodial spaces that would be both accessible and salubrious
enough to maintain more inmates for longer periods.

Given's study of inquisitorial prisons and Jacques Chiffoleau's work
on criminality in papal Avignon were the first major works by medieval historians seriously to engage Michel Foucault's *Surveiller et punir*
(1975).[30] Foucault's influential thesis, or rather its implications for historians of medieval penal practices, was methodological rather than con-
textual.[31] The chronology undergirding Foucault's discussion ignores
the early history of the prison, as delineated in the series of studies
related above, and which would have been entirely available to him. It
also had the detrimental effect of construing a persuasive (and highly
idealized) model of the modern prison that obliterated the significance of earlier institutions: if the prison was essentially the brainchild
of post-Enlightenment penology, its predecessors were relegated to a
hazy prehistory. Given's work did much to correct this view, especially
by illustrating how the use of prisons fit into and augmented the inquisitors' technology of power and control. There are many similari-
ties between Given's conclusions and those presented here regarding
municipal prisons, but the broader methodological point that I wish to
advance is that premodern prisons are better studied without recourse
to modern penological concepts. Conversely, to understand the development of the modern prison requires a longer historical perspective
regarding an institution that was already hundreds of years old in the
days of Beccaria and Bentham, the fathers of modern penology.

Chapter One

ITALIAN PRISONS: THREE PROFILES

THE PRESENT CHAPTER lays the groundwork for an investigation of incarceration and prison life in late-medieval western Europe. It marshals three local studies, progressing from historiographical terra firma to terra incognita, and from the exceptional to the common: from Venice, probably the first polity to formalize the use of punitive incarceration, to Florence, home of an original, purpose-built prison, to Bologna, a more modest and less eccentric city-state, whose prison history is known only in its general contours. Although the following profiles owe much to the few existing studies on medieval Italian prisons, they advance beyond the latter's scope both in terms of chronology and in breadth of archival research. Apart from delineating the development of local facilities, each profile elaborates the material, legal, administrative, and financial aspects of incarceration and their changes over a period of roughly 150 years. Jointly, these case studies considerably augment our knowledge of premodern continental prisons and practices of imprisonment.

One of the many advantages of laboring in the archive of a former Italian city-state is the relative wealth and accessibility of the extant records. During the course of my research, I was able to tap into many previously unutilized sources, especially the registers produced by prison notaries and which aided wardens in monitoring inmate traffic and prison expenses (see full discussion in chapter 2). These logs, especially for Florence, provided much of the data analyzed in the following chapters.[1] Relatively fewer documents illuminate the Bolognese (and Sienese) facilities, but it is clear from both the archival inventories and the extant registers that comparable records were produced there prior to the late fourteenth century and have now been lost.[2] The same observation applies to other archives across central and northern Italy, as Beltrani-Scalia's early study suggests.[3] A further type of prison-related documentation is lists of and debates concerning inmates nominated for release during major feasts or victories, either conserved independently or integrated into the city council's minutes.[4] A singular set of records that Florence alone can boast tracks the prison's supervisory committee's activities. These weekly surveys, whether in their monotony or occasional interruption, preserve precious information about the inmates' interaction among themselves and with the staff, the prison's internal organization, and patterns of inmate dissidence.[5]

No parallel records exist (and probably never did) for Venice. It thus proved necessary to blaze a different trail through the available sources, especially the well-kept and in part published deliberations of the governing councils, which, among other tasks, legislated and acted as a court of appeals. I have also examined a number of collections of individual notaries, the pertinent documents of a few executive bodies that maintained close ties with the prison, and several caches of testaments. All of these "nonorganic" sources, along with statutory legislation, public account books, court registers, records of charitable organizations, and those of confraternities involved in some aspect of prison life were likewise studied at the archives and libraries of Bologna, Florence, and Siena. Together they form the backbone of each of the following profiles.[6]

VENICE

The chronology of Venice's prisons is fairly well known. Prior to the late thirteenth century there were official holding rooms (*casoni*) in each of the city's sixths (*sestieri*), a debtors prison near the Rialto Bridge, and cells in and around the Doge's Palace, appropriated piecemeal at least from 1173. During the thirteenth and fourteenth centuries further spaces were carved out within the palace, eventually occupying the entire ground floor of its southern wing (see fig. 1.1). Several cells were simultaneously constructed beneath the roof of the palace's eastern wing, including a ward for female miscreants, until then incarcerated in nearby monasteries.[7] Several decades later Venice's Council of Ten commissioned more cells (or expanded the existing ones) on the palace's top floor to serve as holding rooms for men under investigation. Theoretically, the act created a separation between the detainees of the upper prison and the debtors and convicts of the lower ward.[8]

The prisons' layout remained intact until around 1540, when a new compound on the ground floor of the eastern wing was built. These *camerotti* came to be known as the Pozzi (wells), alluding to their darkness, dampness, and isolation. In 1591 more cells were built in the palace's upper eastern wing, most probably replacing or augmenting the existing upper prisons. The cells' position directly under the lead roof gave them the name Piombi, and it is from this wing that Giacomo Casanova (1725–98) later made his famous escape.[9] Finally, following

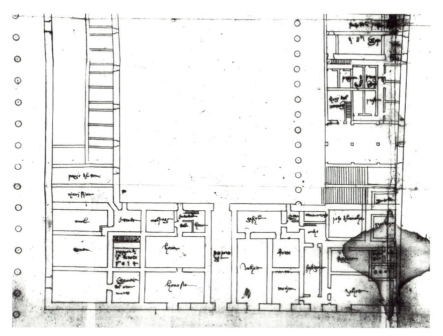

Fig. 1.1. The prison wards of the Doge's Palace, Venice. Detail from a sixteenth-century ground plan (Biblioteca Nazionale Marciana, Venezia, MS It. VII 295 [10047], plan 6). Ward names, counterclockwise from the left, are Prigione delle Donne, Nuovissima (built 1519 over the Nuova, and later renamed Vulcan), Mula, Trona, Malpaga, Liona, Lionessa, Valiera, Forte, Mocina, Armamento, Giustiniana, Schiava, Galiota, Fresca Zoia, Gradonia, Catolda. The Pozzi compound (ca. 1540) is depicted toward the top-right corner. (By kind permission of the Biblioteca Nazionale Marciana, Venice.)

the outbreak of typhus among the inmates in 1563 and a dangerous fire within the palace, and given the constant rise of inmate numbers at the Pozzi and elsewhere, the Great Council commissioned plans for a new and independent building, soon linked to the palace by the infamous Bridge of Sighs. After long delays the new prisons were opened in 1610 and functioned until the early twentieth century. Venice's main present-day prison, incidentally, is located at the city's southwestern outskirts, and a women's prison still operates on the Giudecca, due south of the city's erstwhile political center.[10]

Although familiar, this chronology is often misleading. At base, the stages it discerns overlap substantially; as Casanova's case illustrates, some facilities continued to function decades and even centuries after the establishment of their supposed substitutes.[11] More importantly, the succession of individual prison spaces does not neatly correspond

with key developments between the late thirteenth and mid–fourteenth centuries, culminating with the formal adoption of punitive
imprisonment by the Great Council. By the mid–fourteenth century
a basic jurisdiction over the prisons is observable, since a transition from semi-improvised to rudimentary prison administration
was complete: with around a dozen prison spaces inside the Doge's
Palace, and scores of inmates even by conservative estimates, prison
government became a significant aspect of the Venetian justice system
well before 1610.

Let us illustrate this transition. In 1275, Simone Steno, a convicted per-
jurer, was sentenced to public shaming, the loss of his property, and
perpetual exile. He was also fined the substantial sum of three hundred
lire *grossi*, payable within fifteen days. The Great Council's condemnation specified that Simone was to be incarcerated in the palace's great
prison (*maior carcer*) should he fail to pay his fine duly, and in which
case he was "to compensate his guards and those charged with his
custody by the lord Doge and his Council."[12] Since no individual or
committee was appointed to monitor the execution of the sentence—as
was customary in precarious or extraordinary cases—it is plausible that
even the exceptions made in this case were somewhat customary. In
other words, if Simone's guards were to be assigned or enlisted specifically for his custody, he would have probably been expected to pay
their salaries as a matter of course, perhaps also as a potential way of
aggravating his punishment. In any case, the condemnation assumes
the existence of basic mechanisms to enforce the payment of debts, incarceration, public castigation, confiscation of property, and, if need be,
exile. By implication, the Great Council could rely on a limited routine
of prison administration—for whatever purpose—even if this routine
had to be set in motion every now and then.

The semi-improvised nature of administering imprisonment reflects
the limited legislation on and recourse to punitive incarceration in this
period. Despite the existence of both designated spaces and a modest
prescriptive basis, prison sentences prior to the early fourteenth century
were rare in Venice. Presumably, since most prisons were inside the
Doge's Palace, and given their intermittent utilization, it was more convenient occasionally to divert palace guards to prison duty rather than
create an independent outfit. Accordingly, no need arose to develop an
explicit economic rationale for prison administration or to enlist personnel and service-givers, as was done for instance in contemporary
Florence. The doge and councilmen's weekly prison inspections were
themselves geared more toward securing judicial expediency than supervising inmate conditions or the guards' conduct.[13]

All this, however, was soon to change, as prison routine shifted from semi-improvisation to rudimentary administration. This process coincided with a marked increase in finite and perpetual prison sentences,[14] a continuous expansion of prison spaces,[15] the creation of a formal calculus to convert fines into jail time,[16] a growing interest among magistrates in prison conditions, regulation, and the inmates' well-being,[17] and a proliferation of charitable bequests earmarked for aiding prisoners.[18]

Although various officials, councils, and executives could and did make use of the palace prisons, the Night Lords in particular appear to have gained a fuller and more direct responsibility.[19] Created shortly before 1250 and soon after expanded, this body's original mission of enforcing the city's nocturnal regulations (especially curfew and the prohibition on bearing arms) quickly branched out into many areas, including the collection of debts, the investigation of fornication, bigamy, tax evasions, and counterfeiting, the enclosure of lepers, and the detection of walls that were in danger of collapsing. In 1297 the Night Lords were charged with a weekly visitation of prisoners, traditionally a duty of the doge and the councilmen.[20] By 1321 they were responsible for paying equal salaries to the guards of the upper and lower prisons,[21] and it is their 1339 statutes that first mention a warden or *capitano* of the lower prisons. By that year the number of lower prison guards increased from six to eight (including the warden), and the guards' monthly salaries were raised from four to five lire.[22] A notary joined the permanent staff in 1343 at the latest.[23] Around 1398 the number of guards in the upper prisons, mostly used by the Council of Ten to hold suspects under investigation, reached six, one from each of the city's *sestieri*, and each guard earned thirteen lire monthly, possibly reflecting (or prompting) a rise in the salaries of the lower prison guards as well.[24]

Within fifty years of Simone Steno's 1275 trial a distinct administrative routine was beginning to settle into place among the Venetian prisons, albeit not without its idiosyncrasies. Unlike in most contemporary facilities, Venetian inmates were exempt from specific fees for entry, exit, and upkeep, regardless of their social status or the grounds of their arrest. As elsewhere, however, poor prisoners received some food from the commune and financial aid from individual benefactors.[25] And although Venice instituted a public advocate for such inmates only in 1442 (shortly after Padua, Vincenza, Verona, and Ravenna), basic legal aid was available throughout the late thirteenth and fourteenth centuries.[26]

In contrast to the cities of Tuscany and Emilia-Romagna, Venice rarely liberated prisoners during religious feasts.[27] Some inmates, however, could regain their liberty after providing pledges and on condition that they pay their remaining debts in annual installments.[28] Aid to prisoners, whether supplied by individuals, guilds, or ecclesiastics, was still embryonic in the fourteenth century, and charitable functionaries were seldom involved in prison life before the late sixteenth century.[29] There was likewise no prison infirmary prior to the outbreak of typhus in 1563:[30] sick prisoners could be released, separated, or kept under ameliorated conditions.[31] Abuse of this status, however, soon led magistrates to specify that time spent under improved terms could not count toward the completion of a prison sentence.[32] Still, limited medical aid was available,[33] and at times the inmates' families were granted extended visitation rights on medical grounds.[34] Death among Venetian prisoners appears to have been rare.[35]

From an organizational perspective, then, most elements of prison administration were in place by the middle of the fourteenth century: a growing body of legislation and regulations, a basic but stable staff, designated facilities, and a routine supervisory mechanism. Prison upkeep was financed mainly by the commune, yet it also relied on the inmates' families and to a lesser extent on individual charity. Scores of prisoners inhabited the dozen or so cells of the lower prisons, and others were held (and occasionally tortured)[36] at the upper ward. Given each inmate's social ties, the central location of the prisons, and their visibility, it is safe to conclude that most Venetians could witness prison life, however reluctantly, from the beginning of the fourteenth century. At least to some extent, this visibility underwrites local magistrates' occupation with prison conditions and as such it is reflected in contemporary records.

The Venetian case challenges the view that sees the foundation of prisons as a mere by-product of political autonomy.[37] While most communes across the central and northern peninsula were engaged in protracted and often bloody struggles for independence (and later for internal definition), contemporary Venetians enjoyed remarkable liberties and internal stability. Subordinated to neither pope nor emperor, Venice was a centrally run polity from the early ninth century, when the seat of government was moved to Rialto and work began at San Marco on the Doge's Palace.[38] True, Venetian politics did undergo a process of semi-democratization with the entry of rich immigrants and local nonnobles into the governing councils. But while this expanded local participation in government and significantly curbed the doge's independence, the point of departure for the Venetian commune was an already autonomous and centralized regime.[39] Moreover, subsequent restrictions of access to political power, leading to and following from the famous 1297 *Serrata*, or "Closing" of the Great Council, only increased the role of the state in Venetians' lives.[40]

Unlike most other Italian city-states, Venice never witnessed a process "from tower to palazzo." As long as the city remained independent, the Doge's Palace operated as the center of government. It is no accident that the history of local prisons is intertwined with the building that more than anything symbolized the *Serenissima Repubblica*. On the other hand, given Venice's relatively early independence, the advent of punitive imprisonment there appears to have been late in coming. Judging by the available records, it roughly coincided with similar processes among peninsular cities, whose autonomy was only more recently gained. To notice this peculiarity is to underscore a broad, if complex, regional development rather than an inherent penal logic operative in any "mature" polity.

FLORENCE

The Florentines created the flagship prison of late-medieval Italy, and a unique facility in all of continental Europe. Within two decades of its foundation, Le Stinche—as the compound soon came to be known—was run by three to four wardens, three to six guards,[41] a chamberlain,[42] a scribe, and one or two lay penitential friars (*pinzocheri*), who attended to the prisoners' needs.[43] Additionally, a number of permanent service-givers were enlisted: a chaplain from the adjacent church of San Simone,[44] a water-carrier,[45] and, somewhat later, a physician[46] and a laborer responsible for removing the bodies of dead inmates.[47] A third layer of officials occupied with prison management were its supervisors, or *sindaci*,[48] whose responsibility was later assumed by officials of the Esecutore degli Ordinamenti di Giustizia.[49] By 1355 four *buonuomini* (one from each newly designated quarter) formed a lay supervisory committee that worked closely with the lay friars to distribute alms.[50] Toward the end of the fourteenth century these men were joined by a further, legally trained and salaried supervisor.[51]

This elaborate organization marks a new chapter, rather than the first, in the history of Florentine prison administration. A nebulous basis for this structure already existed in previous decades, since late-thirteenth-century Florence was home to a variety of prison facilities, such as the Burelle and Pagliazza, and quite a few inmates.[52] The accumulated experience of their management informed the definition and regulation of the wardens' office as well as the remainder of the minor and adjunct personnel. The process entailed the conservation of traditional elements as well as the introduction of significant innovations, both of which affected the prison's management culture and the daily life of its inhabitants.

Prominent among the innovations was the erection of an independent building to house the commune's prisoners and staff. Situated near Florence's emerging civic center, the somber, trapezoid compound of Le Stinche superseded all but one of the existing facilities:[53] it was probably the first purpose-built prison in Italy, perhaps even on the Continent.[54] The available records betray a minor excitement over this fact through a reassertion of the prison's novelty and the repetition of its symbolic anti-Ghibelline name: the Cavalcanti stronghold in the Val di Greve, a castle known as Le Stinche (Italian: shin, or crest; probably alluding to the castle's imposing location over a cliff), was razed and its soldiers captured in August 1304, by Guelf forces. The ironic fate of the Ghibelline warriors, who were led from Le Stinche castle to its namesake prison, compelled most contemporary and later writers.[55] By 1358 the compound consisted of seven sections: the old prison, the new prison, a women's ward, the *magnati* ward, the upper malevato, the lower malevato, and an infirmary.[56] A separate facility for the insane was established a year later.[57]

Contemporaries justly associated Le Stinche with Guelf supremacy, since founding the prison enabled the commune to dispose of some imposing physical remains of Florence's oligarchic past. Yet the act carried antimagnate undertones as well. For instance, not only was Le Stinche removed from the city's traditional (Roman and later ecclesiastical) center, but it was also built on lands confiscated from the Uberti family, scions of Florentine oligarchy. In 1293, following the promulgation of the Ordinamenti di Giustizia, which aimed at a more rigorous curbing of oligarchic power, the commune created the so-called Magnati Prison, which was run for and by members of the designated magnati clans.[58] Yet by circa 1307–8 the facility was abandoned, for symbolic as well as for practical purposes, and magnati inmates henceforth dwelled in a designated ward at Le Stinche, which was run exclusively by non-magnati. In fine, the process that Italian historians have dubbed "from tower to palazzo" characterizes the history of local prisons as much as it does the city's grander and more famous civic edifices.

A further, equally significant departure from tradition was the introduction of salaried personnel, paid directly and exclusively from communal funds.[59] The choice may indicate a general satisfaction with the finances of the Burelle and Pagliazza, prisons that only recently shifted from private leasing to public administration.[60] Additionally, set wages were an attempt to reduce corruption among the wardens and guards. Yet regular salaries also signaled the commune's commitment to maintaining the prison's staff. The gesture is understandable—and was perhaps even desirable—given the personnel's frequent appeals for unpaid wages.[61] But however well-intentioned Florentine magistrates

Fig. 1.2. Le Stinche, Florence. Detail from a 1584 map by Don Stefano Bonsignori, in *Stradario storico e amministrativo della città e del comune di Firenze* (Florence: E. Ariani, 1929), between pp. xx and xxi.

were in this respect, Le Stinche's wardens, guards, and other staff members continued to wait for their salaries, sometimes for months on end, during the following decades.[62]

The hiring of caretakers, chaplains, a physician, and a coroner suggests a growing sensitivity to the prisoners' needs, perhaps partly born out of the less intimate atmosphere engendered by a large, central institution. Le Stinche's physician also acted as the commune's *medicus pauperum*,[63] but the creation of his position was not merely a compassionate act; it also made economic sense: at fifty lire a year, the prison physician could attend to a range of cases on the commune's behalf, including the supervision and post-traumatic care of punitive amputations.[64] Thus, the physician exemplifies, on the one hand, the basic conservation of medieval multitasking, and on the other, the introduction of a more efficient utilization of professional skills. Despite his diverse clientele, the physician eventually based himself at the prison,[65] quite possibly at the little hospital or "sickroom" founded there later that century.[66] To be sure, his was not a prestigious position, nor was the salary particularly attractive, but physicians tended to remain at Le Stinche for relatively long periods.[67] It is hard to say if these men's choice of career stemmed from a lack of options, a charitable bent, or both, yet the low death rates recorded among inmates, whether from disease, violence, or suicide, may attest their basic competence.[68]

The prison's minor staff were a more stable group in comparison to the wardens, scribe, and chamberlain, who all served fixed terms of one semester or a year.[69] Andrea di Brunello, for instance, served as the prison's chaplain consecutively from 1362 to 1375; Bartolo di Michele acted as almoner there from 1367 to 1374; and Jacopo di Piero, known as il Grasso, "carried water" from 1374 at least until 1392.[70] These long tenures influenced the prison's management culture by allowing much knowledge and experience to accumulate among a limited number of low and middle functionaries: if scribes and chamberlains enabled a smooth transition from one semester to the next, the presence of permanent personnel shaped many aspects of the prison's daily running.

The permanent staff's competence probably increased their value in the eyes of their superiors. One unofficial way to reward such men (and curb corruption) was to employ them in occasional tasks such as repairs and running errands. Between April and October 1387, for example, the aforementioned water-carrier, Jacopo di Piero, augmented his modest monthly wages of 6 lire, 10 soldi by some 188 lire (over 480 percent!) in this way; and in one semester during 1392, while earning 7 lire monthly, the same employee received more than 49 lire (over 115 percent) in additional income.[71] In other words, Le Stinche's water-carrier could earn nearly as much and at times well beyond the wardens, and certainly more than any other prison official. And it is likely that his rather high income reflects remuneration for services other than mere labor.

Beyond serving as a symbol of Florentine independence and a tool in its machinery of justice, Le Stinche was intended to generate some income for the commune and to render the collection of fines and debts more efficient. Like most of their contemporaries, Florentine inmates paid for their incarceration. While basic processing fees (*pro introitu et exitu*) were set at five soldi per person, other fees depended on an individual's status, the grounds for his or her arrest, whether the arrest was carried out by a communal officer or by a private person, and the amount that he or she owed to the commune or a private creditor. Imprisonment for a private debt was a service—however obligatory, given the official ban on private prisons—offered by the commune to private creditors. Accordingly, the latter had to pay the commune either one-half or one denar for each lire they were owed, depending on whether they brought the debtors into custody themselves, or relied on commune officials for the arrest. Once inside, most prisoners could upgrade their living conditions by paying an additional *agevolatura* fee of between one and five soldi, determined by the value of their fine or debt.[72] In principle, paying for agevolatura simply meant greater spatial freedom. However, those who could afford it sought to re-create external hierarchies within the walls, and in fact lived in a separate ward called the malevato, which was divided into upper and lower rooms. Financial means even overrode traditional status divisions, as the former Magnati Prison (once incorporated within Le Stinche) did not remain exclusive to magnati, however loosely this group came to be defined outside the prison.

Le Stinche's inmates and staff constituted a separate jurisdiction. For the duration of their stay, prisoners were subject to a distinct scale of fines, and were adjudicated weekly by the Esecutore degli Ordinamenti di Giustizia "under the roof of the upper malevato [ward], located within Le Stinche's walls" (*sub volta malevolatis superioris posita in muros stincharum*).[73] Most documented offenses were gambling, blasphemy, drinking, brawling, and sexual intercourse, all of which were strictly forbidden at Le Stinche. The inmates' penalties were usually pecuniary, and as such they were quite low by "outside" standards. Compared to regular fees such as processing and agevolatura, the Esecutore's fines contributed little to the prison's income (see chapter 2). The Esecutore also monitored the staff's conduct, fining them for the escape of prisoners or illicit entries of prostitutes, for exacting inappropriate fees, or for embezzling the inmates' alms.[74] Though imperfect, the Esecutore's supervision was the most rigorous of its kind, at least among our case studies.

Founding Le Stinche was an exercise in political centralization and administrative efficiency. Its planning involved a reexamination of the roles and responsibilities of prison staff, an assertion of the latter's prestige vis-à-vis their disparate predecessors, and the establishment of an administrative mechanism to integrate the institution into the commune's judicial and political structure. In the process, Florentine magistrates strove to tackle the prison's perennial problems of security and corruption, but eventually encountered and inadvertently created new ones: a trickle-down process of control, deteriorating hygiene, increasing violence, and an imbalance between expenditure and income. At the same time, the foundation and regimentation of a central institution was pregnant with implications for the socialization of debtors and convicts—among themselves and with the prison's staff, random service-givers, and licit and illicit visitors.

Bologna

As elsewhere, so in Bologna, early prisons were initially appropriated from among the existing aristocratic *torri*.[75] The first permanent cells were designated sometime between the completion of the first communal palace in 1203 and the construction of the so-called Palazzo Re Enzo, the lifelong prison of Frederick II's son, captured in 1249.[76] Bologna's new communal prison only gradually rendered existing facilities obsolete, especially due to sporadic influxes of war captives. In 1254, for instance, the commune still financed repairs of private prisons and occasionally paid for their guards.[77] Nevertheless, the overlap was minor, especially when compared to larger cities such as Venice, Florence, or Milan.[78] Within several years Bologna's prisons were exclusive to its new center of government on the Piazza Maggiore, where they remained well into the nineteenth century.[79]

Although the original prison was probably of modest size, it was supposed to meet two basic requirements. The 1250 statutes forbade

the joint incarceration of men and women, and insisted on a separation of "banniti pro debito capti et pro condempnationibus" from those
imprisoned "pro maleficio." It appears, however, that this separation
initially failed to translate into three distinct wards (or rather, four, if
female debtors and delinquents were to be kept apart), since the same
statutes mention only one general prison, that of the "thieves" (carcer
latronum communis). According to the same rubric, moreover, all other
prisoners were to be held elsewhere (in alio loco) should the podesta and
judges insist on their incarceration.[80] This situation changed around
1260 with the establishment of the Malpaghe Prison, where the commune and private persons could detain male and female debtors. The
pertinent statute is also the first to mention processing fees "for chaining or entry and unchaining" (pro inferiata vel intratura et deferiata; 12d.)
and daily fees (6d.) to be collected from each prisoner, and whose payment was a prerequisite for release.[81]

Later redactions of the statutes (1262, 1264, and 1267) reserved a
separate rubric for the Malpaghe Prison. Even if this signaled a legal
distinction rather than a physical separation between the latter and
the "carcer communis," the new ward (if such it was) was still run by
the same four custodians in charge of the general prison. The 1262–67
statutes also required that the debtors prison be sold, or rather leased
to private hands and be subject to the same fees as mentioned before,[82]
but there is no indication that the suggested privatization ever trans-
pired. In any case, by 1286 two groups of salaried custodians were
running the older upper prison (carcer camere superioris) and a newer
lower prison (turris de subtu), both located inside the podesta's palace,
somewhere in or around the Arengo Tower.[83]

Neither the 1288 statutes nor any available record suggests a func-
tional-administrative distinction between the upper and lower prison
locations. On the other hand, occasional lists of prisoners reveal a
growth in the number of inmates—arguably a stronger motivation for
expanding prison spaces than any maintenance of legal categories.[84]
None of these spaces survive intact today. Their general dimensions
can only be conjectured from subsequent ground plans that are en-
cumbered by centuries of extensive renovations.[85] A rare glimpse of
the prison's layout emerges from a 1305 inventory that mentions an
administrative quarter (including the custodians' room), a kitchen
and dining hall, a storage space, and two rooms for prisoners, capable
of holding around forty men.[86]

Throughout the early fourteenth century, the proliferation of prison
locations accompanied the commune's rapid centralization, and this
despite a continuous demographic decline.[87] Sometime prior to 1318 a
new space, the Predacolaria, was created, yet it is once again impossible

Veduta della Dogana, e Carceri della Città di Bologna.

Fig. 1.3. The Torrone Prison, Bologna (*front right*). Reproduced from *Diario bolognese ecclesiastico e civile* (Bologna: Lelio della Volpe, 1774).

to identify a specific function for this ward.[88] In late 1326 two engineers began constructing several cells at the Palazzo della Biava, the original nucleus of the Palazzo Pubblico, erected on the southwestern corner of the Piazza Maggiore between 1293 and 1295.[89] These cells originally served for holding Milanese war captives sent there by the papal legate—soon to become Bologna's ruler—but later probably used as regular prisons.[90] Two years later, an independent women's prison was appropriated at the foot of the Palazzo del Capitano's tower (see below). Last, around 1352, the northwestern tower of the Palazzo Pubblico became the site of a new set of prisons, later known as the Torrone.[91]

It remains unclear whether the Torrone immediately replaced the recent cells at the Palazzo della Biava in name and function, or rather did so over time. In any case, the 1327 cells eliminated the original distinction between "upper" and "lower" wards, creating a new division between "old" and "new" prisons.[92] Accordingly, the Torrone became the new "new" ward, in conformity with the existing administrative structure. Throughout the remainder of our period two groups of custodians continued to operate the two prison compounds, one at the podesta's palace, the other at the Palazzo Pubblico;[93] the former facility operated well into the fifteenth century, the latter until 1830.[94]

Prisoners lists and other court documents reveal that female inmates were a small minority in Bologna. For decades local magistrates refrained from establishing a separate prison for women, preferring instead to utilize female convents, as was done, for instance, in Venice.[95] The practice did have its shortcoming, however, for by the early 1290s local nuns refused to receive female convicts on the grounds that the latter, often being prostitutes, were trailed by their clients. Thus the statutes' insistence on gender separation, the nuns' refusal to accommodate female culprits, and the magistrates' neglect to build a women's ward threatened to paralyze female incarceration.[96] Perhaps in an attempt to alter this situation (and to preserve the reputation of local nunneries), in early 1328 the papal legate, who already ruled the city, ordered the base of the tower of the Palazzo del Capitano to be converted into a special prison for women who "in aliquo delinquerent usque ad quantitatem decem ll. bon."[97]—a formulation that discloses the presence of convicted female offenders, but not necessarily debtors, as was previously assumed.[98] Still, the provision offers no ostensible solution for women who were fined (or in debt for) over ten lire. One hypothesis is that at least female debtors were imprisoned at the Malpaghe Prison.

The statutes of 1252 mention four "boni et probi homines et fide digni" who were elected as the then single prison custodians. These men were nominated from each of the city's four quarters and were to earn twenty-five lire each for a nonconsecutive one-semester term; they had to own property valued at two hundred lire or provide sureties for that amount; and they were obligated to sleep in the prison (*ibi in domo carceris*), where no less than two of them had to be present at all times. One penitential friar, elected each month, was to supervise the distribution of bread (or its cash equivalent; in any case provided by the commune), preach, and monitor the inmates' welfare.[99]

The 1288 statutes modified these rudimentary provisions to fit the prison's changing needs, and it is these emendations that persevered throughout the fourteenth century. Two groups of four salaried custodians (one from every quarter in each group) supervised the two prisons (upper and lower) respectively. The eight men[100] were elected "ad brevia" each semester. Two separate custodians were put in charge of the women's prison once it was founded in 1328, and in 1334 their salaries, fees, and terms of employment became subject to the general statutes governing all other communal prisons.[101] It appears, however, that this group of wardens was short-lived; given the physical proximity of the two locations, it is likely that the custodians of the old prisons eventually took over their responsibilities.

Contrary to Florence, where the creation of a new compound prompted an administrative reform, the revisions described in Bologna's 1288 statutes suited (or shaped) most future developments. When, for instance, the new cells were completed in 1327, one group of custodians was left in charge of the upper and lower prisons as one outfit, while the other assumed responsibility over the new compound. As mentioned above, this division remained in place even when the Torrone took over the Biava cells, sometime around 1352.

Administrative know-how continued to accumulate. If first-generation custodians were responsible for counting the inmates every night,[102] by 1288 a designated notary, elected once every semester, assumed this responsibility as well as that of supervising the custodians' conduct, and a further scribe had the unnerving job of recording the inmates' confessions under torture.[103] To complete the list of personnel, all statutes from 1335 on mention the custodians' *familiari*—an unknown (and likely fluid) number of caretakers and perhaps a cook. A final functionary, this time a private individual, involved in prison life was responsible for collecting the prisoners tax, a set fee of eight soldi per person. Like all other tax rights in Bologna, the office (established by 1289)[104] was purchased from the commune for a fixed period, usually one year.[105] All statutes specify that the prisons were under the direct jurisdiction of the podesta and *capitano del popolo*, who audited its registers and nominated supervisors to support the notary's monitoring functions.[106]

In order to consolidate his nomination, every custodian had to provide securities of two thousand lire from 1288, and of five thousand lire from 1352—a steep rise from the two hundred lire specified in the 1250 statutes.[107] A further change from earlier regulations concerns the custodians' income. Between 1250 and 1267 they each earned twenty-five lire per term and were prohibited from receiving any other payment, direct or indirect. By 1286 this modest salary was further reduced to twenty lire,[108] but the wardens became eligible for certain fees that were first mentioned in 1262: a processing fee of twelve denari per prisoner and daily charges of no more than two denari per prisoner. It was no more than a modest improvement; beyond reducing the daily fees from their 1262 rate of six denari to two denari, the 1288 statutes also specify for the first time that such fees were to cover lighting and other basic necessities. On the other hand, custodians could now earn further wages by executing capital punishments, dismemberments, and floggings at the rates of twenty, ten, and five soldi, respectively.[109] Among our case studies, this "perk" appears to be uniquely Bolognese.

The custodians gradually became more dependent on the prisoners' payments, which were formally raised by 1335: processing fees were doubled to two soldi, and daily fees increased to three denari (and again to six denari in 1376). Furthermore, every inmate paid twelve denari for each eight-day period "for light, water, bath, and other necessities" (*pro lumine, aqua et mastello et aliis neccesariis*), a registration fee of six denari to the notary, and the sum of three denari (raised to six denari in 1376) to the custodians' *familiari*.[110] Prison meals (lunch and dinner) cost eighteen denari each, but were not obligatory.[111] In short, excluding food and legal expenses, merely setting foot in prison between 1335 an 1376 amounted to twelve soldi (including the prison tax of 8s.), roughly a day laborer's weekly salary.

The custodians' unusual power, compounded by their intermittent role as communal executioners, called for some precautions. While ordinary officeholders had to wait a year or two before they became eligible for reelection, prison custodians had to wait five years between terms.[112] Tellingly, in the intervening period they could bear arms,[113] and the statutes stress the use of caution regarding their imprisonment.[114]

As elsewhere, the Bolognese commune employed regular and lay friars to care for the inmates' material and spiritual needs. Prior to 1288 these men distributed bread daily, preached, and monitored prison conditions, much like their Florentine or Perugian counterparts.[115] The friars were formally omitted from the 1288 statutes, but were reinstated by 1320,[116] all the while continuing to frequent the prisons in their capacity as confessors and executors of wills.[117] Whether the inmates regularly celebrated mass is unknown, yet in the aftermath of the Fourth Lateran Council (1215), which numbered it among a Christian's obligatory rites, it is likely that they did. In any case, only in 1371 did the papal legate found a small chapel for prisoners in the courtyard of the podesta's palace. It was run by the local Celestine monks, who received fifty lire annually for their services.[118] By the century's close the chapel served as a center for the officers of the confraternity of Santa Maria della Morte, which initially focused on convicts' spiritual preparation for execution, but later expanded its activities to include the inmates' general welfare.[119]

Prior to the confraternity's involvement there was a trickle of individual bequests—some of them quite substantial—aimed at ameliorating the inmates' conditions.[120] Another aspect of charity toward inmates was the "offering" of prisoners, already attested in the late thirteenth century.[121] However, only the 1376 statutes specify the routine release of inmates during four separate feasts: Christmas, Easter, the Feast of St. Peter, and the Feast of St. Petronius, Bologna's first bishop and patron saint.[122]

By the end of the fourteenth century, and seemingly regardless of the city's political unrest, a nascent prison system was installed in Bologna.[123] Its accommodation of a variety of inmates reflects the different services it performed in the administration of local justice, from custody and coercive detention, to the execution of corporal and capital punishments, to punitive incarceration. The physical arrangement would continue changing, but the Torrone and its satellites remained the system's focal points for centuries to come. Thus, it was concerning these spaces that Bolognese magistrates went on promulgating regulations for staff, inmates, and auxiliary services; and it was in view of their conditions that charitable institutions and individuals developed in order to assist

inmates and their families. Above all, however, the system's crystal-
lization meant that imprisonment turned into a coherent experience, at
least by repute. When a defendant was arrested or when a judge sent a
culprit to prison, both had a solid sense of what was in store.

CONCLUSIONS

Shoehorning the foregoing case studies into one model would be a
futile exercise. Despite their geographical proximity and frequent, mul-
tidimensional exchange, these sites offer a kaleidoscope rather than a
unified picture. Moreover, and as the next chapter demonstrates, the
farther one looks, the greater the diversity among facilities becomes
apparent. For several equally detailed studies exist for other Italian,
English, and French cities, and dozens more can be written from local
archives across western Europe.

But whatever their individual paths, each city-state reached similar results in a process underpinned by a common chronology. At the
end of the fourteenth century, the prisons of Siena, Venice, Florence,
Bologna, and many other urban centers stood complete, their edifices
visible and physically central; regulations governing their personnel's
constitution, conduct, and selection procedures were firmly in place;
and the inmates' obligatory fees (at least outside of Venice) were fixed.
Next, inmate populations were stable or growing due to an unprecedented recourse to imprisonment in all of its modes. Last, there was
a budding activity—individual, institutional, civic, and ecclesiastical—
designed to improve the prisoners' welfare. These ubiquitous processes
characterize a period of intense activity in and around prisons: nothing
remotely similar is evident beforehand, and its impact (physical, administrative, financial) shaped the penal and administrative practices
of prisons well into the modern era.

Chapter Two

ASPECTS OF IMPRISONMENT

Founding and maintaining prisons introduced numerous challenges. We now move to examine local responses to these challenges in greater depth and from four different perspectives: urban development, administration, finance, and law. The discussion is based on the prison profiles related in the previous chapter, while gradually introducing information gathered at the Sienese archives and drawing on published studies on other Italian, French, and English case studies.

While focused on topics rather than specific sites, the present chapter continues in the vein of its predecessor in seeking to underscore the variety of approaches to common problems rather than to present a unified picture. Nonetheless, the concerted attention awarded to prisons throughout western Europe during the late thirteenth and fourteenth centuries confirms once again that this was a watershed period in the history of the prison.

Urban Development

In present appreciations of the medieval urban panorama prisons are mostly blind spots. The oversight is surprising given the close link between the foundation of prisons and a rather familiar phenomenon, namely, the explosion of civic architecture and urban planning during the communal era.[1] As new walls, bridges, hospitals, and especially public squares and government palaces mushroomed across central and northern Italy, local magistrates began carving out prison spaces as well, mostly—or at any rate initially—within the courts and towers of communal palaces. What is most typical of prisons in our period, then, is their physical centrality and visibility: whether built anew or gradually appropriated from existing structures, prisons were located almost exclusively within central government buildings that, in turn, habitually flanked the city's main square.

Since the mid–fourteenth century the prison was fixed as a sine qua non of urban space. It featured in encomiums of civic pride,[2] testified to a people's charity or depravity,[3] and occupied early urban theorists such as Leon Battista Alberti (1404–72) and Antonio Filarete

(1400–1469/70?).[4] Medieval prisons' conspicuousness, moreover, has been durable; many of them remained in their original locations until the nineteenth and even twentieth centuries, when their dimensions, disrepair, and dysfunction finally rendered them obsolete. Even then, however, many facilities (new or renovated) remained physically central. The present-day extraction of penitentiaries from European metropolises is increasing, while the "ruralization" of prisons in North America continues apace.[5] But until this process ends on either side of the Atlantic, the link forged between prisons and city centers remains a palpable legacy of urban developments in the late thirteenth and fourteenth centuries.

Notwithstanding their similar location, municipal prisons took many shapes and sizes. To offer a physical taxonomy of these structures is perhaps to draw too sharp a distinction among architectural forms that were, for the most part, improvised solutions. Nonetheless, most prisons in our period fall into one or occasionally two categories. In decreasing order of ubiquity, these structural types are the following:

Appropriated. A preexisting facility or space, converted permanently or temporarily for purposes of incarceration. From Hanani the Seer's up-turned basket (II Chron. 16:10), through various city walls, gates, and amphitheaters, to castle dungeons, confiscated aristocratic towers, and even chapels and bell towers, appropriated prisons are perhaps the most common throughout history.[6] Other occasional prisons were created to hold war prisoners below inns, over rooftops, and in vacated courtyards. Virtually all of Bologna's prisons, from the twelfth to the nineteenth century, fall into this (and partly into the next) category.

Embedded. Cells or rooms, whether appropriated or purpose-built, incorporated within a greater edifice. This category overlaps with the former, especially since it is rarely known whether the decision to define such a space went into a building's planning or predates its construction. The distinction is useful, however, to separate random or occasional quarters from those that, at least over time, became permanent facilities. Embedded prisons include designated monastic cells (especially after the twelfth century), ecclesiastical jails attached to episcopal palaces, and prison wards in many communal palaces. Embedded prison spaces existed in each of the cities examined in chapter 1; even after the construction of Le Stinche, Florence maintained one such prison—the Volognana—inside the podesta's palace.

Separated. A prison facility, usually purpose-built, but occasionally appropriated, constructed as a wing of a new government compound. Siena's communal prison, joined to the Palazzo Comunale in the early fourteenth century, is one such example; others are Paris's Châtelet prison and the municipal prison at Arras.[7]

Independent. A self-standing, purpose-built prison. Among these rare compounds were Le Stinche, the Paduan and the Parmese prisons, as well as
several English facilities.[8]

It is a common but inaccurate view that, prior to the late sixteenth
century, Italian prisons were "always and only" appropriated structures.[9] True, purpose-built facilities such as in Florence, Padua, and
Parma (and, later, in Venice and Milan) were exceptional, although
they certainly indicated a general future trend.[10] Eventually, overpopu-
lation and deteriorating conditions in the appropriated facilities led to
the construction of new wings or entirely new structures: Siena and
Modena exemplify the former solution, Venice the latter.[11] Bologna, by
contrast to both, continued to employ existing spaces—mostly expropriated aristocratic towers—throughout our period, but even there
the progression was toward one central facility, namely, the Torrone.
A telling exception to this rule was Verona, where centralization was
temporarily "interrupted" during the reign of Ezzelino (1226–30 and
1232–59), who granted his partisans the right to incarcerate in their
own residences, thereby reinstating a former practice. However, spatial
centralization was soon reestablished under the Scalieri, and maintained under the Visconti and Carraresi. The public administration of
Veronese prisons was introduced under Venetian rule.[12]

Despite the chronological overlap between a city's various prisons,
the above list delineates, *grosso modo*, the trajectory of prison architecture from antiquity to modernity. Modern penitentiaries serve diverse
functions, but the seminal designation of structures for long-term incarceration and the construction of purpose-built facilities mark their
early physical and administrative beginnings. And although slow in
coming, it is precisely this process that begins to unfold between the
late thirteenth and fourteenth centuries, especially in urban centers.

At the same time, the physical typology of prisons does not necessarily
correspond to the development of practical distinctions among custodial,
coercive, and punitive incarceration, let alone to the growing employment of the latter measure. In fact, the nearly diametrically opposite
cases of Florence and Venice demonstrate that, where no rupture existed
between the theory and practice of penal incarceration—as in Venice—a
separate building was deemed unnecessary, at least for the time being;
whereas Florentine magistrates, who largely refrained from meting out
punitive sentences, went to considerable lengths to found an independent facility, ostensibly in order to secure higher revenues from debtors
and to increase administrative expediency, rather than prepare for the
implementation of punitive imprisonment.

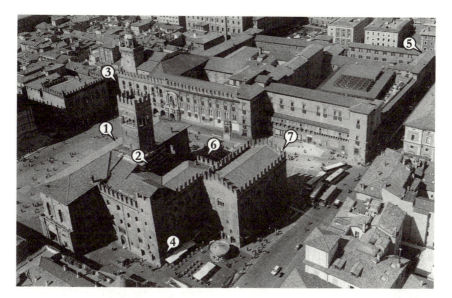

Fig. 2.1. Prison facilities around the Piazza Maggiore, Bologna. 1. Upper and lower prisons (before 1256). 2. Predacolaria (before 1318). 3. Biava cells (1327). 4. Women's prison (1328). 5. Torrone (ca. 1352). 6. Prison chapel (1371). 7. Re Enzo's prison (mid–thirteenth century).

Prisons' location and layout and their variety of functions could and at times did influence one another. This topic will be explored in subsequent sections in greater detail, but suffice it to say here that the prison's traditional role as a place of custody and coercion influenced its choice of location. Physical centrality meant better access for court officials and private creditors, both of whom had frequent dealings with inmates. Conversely, the availability and accessibility of prison spaces operated as a catalyst for employing coercive and punitive incarceration on an unprecedented scale. Like other institutions, the prison too created its own momentum.

Less common but still a dominant characteristic of late-medieval prisons is their increasing physical (rather than social) exclusivity. Sooner or later, magistrates sought to condense all prison facilities into one space or, as in Bologna and Venice, one area at the city's political center. The endeavor was both practical and symbolic. After a modest initial investment, polities would rather own than rent a facility, whose proximity expedited the work of the courts and rendered monitoring the wardens and inmates simpler and less costly.

In Venice, for instance, the Ten's torture chamber and investigation room was positioned directly above the committee's offices; and the lower palace cells were linked to the Great Council's deliberation hall by a special stairwell. This vicinity did not come without a cost: on one occasion the Venetian councilmen complained of the stench rising from the lower cells.[13] They could not ignore the inmates' conditions.

Under the previous aristocratic regimes of most Italian city-states, public space was divided among the *torri* of several powerful families.[14] Just as most political activities in the precommunal era were presided over by a handful of scions, so incarceration (usually of a political or military nature) was limited to private compounds. As noted above, with increasing participation in government and its concomitant centralization, public space was reorganized around the communal piazza. And the process, commonly dubbed "from tower to palazzo," also entailed the incorporation of prisons within the new civic centers, to the exclusion of aristocratic towers. Communes such as Siena, which initially rented noble residences to serve as prisons, later decided to abandon them in favor of one central facility. In Florence, the Magnati Prison remained independent for just over a decade before it too was transferred into Le Stinche's grounds. It was only the last tower to be abandoned; in its previous incarnation, the women's ward at Le Stinche was located at the Pagliazza, another expropriated aristocratic tower.

The unification of prison spaces holds true even for Venice, where a feudal aristocracy never existed. Although the *Serenissima* underwent no process from tower to palazzo, centralization had other goals. For instance, as Edward Muir has argued, political developments in thirteenth-century Venice eradicated the traditional parish structure.[15] Correspondingly, the use of *casoni*, the original prisons in each *sestiere*, was suppressed or limited, theoretically, to overnight custody. As a rule, all prisoners had to be marched to the Doge's Palace.

Although mostly unnoticed by historians of medieval architecture and urban planning, the creation of prisons participated in the transformation of public space.[16] Like the central piazza, the communal palazzo, and the purpose-built hospital, the prison too was a political sign of its times: its presence and location affirmed local hegemony, reified dissidence, and reminded passersby of the importance of civic charity.[17] As a political symbol the prison would continue to assume and shed meanings in the centuries that followed. With every major regime change, crucial victory, or environmental disaster, the prison reemerged as a key point of reference, whether through its storming, triumphant emptying, or sending aid to its inmates during trying times.[18]

Fig. 2.2. The Pagliazza Tower, Florence. Formerly the women's prison (2d. per day); today the Hotel Brunelleschi (Euro 250 per day).

Administration and Bureaucracy

"The escape-proof prison," wrote Leon Battista Alberti, "is in the eye of the vigilant custodian."[19] Wise and still relevant, the admonition is nonetheless one-dimensional. Well before Alberti's time, running a prison amounted to much more than ensuring that inmates stayed put. The grounds and goals of incarceration pertained to various populations, each with its own set of needs and internal tensions. And rising turnovers meant more custodial spaces to maintain and a greater demand for food and medical, legal, and religious services. Furthermore, inmates were kept in different areas at different rates for different periods of time, a fact that partly explains why their labor force was never exploited. As was becoming apparent in other areas of urban government, operating these facilities required coordination among many bodies and individuals.[20]

To meet such demands, communes established executive hierarchies among the prison's staff and developed mechanisms to help ensure that the latter conduct themselves according to written regulations They also introduced methods of record-keeping to monitor the prisoners' movements and account for the facility's income and expenses. As we shall see, these measures varied enormously between polities, in terms of both scope and execution. Further, the (theoretically) increasing supervision over prison spaces did not always and everywhere translate into a more efficient government. Nonetheless, if centralized government was a prerequisite for prisons, bureaucracy and regulated personnel enabled them to function and expand.

There was a range of prison governments, from the rudimentary to the elaborate. Since its establishment in 1330 and throughout most of the fourteenth century, Siena's prison was run solely by two custodians and possibly by a part-time notary.[21] Two groups of four wardens, a notary or two, several *familiari*, and an almoner maintained the Bolognese upper and lower wards—an outfit that remained intact throughout the prisons' periodic reorganizations. Six to eight guards worked at the lower Venetian prison complex, a group headed by a *capitano* at least from 1339, while each of the city's *sestieri* furnished one guard for the upper prisons by the century's close. The most elaborate administration operated in Florence: circa 1360 Le Stinche's permanent staff comprised four wardens, six guards, a chamberlain, a notary, an almoner or two, a chaplain, a physician, and a water-carrier.[22] Most prison functionaries in Florence and elsewhere served nonconsecutive terms of six months and earned modest but reasonable salaries.[23]

In Siena and Bologna prison oversight was entrusted to the podesta and the *capitano del popolo* (or their delegates)—a task that constituted one criterion by which these functionaries were evaluated at the end of their terms.[24] While this is true of Florence as well, monitoring Le Stinche's inmates and staff appears to have been more elaborate and better structured. First, the prison almoners acted, at least in theory, as a safeguard against the wardens' potential corruption. They also had to witness incarcerations and releases, actively supervise the separation of men and women, and arrange for the collection and distribution of alms. Next, the Esecutore degli Ordinamenti di Giustizia conducted weekly inquests at the prison, gathering testimonies from the prisoners regarding their welfare and the staff's conduct, and adjudicating inmates and personnel who violated prison regulations. Last, by 1355, the commune nominated a lay committee to aid the almoners, and a further, legally trained supervisor began collaborating with the committee toward the end of the century. This variety of checks was exceptional, especially at such an early stage. On the other hand, monitoring by almoners, a notary, and, somewhat later, an external supervisor are attested in Bologna as well, and throughout the thirteenth century the Venetian doge and an ad hoc group of councilmen frequented the palace prisons, a responsibility assumed, starting from 1297, by the Night Lords.

The diversity of prison administrations and methods of oversight reflects more than a difference in scale. Siena, Bologna, and Venice had similar inmate turnovers, and yet each city maintained a different number of guards: two, eight, and twelve to fourteen men, respectively. At Le Stinche, where inmate numbers were markedly higher, the number of guards never exceeded six, although admittedly staff members were more numerous than elsewhere. Location and internal divisions also created certain demands: two custodians sufficed for Siena's embedded compound, while Bologna's and Venice's cell-clusters required distinct groups of guards in greater numbers. Furthermore, as in many areas of urban government, the topography of a city's internal politics informed the staff's constitution: Le Stinche's chamberlain "rotated" between the city's sixths (and later quarters), and the same municipal unit determined the number of wardens in both Bologna and Florence. Each of Venice's sixths supplied one guard to the upper prisons. Perhaps these arrangements were excessive, but sacrificing efficiency on the altar of harmony was (and pretty much still is) a common practice.

The notary and, where this functionary existed, the treasurer best embody the shift from a semi-improvised to a rudimentary prison administration. Under communal regimes, whose officials changed substantially every semester, notaries' records enabled a smooth transition from one administrative term to the next. This holds true for prisons as well, where wardens, custodians, and guards usually served nonconsecutive, six-month terms.[25] By comparison, a notary's tenure could be longer. In Florence he often served for one year, as did the chamberlain.

The registers kept by prison notaries were mainly of two kinds.[26] The first was a chronicle of inmate traffic, where a typical entry would contain information such as the date of and the grounds for a prisoner's arrest, the arresting officer or private individual, the amount of a prisoner's debt or fine, and basic biographical information such as occupation, status, original provenance, and present residence.

This record served prison governors as a point of reference (a "personal file") throughout the inmate's period of incarceration: charges that were added, dropped, or modified; full or partial payments toward the cancellation of a specific fine or debt; a prisoner's death, execution, or the circumstances of release—all or some of these would follow the original entry. The data also helped to determine which inmate was eligible for charitable release. In distilled form such lists were presented to the deliberating councils prior to every major feast.[27]

Inmate traffic records usually passed from one group of wardens to the next in modified form. As each semester drew to a close, the notary

Fig. 2.3. An inmate traffic register, Siena. Archivio di Stato di Siena, *Soprastanti alle Carceri* 1, fols. 3v–4r (1395). (By kind permission of the Archivio di Stato di Siena.)

prepared a revised register or simply drafted a list of the remaining inmates, omitting terminated cases from the new record. In Florence, a list of cases lingering from the previous semester opened each new register, while incoming prisoners were entered separately in the second part.

The notary also monitored the prison's income and expenses. Inmates were subject to a variety of fees and taxes whose payment constituted a prerequisite for release. The prison's fiscal records could ensure that each prisoner paid precisely what was due, thereby curbing (but not eliminating) the wardens' capacity for extortion or collusion with private creditors. The notary likewise logged the wardens' expenses for supplies, repairs, and salaries. Since the prison lacked a formal budget, the information allowed the communal treasurer to ensure that sums allocated for the prison's maintenance were being spent properly, and that the employees and service-givers received salaries that were adequately taxed.

Apart from registers of inmate traffic and general finance, occasional documents were produced by or in connection with communal prisons. These include prisoners' petitions,[28] periodic inmate lists,[29] prison inventories,[30] and registries of inmates who left the prison temporarily to attend to their personal affairs.[31] Although sporadic, such records illuminate more than the margins of a prison's routine; they give us a glimpse of preparations for festive releases, of business transactions between imprisoned debtors and their creditors, and of inmates

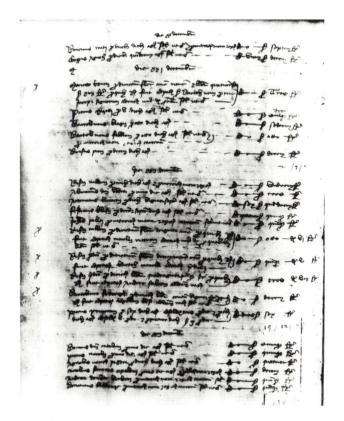

Fig. 2.4. A register of prison expenses, Florence. Archivio di Stato di Firenze, *Soprastanti alle Stinche,* Entrata e Uscita 380, unnumbered folio (1359). (By kind permission of the Archivio di Stato di Firenze.)

walking to and from the courts. Jointly, both "organic" and occasional documents bear witness to the prison's budding routines.

Around the middle of the fourteenth century, prisons completed a transition from a semi-improvised to a rudimentary government. Just as prison facilities were no longer designated ad hoc, so their administration settled into a steady routine, even if a varied and imperfect one. Occasionally, as in Florence and Bologna, the organization of local facilities, staff, and supervisory mechanisms attained a high level of sophistication, yet many other polities kept systematic records of the prison's human traffic, income, and expenses, and determined the salaries, norms, and nomination procedures of prison functionaries. This attention to prison government was unprecedented across western

Europe. Its achievement was a structural organization of prisons that would persist for centuries to come.

FINANCE AND ECONOMY

Communes founded and developed prisons as cogs in their machineries of justice. Beyond facilitating the work of courts and magistrates, custodial spaces expedited the collection of fines and debts—the latter a crucial mechanism in any credit-using economy. In these polities "of businessmen, by businessmen, and for businessmen,"[32] constructing and maintaining prisons was another sound investment in infrastructure. As such, prisons were rarely expected to yield a direct profit.[33] In Venice, for instance, imprisonment was free of charge, although this was anomalous. But even small and medium-size prisons, where inmates were subject to a range of fees, never generated much income for a city's coffers. Lack of profit, in turn, may help explain why prison management was seldom privatized in our period: there was simply little or no money to be made. Temporary exceptions such as those documented for Siena were prompted by extreme financial distress.[34] And what probably aided (if not altogether enabled) periodic privatizations was an implicit understanding that the government would turn a blind eye to the lessees' entrepreneurial activities within the "gray area" of a prison's administration. At any rate, to judge by the Sienese case, even income from leasing the prison was fairly low, as the commune stood to earn a mere three hundred lire over a period of two years.[35] A final obstacle to profiting from the prison was the strong presence of debtors, whose incarceration could have been interrupted at any moment, thereby inhibiting the organization of prison labor.

But if prisons were never promising capitalistic endeavors, it is likely that local governments still aspired to some remuneration from the inmates.[36] Venice aside, there appear to have been two alternative rationales governing prison finance, one based on high turnover, the other on long sojourns, in a manner reminiscent of the present-day models of a Chinese and a French restaurant, respectively. Among our case studies, Bologna clearly followed the "Chinese" model, as the fees' distribution over time reflects a preference for brief sojourns, or at least provided little economic incentive to prolong them.[37] A prisoner's fees for a one-day incarceration (12s.) constituted over 50 percent of his or her expenses even after thirty-two days, when the daily fees finally matched the prisoners' tax (8s.), until then the largest single component.[38]

In Siena, by contrast, there was no prisoners tax, and although processing fees were markedly higher than in Bologna (5s., 4d. vs. 2s.),

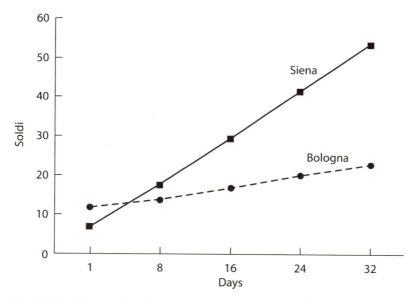

Fig. 2.5. An inmate's daily expenses in Siena and Bologna (cumulative).

the overall cost of setting foot in prison was much lower: six soldi, ten denari versus twelve soldi. At the same time, a full day's agevolatura was six times as expensive as the Bolognese obligatory daily fees: eighteen denari versus three denari.[39] Thus, an inmate paying for a full agevolatura surpassed the initial processing fees within four days. These high rates and their uniform distribution across time translated, theoretically, into a rapid progression of expenses and a potentially costly incarceration.

In order to convey the scale of these prisons' income within the general scheme of their finances, let us compare their revenues with the staff's salaries, a city's greatest single expense over its prison. By the late fourteenth century, the eight custodians and one notary running the Bolognese prisons jointly earned 370 lire a year; in contemporary Siena, maintaining the two prison wardens cost the commune 154 lire annually.[40] To meet these costs, Bologna theoretically required a monthly turnover of twenty-seven paying inmates with an average stay of just over one month. Siena's high fees and rudimentary administration meant that as little as two paying prisoners per month (according to the aforementioned configuration) would have covered the wardens' salaries. Prima facie, then, the modest Sienese administration and its financial rationale could easily increase the commune's income, while at Bologna only a relatively high turnover would generate real profit.

As it happened, however, reality interfered with theory. Each of the 249 inmates processing through the Sienese prison between January and July 1395, left behind an average sum of twenty-five soldi. After deducting the processing fee, this sum would have sufficed for thirteen full days of agevolatura, at eighteen denari per day. The prison's income that semester was two hundred lire, or a mere ten lire more than the cost of the custodians' salaries, compounded by miscellaneous expenses adding up to thirty-six lire.[41] The Sienese prison, in short, barely made ends meet.

Assuming these figures were not exceptional, how to account for the discrepancy between a potentially profitable facility and its actual income, despite its low maintenance costs and what appears to be a solid average monthly turnover of over forty-one inmates? The most plausible explanation is that few inmates were paying to ameliorate their conditions, probably out of indigence rather than choice. As in Florence, Pisa, and Lucca, prison finance in Siena was based on a strong presence of propertied debtors who could afford to pay for better conditions.[42] (Was the state of standard wards purposely neglected in order to encourage this tendency?) The imprisonment of poor debtors or offenders who could not sustain themselves at the standard agevolatura rates completely undermined this rationale. Before exploring what may account for the incarceration of poor offenders in the first place, it appears that their growing presence hastened the decline of even economically viable prisons such as the Sienese.

Among our case studies, only Le Stinche generated some profit—a remarkable achievement given its high running costs.[43] Compared to either Siena or Bologna in terms of potential income, Florence had the best of both worlds: on the one hand, a high turnover of inmates, on the other, long average incarceration periods.[44] As in Siena, the largest single component of Le Stinche's revenues was the income from agevolatura fees, one to five soldi per day, determined according to the cumulative amount of an inmate's fines or debts.

For the three semesters analyzed below, the average daily agevolatura rate was two soldi, six denari, applicable to roughly 53 percent of the inmates. The second largest component was an item missing from both Siena and Bologna, namely, the income from taxation on private debts, prorated at one-half or one denar for each lira owed—depending on whether the creditor or the commune apprehended the debtor. The average tax during these semesters was sixteen soldi, two denari, applicable to 36 percent of the inmates.[45] Income from processing fees (5s. per person) is the third largest component, trailed from afar by the occasional fines imposed by the Esecutore, who oversaw prison administration and the inmates' conduct.

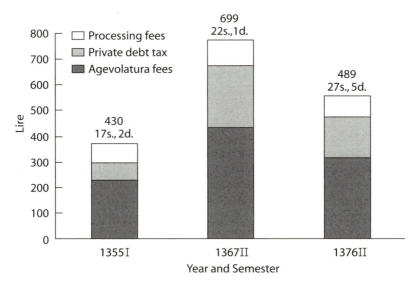

Fig. 2.6. Major income components at Le Stinche. Based on Archivio di Stato di Firenze, *Soprastanti alle Stinche*, Entrata e Uscita 376, 382, 388. The upper figure above each bar relates inmate quantities; the lower figure represents the average expense per inmate during each term.

A Florentine prisoner who was not a private debtor, paying the average agevolatura rate mentioned above, would have spent eighty-five soldi for a thirty-two-day imprisonment: over one and a half times more than in Siena, and nearly four times more than his Bolognese counterpart. The agevolatura fees constituting this figure are particularly prominent (nearly 95 percent), reflecting their proximity to the processing fee. We have seen that it would have taken a Bolognese prisoner thirty-two days to match his or her processing fees in daily fees, and that in Siena equilibrium would be reached after four days. In Florence agevolatura fees would outweigh processing fees within two days only.

Around 1360, the salaries of Le Stinche's elaborate personnel amounted to 1,460 lire annually. To shoulder this burden, 343 inmates (according to the above configuration) would have been required: a monthly turnover of nearly 29 inmates, just above Bologna's 27 and far higher than Siena's (theoretical) 2. However, according to this analysis, an inmate's average expense at Le Stinche was twenty-two soldi, three denari, that is, nearly 75 percent lower than the desired eighty-five soldi. The average annual turnover, despite being over three times *higher* than that theoretically required for meeting the staff's salaries, still leaves a gap between the potential and actual income. What partially compensated for the shortfall was the income

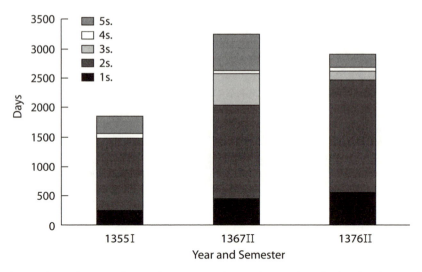

Fig. 2.7. Distribution of agevolatura rates (1s.–5s.) at Le Stinche (in days). Based on Archivio di Stato di Firenze, *Soprastanti alle Stinche*, Entrata e Uscita 376, 382, 388.

from the private debtors' tax and, to a lesser extent, the Esecutore's occasional fines. Still, Le Stinche's income barely covered the cost of its personnel's salaries even in a busy semester.

A pattern of economic imbalance is beginning to emerge. For as elsewhere, so at Le Stinche, the discrepancy between potential profitability and actual income was tied to the low revenues from agevolatura fees. In the registers analyzed above, just over half the prisoners paid to ameliorate their conditions. Presumably, more inmates would have done so had they been capable of paying. A comparison between these three registers reveals that (*a*) paying inmates were mainly divided between two major fee-groups; and (*b*) there was a growing asymmetry between the two. The vast majority of agevolatura payments (66, 49, and 65 percent, respectively) were for two soldi, the daily rate fixed for accumulated fines or debts of between one hundred and five hundred lire. The second largest group (daily 5s., corresponding to fines or debts of one thousand lire and above) accounted for 16, 20, and 8 percent, respectively, of all agevolatura payments in each semester. Although both groups remained dominant, the former expanded, while the latter ultimately shrunk. There was a marked rise of the less expensive agevolatura rates as opposed to a sharp decline in maximum-rate payments: between the second semester of 1367 and the parallel term in 1376, agevolatura payments of five soldi dropped by over 60 percent, from 652 to 242.

The expansion of low-rate agevolatura is all the more telling given that even these rates were a difficult compromise on the commune's part. For at least thirty years agevolatura at Le Stinche cost nominally double the amounts related above.[46] The reduction is first attested in the 1355 statutes, where the commune signed off half of its potential income from agevolatura fees, the prison's single largest income component.[47] Although the motivations for the act are nowhere stated, the reduction probably reflects the deflation or contraction of Florentine economy in the aftermath of the 1348 plague. If so, however, the reflection is a partial one at best, since the same statutes contain no parallel adjustment to the staff's salaries. On the other hand, it is likely that the reduced range of fees corresponded to the continuing impoverishment of the prison's population or even a certain deflation in pecuniary penalties. According to this interpretation, the rates were slashed in order to salvage the income from the agevolati wards, whose population would have otherwise diminished.

By updating the scale of agevolatura rates the Florentine commune sought to maximize the prison's income under changing economic circumstances. This attentiveness paid off, at least temporarily: to judge by the 1367 register, both high- and low-rate agevolatura payments increased. The number of optional-fee payers itself grew from 221 (51 percent of all inmates) to 404 (58 percent). This trend reversed, however, within less than a decade, as the 1376 register reveals: payments of five soldi plunged from 20 to 8 percent of all agevolatura payments, while payments of two soldi climbed from 49 to 66 percent. The number of agevolati itself fell from 404 to 236 (from 58 to 48 percent of all inmates). In graphic terms, what was beginning to look like a symmetrical hourglass division circa 1367, turned into a broad-based pyramid by 1376: the ratio between payments of one or two soldi and those of three to five soldi shifted from 62/38 (2,035 vs. 1,225 payments; 182 vs. 250 lire) to 85/15 (2,459 vs. 460 payments; 217 vs. 97 lire)! Thus, from the middle of the fourteenth century, wealthy debtors were a shrinking minority among Le Stinche's inmates.

Although prisons were not designed to be profitable, over time their income declined to levels that were lower than had probably been anticipated. This was especially true where the bulk of income was expected to come from prisoners' amelioration fees, as in Siena and Florence. The shortfall was due neither to low prisoner turnovers nor to oversight: inmate numbers remained steady even after the onset of the plague cycle in 1348 and throughout the political and military turmoil of the second half of the fourteenth century—a stability that in fact signifies a substantial relative increase; and governments routinely updated prison fees in keeping with financial circumstances. Furthermore, where the prison's balanced "budget" depended on a combination of high entry fees and a modest but rapid inmate turnover, as in Bologna, income continued to be stable but low. In Florence, by contrast, the growing presence of nonpaying inmates and of prisoners who only paid low agevolatura rates undermined the prison's income base. The impoverishment of the inmate community, in turn, depended on a growing recourse to the incarceration of poor debtors or those who defaulted on minor sums. In Florence and elsewhere, many of these inmates were not in a position to pay their fines or debts to begin with, let alone maintain themselves in better wards, even after the halving of agevolatura rates in 1355. It is also possible that the growing presence of poor inmates deterred wealthy merchants from getting incarcerated, a development that, although in certain respects welcome, could have reduced the prison's income even further. But was this gradual impoverishment of inmates and the attendant economic decline of prison finance unwitting? What accounts for the growing presence of poor prisoners over propertied debtors? The following section offers some clarifications.

PUNITIVE IMPRISONMENT: JURISPRUDENCE, LEGISLATION, AND PRACTICE

There are laws in books and laws in action.[48] Punitive imprisonment was mostly abhorred by medieval jurists and is uncommon in the period's penal legislation. In practice, however, judges applied the measure on various occasions, typically for minor crimes such as gambling and bearing arms, in conformity with a master's desire to punish a domestic slave or a paterfamilias his child, or as a substitute penalty for fines. It is not simply the case that prisons were more numerous in the fourteenth century—the volume of culprits effectively serving prison sentences was substantial.

But in what sense were these *legal* developments? The relationship among jurisprudence, legislation, and practice is complex and contingent and obeys no fixed set of rules. Whether or not laws are "born old," the shortcomings of enforcement and the politics of lawmaking mean that practice seldom follows directly from written laws, or legislation from theory. In the case of punitive imprisonment in the Middle Ages, legislation lagged behind practice, and both departed from contemporary, mainstream penal thought. This picture, however, emerges only when all three realms are considered jointly and without privileging normative texts over documents of practice, as has so often been done in this case.

Until recently, studies on the so-called birth of the prison tended to focus on the theoretical and prescriptive basis of penal incarceration. An apparent lack of pertinent discussions by medieval (and earlier) jurists allowed modern scholars to associate the development of imprisonment with the implementation of penal reforms promoted by men such as Cesare Beccaria (1738–94) and Jeremy Bentham (1748–1832). Accordingly, a prevalent view identifies the "real" birth of the prison as a product of either Enlightenment penology or bourgeois mentality, thereby relegating modern discussions of the prison in earlier periods to a prehistory of sorts. However, since the 1940s and increasingly in recent decades, the traditional chronology has been challenged, not merely by medievalists, but even by social and legal historians of Late Antiquity.[49] Even those scholars working within the confines of normative texts have demonstrated that virtually every period since the dawn of Greek civilization recognized and employed penal incarceration, however unsystematically.[50] Moreover, the category of imprisonment for debt, commonly practiced throughout the Middle Ages, is misleading insofar as it purports to describe a squarely coercive measure. As Richard Ireland contends, imprisonment for debt had intrinsic punitive goals against a breach of faith, not mere "punitive overtones," as was previously conceded.[51] The impact of modern penology, then, was not in devising or applying punitive imprisonment per se, but rather in establishing the measure as the *basis* of state penal systems and, equally important, as a means to effect culprits' personal reform.

The revised chronology holds true for late medieval Italy, although it would be hard to illustrate these developments solely by recourse to jurisprudential literature. Indeed, both theoretical and prescriptive texts offer a skewed view of penal practices in the period. And while it would be wrong to dub late-medieval lawyers, especially in Italy, as detached or "academic,"[52] it seems that they only gradually came to grips with the use of punitive imprisonment outside ecclesiastical jurisdiction. The literature of medieval jurisprudence—glosses and, later, commentaries on Roman and canon law, individual treatises, *quaestiones*, and monographs—is mostly silent on the matter;[53] and when it is not, the pertinent writings exhibit a shared aversion to penal incarceration, in keeping with the ancient dictum by Ulpian (d. 228) that "the prison is meant for the detention of men, not their punishment."[54]

What appears to be a *communis opinio* among medieval jurists did not stem from ignorance or detachment. Outside Venice imprisonment was not a frequent penalty precociously introduced into local statutes: most inmates were, at least technically, debtors or prisoners awaiting their sentences. Such limited *formal* recourse to penal incarceration generated no major public or learned debate on the matter, and it is likely that most academic lawyers perceived (or wished to regard) it as a minor, if not altogether temporary, phenomenon: insofar as jurists discussed imprisonment, their focus remained its coercive and administrative aspects.[55] However, sensitive as these authors were to the arbitrary distinctions among custodial, coercive, and (outside the church, illicit) punitive incarceration,[56] they were uniquely privileged to detect and admonish against shifts from custodial and especially coercive to penal incarceration. In Bologna, for instance, it was common for doctors of jurisprudence to act as the prisons' external supervisors.[57] Such men likely knew that in reality an inmate's experience depended heavily on the wardens' attitude and the quality of external supervision, and less so with the explicit goals of one's incarceration. In fine, the occasional but uniform reminders regarding the licit use of imprisonment and the emphasis on the staff's responsibilities can be read as cautionary if not reactionary.

Only one medieval jurist dedicated an independent discussion to imprisonment—the treatise *De carceribus*.[58] Drawing on a range of authorities, from Ulpian to Bartolus de Sassoferrato, the work addresses traditional questions such as the prison's definition, who may be held there and on what grounds, how an escaped prisoner is to be punished, and who is eligible to run the facility. Treating imprisonment in monograph form was seminal in itself, yet *De carceribus* departs from earlier and indeed sporadic discussions in another important way. While stressing the illegality of penal incarceration, the author acknowledges the potential "sliding" of coercive into punitive imprisonment, particularly in the case of poor prisoners. In the treatise's opening words, "The precepts of laws were developed mainly so that poor persons would not be molested. Therefore, among the poor, no one appears to be more miserable and destitute than an imprisoned person."[59]

Like most jurists down to Ulpian, the author of *De carceribus* too believed that "the prison is a secure and dreadful place, devised not for punishment but for the custody of offenders and debtors."[60] Yet the dangers attendant upon the incarceration of poor debtors in particular threatened to undermine the prison's conventional role as a place of custody and coercion. The author's solution was to restrict the incarceration of debtors and malefactors to a minimum (including the days in which they might be arrested), limit the charges that could be made against a person already in prison, create pertinent supervisory mechanisms, and institute procedures for appeal. Furthermore, in a key passage he argues that it is licit to imprison public debtors only upon refusal to pay from their *available means*. The exhaustion of a debtor's funds, in turn, signals the termination of a lawful coercive arrest, although the author does grant the judge some leeway in determining this moment by considering the debtor's broader social networks.[61] In any case, it is contended that poverty should provide legitimate grounds for canceling the process.[62]

De carceribus underscores a problematic principle: a debtor's financial resources determine the limits of his or her penalty. On one hand, it is an obvious guideline given that the coercion of debtors presupposes a capacity to pay. On the other hand, an *ad personam* approach opens the floodgates to shrewd business maneuvers calculated to reduce legitimate fines and, potentially, a polity's income. The treatise's broad definition of a debtor's means sought to address this tension, but never at the cost of curbing a deep-rooted aversion to punitive incarceration. The suffering of poor debtors evidently concerned the author more than safeguarding equity, the legal system's efficiency, or its deterring power.

The preoccupation of this author and of other jurists seems justified. In the expanding monetary economy of the Italian city-states, pecuniary penalties were becoming common and more burdensome. Rising fines went hand in hand with the growing number of poor debtors, whose coercive imprisonment was practically indefinite. So much so, that the coercive value of incarceration was coming into question. One solution was already suggested by the influential French jurist Pierre de Belleperche (d. 1308), who advocated the commutation of fines into corporal punishments.[63] De Belleperche's original intention was to refrain from innovating or condoning an illicit measure such as punitive incarceration, yet the initiative had the further advantage of not throwing out the baby (punishment) with the bathwater (incarceration). In his view, seeking to avoid "hopeless" coercive incarceration should not forgo punishment altogether: whoever could not pay would suffer bodily harm. *De carceribus* offers a different solution, but the motivation was similar: without nipping punitive imprisonment in the bud, the measure would "contaminate" civic law, causing much undue suffering. This, after all, is precisely what occurred in Venice, where magistrates introduced a formal calculus to convert fines into prison sentences, effectively legitimizing penal incarceration for almost any offense. True, the Venetian 1303 calculus was exceptional, but only insofar as it could be applied so generally. As we shall see, commutations of fines into jail time were already instituted in Florence and elsewhere,[64] and the reaction of contemporary jurists may disclose a growing fear of their spread.

But what stood at the base of this anxiety? After all, not everyone could pay a fine, but anyone could serve a prison sentence. Imprisonment was accessible and applicable and provided urban magistrates with a formula to bridge socioeconomic gaps among citizens. The measure no doubt privileged the propertied, but poverty would no longer serve as an excuse to avoid punishment: as a temporary, internal exile that did not deplete a community's resources and was enthusiastically supported by the church, incarceration offered a viable alternative to corporal punishment and inflated fines. Above all, applying it as a licit penalty could have signaled a real extension of civic justice among the growing urban citizenry.

Seldom did any of these arguments find expression in the jurisprudential writings of the later Middle Ages. A typical compendium of legal *consilia* from the fourteenth and fifteenth centuries contains a discussion attributed to Baldus de Perusio (likely, de Ubaldis) that denies a judge's right to impose perpetual incarceration, citing the standard range of proof-texts. However, the author immediately adds that a finite incarceration can be meted out for offenses that still lack a prescribed punishment.[65] The relevance of such a statement largely depends on a judge's capacity to interpret or rather identify a particular offense—an unrealistic assumption, if such it was. Yet whatever his ideological or professional motivations, whoever produced this legal opinion clearly sought to justify punitive imprisonment without overtly dismissing the venerable dicta of Roman law.

But this of course was an exception. As Nicoletta Sarti has amply shown, the formidable gallery of contemporary jurists such as Bartolus de Sassoferrato, Lucas de Penna, and others never explicitly reconsidered punitive imprisonment in a new key.[66] Time and again they defended the Roman tradition, which detested punitive incarceration. Yet the jurists' enemies were real: local statutes and, to a greater extent, judges' actions, which tended to overcome the lawyers' purism and sense of taboo. It was probably in recognition of these forces that some jurists took up the issue—however sporadically—and with moderate success. Outside of Venice, the formal reception of penal incarceration was perhaps delayed and its practice curbed, but no lawyer was able to impede the sanctioning of punitive imprisonment by urban statutes or eradicate the "sliding" of coercive into punitive imprisonment. A gap between legal theory and legislation was beginning to open.

While jurists could and often did serve on city councils, the latter's professional constitution was wide-ranging. Occupational diversity, along with a range of preoccupations, helps to explain why, in drafting statutes, urban magistrates were more willing to employ penal incarceration. A fourteenth-century Modenese found breaking curfew would be fined and incarcerated for a minimum of three days.[67] In contemporary Siena, sodomites aged twenty to thirty were to be fined three hundred lire and imprisoned for three years without the possibility of early release; their elderly co-felons could receive five hundred lire in fines and five years in prison.[68] Immediate incarceration and a hundred-lire fine was the prescribed penalty of any Florentine who aided an excommunicate, and the same measure (along with a fine of fifty lire) was prescribed for those who denied the commune's jurisdiction.[69] Violent assaults were punishable in Florence by a two-thousand-lire fine and six months' incarceration,[70] and a non-Florentine caught gambling was to be flogged if he wished to forgo imprisonment, the default penalty in such cases.[71] It was licit, moreover, for a paterfamilias to have his misbehaving sons or nephews incarcerated "until they return to the path of obedience."[72] As in Venice, imprisonment could also serve as a commuted fine: for instance, a Florentine *nuntius* convicted of abusing his office was to pay a hundred-lire fine or else spend six months in prison.[73]

That and more, it was customary in thirteenth-century Venice for those who defaulted on their fines to be confined to the area of San Marco for thirty days. Debtors who crossed the designated boundaries would be imprisoned for a further month in a proper prison on the grounds of disobedience.[74] Prison sentences could also be meted out as individual or joint penalties for a variety of offenses: sailors aboard Venetian galleys who failed do defend their ships from enemies (including pirates) faced a two-year sentence;[75] a night guard discovered to have a side job was to be incarcerated for a month;[76] gamblers were fined but could also spend up to eight days in prison;[77] and bakers and butchers who repeatedly transgressed the regulations governing their trades could lose their stalls and find themselves behind bars for several months, along with their apprentices.[78] Venetian rulers also approved imprisonment as a secondary measure to be applied against convicts who broke the terms of their condemnation. For instance, anyone who failed to pay the fixed ten-lire fine for bearing arms around San Marco (fifty lire around Rialto) was to be imprisoned for six months;[79] and a merchant who exported goods from Venice without permission was to pay the commune half the value of the merchandise or else go to prison for one year. For a repeated offense the fine-rate remained the same but the merchant's prison sentence would be doubled, and for a third consecutive offense the merchant would again have to pay the same fine or suffer perpetual incarceration.[80]

In the above cases the Venetian councilmen drew a clear distinction between primary and secondary penalties. And in fact, it would be wrong to place imprisonment on par with fines or exile, at least prior to the early fourteenth century. Eventually, however, formal commutations were introduced as the Great Council devised a calculus to convert pecuniary penalties into jail time. According to the decision, dated 8 November 1303, one could erase a fine of 25 lire and below after an incarceration of six months, fines between 25 and 50 lire after nine months, and fines between 50 and 100 lire after one year.[81] The table's upper limit of one hundred lire seems to have been aimed at benefiting poor debtors in particular or those incarcerated for modest fines,[82] but the commutation was soon extended to erase up to 100 lire from *any* condemnation. Thus, sometime in May 1312, Simeon di Sborga was fined 260 lire, which evidently he was unable to pay. After eleven months in prison, he asked the Great Council to deduct 100 lire from the original condemnation once he completed a full year in custody. The remaining 160 lire were to be paid back in annual installments.[83]

From a prescriptive standpoint, the Venetian calculus marks the beginning of a new stage in the history of punitive imprisonment. Whether this development is indebted to the Venetians' greater reliance on local statutes than on Roman law is debatable,[84] yet allowing prison stays to erase fines paved the way for incarceration to become a common penalty for various offenses. To name a few: anyone crossing the Rialto with a horse (even if led and not ridden) could be fined three lire or imprisoned for three days (likewise for anyone galloping or leading a running horse through Piazza San Marco); the penalty for usury was set at three months in prison and banishment from Rialto; and bigamy was to be punished by the restitution of both dowries, a fine, and one year in prison.[85] The penalty for fornicating with a reluctant nun (why this was not considered rape is unclear) was set at three years' imprisonment; with a consenting nun, at two years; for any other offense committed by a layman within a monastery, at one year; and any offense against nuns committed in the vicinity of a monastery, at six months. These penalties could be augmented by a fine.[86] To be sure, Venetian legislation on imprisonment was exceptionally developed, but it was not unique. As shown above, lawmakers elsewhere in Italy prescribed the measure as a punishment in a growing number of cases.[87] The gap between legal theory and legislation was widening. Passing into the realm of practice (and changing the metaphor while at it), even local statutes emerge as the very tip of the iceberg.

Six prison registers from Le Stinche, all compiled in the second half of the fourteenth century, reveal the distribution of initial grounds for the inmates' incarceration shown in table 2.1.[88] The range and distribution of offenses is fairly consistent. Debt is the most common offense among the inmates, trailed from afar by custodial imprisonment with or without bail (*uno processo* and *bene custodia*, respectively), and custody prior to execution (*avere et persona*).[89] Yet beyond serving as a coercive or custodial measure, imprisonment also served as a formal penalty. Fairly common were incarcerations for gambling and the illicit bearing of arms (an average of 3.6 cases per semester) and especially incarcerations *pro amendare* (8.3 per semester), usually inflicted upon delinquent domestic slaves and children. The latter practice was commonly considered the

TABLE 2.1
Grounds for Incarceration at Le Stinche in Six Semesters
(existing inmates only)

	1347 II	1359 I	1369 I	1375 II	1376 I	1395 II
Debt	219	135	159	89	76	102
Bene custodia	50	40	66	3	2	8
Pro amendare	11	4	4	11	9	11
Avere et persona	8	2	2	5	4	10
Gambling	5	1	2	2	0	0
Arms	1	2	5	2	2	0
Uno processo	0	8	2	8	5	0
Homicide	1	0	0	0	0	0
Theft	0	1	0	0	0	0
Unknown	17	8	3	8	13	11
Total	312	201	243	128	111	142

Source: Archivio di Stato di Firenze, Soprastanti alle Stinche, Carcerati, 82–84, 89–91.

prerogative of a paterfamilias: when a Florentine notary entrusted his son to a certain business associate, the latter was encouraged to "make him [the lad] good; and if he obey you not well, beat him like a dog, and cast him into prison, as if he were your own [son]."[90]

By themselves these figures testify to a minor but steady use of punitive imprisonment *de iure*. But numerous cases of penal incarceration are obscured by the category of debt. Debts make up 64 percent of the grounds for arrest in the six semesters analyzed in the table, and these are divided almost evenly between private and public cases. Yet while private debtors constitute a distinct if diverse group of propertied men, it is harder to generalize about the category of inmates who were public debtors. In principle, any person who owed money to the commune was a public debtor or a debtor of the treasury (*debitor fisci*). There were, however, different ways of attaining this status and still others for construing a public debt as grounds for incarceration. Some public debtors owed the government money from unpaid taxes. Others fell behind on their installments from leasing an office or a right such as collecting a certain tax or leasing a property. The latter had to be propertied men and as such could renegotiate their schedule of payments, often by providing new sureties or paying an interim fine. In any case, they seldom went to prison: as long as money kept flowing into the city's coffers, magistrates tended to refrain from applying incarceration as a coercive measure.

Poor debtors suffered a different fate. To begin with, their debts often began as pecuniary penalties rather than unpaid taxes or delayed installments. Unable to pay their fines duly, such men became, technically, debtors to the treasury. They could then be arrested and imprisoned—assuming they were not already in jail—ostensibly as a way to expedite payment. Prima facie, then, we are dealing with a classic case of coercive imprisonment: the culprit's own reluctance prompted the arrest; presumably, once the debt was cleared, release followed. But there is more to this procedure than meets the eye. To offer an analogy, when Quakers in seventeenth-century New England were convicted of missionary activities, the law allowed them to "opt" between flogging and the payment of a five-pound fine. But the choice was more apparent than real, since devout Quakers would not have paid the fine as a matter of conscience.[91] In a way, poor medieval debtors faced a similar nonchoice.

The problem lies with the premise of coercive imprisonment, namely, that the debtor is *reluctant* to pay: poor offenders or those who were fined well beyond their means (or those of their families' and friends') were not reluctant, but simply *incapacitated*. But as long as their sentence was legitimate, poor debtors could expect to remain imprisoned—until they died or until their "debt" was canceled. It was a dangerously slippery slope: by 1415 the Florentine statutes, for instance, specified that those convicted, fined, and then imprisoned for accidental homicide, sexual offenses, grave and minor assaults, private incarceration, theft, blasphemy, carrying arms, gambling, and disturbing the public peace were eligible for charitable release, thereby disclosing the variety of offenses that could lead—as a quick second step after the initial fine—to de facto penal imprisonment.[92] Tellingly, it was in this context that private charity and periodic releases on feast days developed as crucial release valves for prisons overcrowded with poor inmates. At any rate, months and sometimes years could pass before such "hopeless" debtors regained their liberty.

Under the guise of a licit measure, coercive arrests opened a wide back door to punitive imprisonment—precisely the concern of jurists such as the author of *De carceribus*. Yet even beyond legalistic concerns, "hopeless" coercive incarceration created a vicious cycle of debt, since most poor inmates could not meet the costs of incarceration. True, some polities (Venice, Padua) did provide for the very basic needs of poor prisoners, but rarely did such action suffice. As we shall see in the following chapter, in lieu of employment options in prison, poor inmates resorted to gambling, violence, and trickery in order to sustain themselves, and could develop complicit relationships with wardens and guards in order to gain the favor of a potential donor or a place on the next list of oblations. At best, a poor person's incarceration placed an immense burden on his or her family and friends. The proliferation of "hopeless" coercive incarceration, in sum, justly worried jurists, but it also weighed heavy on urban magistrates, charitable officials, and prison administrators.

The situation was different in Venice but only in the sense that incarceration there was not a sub-rosa punishment. It was perhaps a living proof that underscored the fears of contemporary jurists that the number of people serving formal prison sentences in Venice had been constantly on the rise ever since the introduction of the 1303 calculus. Partial and complete commutations of fines into jail time brought into the Venetian prisons a range of offenders: Piero Remario, who kidnapped a young woman in order to marry her;[93] Francesco Abramo, who participated in a brawl;[94] Viviano, a former night guard convicted of assault;[95] Piero, a servant who swore at another man's servant;[96] Johannes, a German, imprisoned for illicit trade;[97] and a certain Michele of Padua, convicted of aiding the escape of six Cypriot slaves.[98] The list could go on and on. Around the middle of the fourteenth century, imprisonment routinely accounted for over half the sentences handed out by the Quarantia, the Venetian criminal court of appeals.[99]

Common to many of the Venetian inmates—as with their peninsular counterparts—was poverty. Erasing a 10-lire fine by subsisting six months in prison is an act of despair; anyone who could afford to avoid it, probably did so. Unfortunately for truly poor inmates, negotiating their terms of release depended on their capacity to pay their original fine, either immediately or in annual installments. Sometime in 1309 the Venetian Five of Peace arrested Avancio, a baker from San Gimigniano, for brawling with another baker. He was fined 107 lire but, unable to pay, he remained in prison. By early 1310 the Great Council approved his release, officially on account of his poverty, but on condition that he repay his fine in annual installments of 10 lire.[100] Avancio was perhaps a poor inmate, yet, probably due to his professional skills, he could guarantee a steady income to the city's coffers once released. This solution was irrelevant to the nonprofessional underclass: in Venice, where charitable releases were not a routine practice, incarceration marked the beginning of a vicious cycle for the poor.[101]

Punitive imprisonment developed among the Italian city-states in the teeth of contemporary legal thought. Outside of Venice, the measure had only a weak prescriptive basis, although in practice local judges routinely meted out prison sentences on a variety of grounds and especially to "hopeless" debtors under the guise of coercive incarceration. Thus, along with a handful of miscreants who served formal prison sentences, many if not most inmates effectively were incarcerated for "defaulting" on fines they could never hope to pay. Formal or informal, sanctioned or not, punitive incarceration was becoming an increasingly common penalty in Italy and beyond.

CONCLUSIONS

Italian urban liberties were sought with great enthusiasm and came at a steep price. But after gaining independence, the greatest challenge to any communal regime still lay ahead, namely, to convince its citizens that it was up to the task of effective government.[102] In contrast to the city's defense from external threats, maintaining order within the walls was everyone's prerogative. Faced with suspicion and a long tradition of private dispute-settling, urban magistrates chose to advocate exclusivity when it came to the administration of justice, albeit with varying degrees of success. In any case, while it was useful to back such claims over jurisdiction with real force, it was no less important to develop an administration on a grander scale and in a new key.[103]

Communal regimes have often been criticized as pretentious. Yet it is easy to forget that their challenges were immense, not least because they attempted to create a more efficient but at the same time more public form of government, one, moreover, that would satisfy their citizens' claim to greater participation without threatening stability. It was a tough balancing-act, and compromises abounded. The insistence on a foreign podesta and the frequent rotation of offices, for instance, were products of strong pressures that often ran counter to efficiency. In this setting, rendering the commune's legal routines more visible and accessible can be seen as yet another response to the reshuffling of local power structures. All this, however, forms only a general background to the great proliferation of urban prisons, and does not account for the parallel process in Venice, whose political stability had been established long before that of any of its peninsular counterparts.

What partly explains both this development and its concurrence across Italy and beyond is the encroachment of inquisitorial on accusatorial procedures in secular courts.[104] For in their quest for political hegemony, communes took it upon themselves to instigate rather than respond to civil and criminal infractions. Based on the ancient techniques of Roman jurisprudence, inquisitorial methods of litigation, including a growing emphasis on witness testimony, documentation, and judicial torture, meant that bringing a defendant to trial required a greater effort, and often resulted in lengthier periods of pretrial incarceration. These procedural demands created an urgent need for more custodial spaces, and it comes as no surprise that such facilities were built or appropriated as close as possible to the main government compound, as the first section of this chapter demonstrates.

But prisons were more than efficient facilitators of a "revived" procedure. In their conspicuousness they served as living symbols of a revolutionary political era and of a new public theater of law. Their creation, expansion, and relocation was a coherent (and so far neglected) strand of the so-called process from tower to palazzo, or the conversion of public space to suit the ideological and practical needs of centralized communal regimes. Centralization went hand in hand with a quest for administrative efficiency and financial security, goals that the prison served in its capacity as a place of custody and coercion. As related in the chapter's second section, prison administration took its cue from the know-how accumulated in other areas of urban government such as nomination procedures, remuneration, record-keeping, and supervision, all devised to address the demands of a mercantile culture. The endeavor was often costly, and urban magistrates took some care to revise incarceration fees and offer certain services to the inmates by which they hoped to increase the city's income from this new facility. As it turned out, however, revenues from inmates' fees rarely even covered the prison's running costs, as the third section demonstrates. And, while it would be misleading to evaluate the prison in terms of a capitalistic endeavor, income rates were unexpectedly low.

What probably weakened prison finance most was a gradual impoverishment of the inmate community. Unlike merchants and artisans, poor prisoners could not afford their own upkeep, let alone upgrade their conditions through agevolatura. Thus, prisons usually became minor burdens on local treasuries rather than sources of even modest income, while dealing a major blow to the lives of its poorer residents, especially in the absence of employment possibilities inside the prison. Ironically, by the time this was becoming apparent, the administration of justice in many cities had come to rely on prisons, not only as places of custody and coercion, but also as punitive facilities. As stressed in the fourth section, the latter development went mostly unstated, for although urban magistrates began incorporating punitive imprisonment into local statutes (mostly against the grain of contemporary legal thought), most prison sentences were coercive arrests gone sour.

There was, in fine, something unwitting about prison economy in general and the growth of de facto punitive incarceration in particular. Neither aspect of the prison's early history was unavoidable, for any given regime could have put a stop to these seemingly unnecessary complications, whether the minor burden on the city's coffers, or the ostensible violation of contemporary penal law. This in turn suggests that there were important enough justifications to maintain (indeed, to expand) these institutions despite their apparently uncomfortable fit with communal finances and Roman law. As indicated, this had much to do with the communes' desire to consolidate their political monopoly and publicize their autonomy. But a further insight into the proliferation of prisons can be obtained from the way in which these institutions were run. And so, it is to examining the daily life of medieval inmates that we now turn.

Chapter Three

PRISON LIFE

ONE TELLING DIFFERENCE between modern and medieval prisons is their typical location. Despite the current consensus on the importance of a structured integration of inmates into free society, most new prisons, especially in the Anglo-American world, are rural, or in any case extra-urban.[1] Security considerations notwithstanding, scholars often argue that by extracting prisons from population centers governments discourage prisoners from maintaining or acquiring key values cherished by contemporary Western society. Community, leadership, competitiveness, assertiveness, self-confidence, pride, and individuality are traits likely to be perceived as threats to any prison's administration, and their suppression, in turn, strongly inhibits the inmates' ability to reenter society once at large.[2] Indeed, some studies argue that it is the less "prisonized" inmate who stands a better chance of adjusting to the free world.[3]

In contrast, due to its central location and its inmates' frequent contacts with the outside world, the medieval urban prison offers a unique counterexample to modern practices. As related in the previous chapters, medieval prisons were founded at the physical heart of cities, were highly accessible, and their routine depended to a large degree on external intervention. In this chapter, we will examine more closely what that routine was like, and how the prison's location, internal organization, and regimen helped shape the inmates' experiences. To do so, we will advance linearly through stations in prison life, from arrest to the end of incarceration. This trajectory is misleading inasmuch as it suggests a uniform prison experience. This is not the case; the inmate's career depended on a variety of factors, from the institutional, to the social, to the biographical. Yet the picture that emerges, if not pleasant, is of a tolerable place, by medieval and certainly by modern standards.

From a modern penological perspective, the visibility and accessibility of medieval inmates helped mitigate a tension between social rehabilitation and social destruction. Anthropologist Claude Lévi-Strauss sketched a theoretical spectrum between "digesting" and "vomiting" the deviant, that is, between literally consuming a culprit and perpetually banishing him.[4] Within this range, medieval imprisonment occupies a median position between the two extremes of cannibalism and

the modern, rural maximum-security prison. Even when compared to
the choice of nonfatal penalties prevalent in the Middle Ages, incarceration reflects a rather complex attitude toward deviancy: exiles could
seldom return; those who were publicly beaten, branded, or amputated
were marked for life, both in body and in reputation; and the payment
of a fine—the most common punishment in the period—was a routine
private affair. Protracted imprisonment, on the other hand, was a less
obvious type of deprivation, whose damage was mostly indirect. It
had the markings of enslavement and an element of corporal punishment, but neither was pronounced and both could be obviated.

Modern prison life is often construed as a liminal state, wherein men
and women live "on hold" between social separation and incorporation.[5] In contrast, the realities of medieval prisons rendered life within
them as only a semi-exclusive and ipso facto semi-inclusive experience.
Thanks to their visibility and accessibility, medieval urban prisons
never became truly liminal spaces, nor their inmates liminal people.
Rather, incarceration in that period can be likened to a prolonged rite of
passage that commenced with an offender's arrest, and usually ended
with his or her release. While arrest never signaled a complete severing
of social ties with the outside world, and release did not mark their full
restitution, these two moments at either end of the protracted corridor
of the prison experience, along with the stations in between, are the
focus of the present chapter.

THE TERROR OF ARREST

Most medieval inmates were, technically, debtors. Like pawns in a great
human bank, they remained incarcerated for unpredictable periods
that tended to drag on. Anyone setting foot at Le Stinche, for instance,
might be fortunate enough to leave that very day, but was more likely
to remain there for months on end, even years. During the second half
of the fourteenth century, the vast majority of Florentine inmates spent
between six and twenty-four months behind bars. Such long durations were common elsewhere: to relieve the overcrowded prisons of
Venice in 1331 the Great Council ordered the discharge of any debtor
who had been incarcerated for more than two years; the decision was
to be applied during the following three years, and was extended *sine
termino* in 1334.[6] All of the twelve inmates offered at Bologna during
Nativity, 1327, had spent at least eight months in prison; on average,
each prisoner languished there for sixteen.[7] And a typical oblation list
from Siena that year reveals that seven of the twelve prisoners sched-
uled for release on Christmas had been incarcerated for over one year,

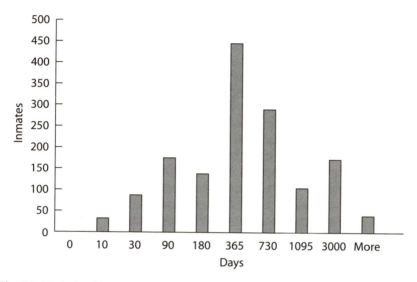

Fig. 3.1. Periods of incarceration at Le Stinche (cumulative). Based on Archivio di Stato di Firenze, *Soprastanti alle Stinche*, Carcerati 82–85, 88–91.

and three others for over two years.[8] Given medieval people's shorter life-expectancies, these typical durations approximate the definition of modern long-term imprisonment.[9]

Various factors contributed to the extension of prison stays. First, inmates became more vulnerable to further accusations once immobilized, whether by other creditors or the commune. Moreover, they could accrue additional debts to other inmates or personnel, and incur fines for offenses committed during their incarceration, thereby risking further postponement of their release. After eight months of incarceration in Bologna, the petty debtor Giovanni Jacobini "could not be released because he could pay neither his creditors nor the wardens."[10] It is no accident that inmate traffic registers typically allocated one half-folio for each entry: additional charges, sometimes in the dozens, were often brought up within days of the initial arrest.

But arrest initiated a hiatus in more than one respect. Convicts and their families had to adjust to a radical and extended disruption of their routines. And the poorer they were, the greater was the risk of entering a vicious cycle of debt and dependency. Once incarcerated, day laborers and artisans turned from main providers into financial burdens. Merchants, in contrast, could continue handling their affairs from prison, albeit not as efficiently as when at large.[11] To pay back debts, men of means could rely on business connections or family members, and in any case, as the greatest contributors to the prison's coffers, they feared

no grave ill-treatment. Thus the wealthy merchant of Prato, Francesco
Datini, resigned himself rather calmly to the idea that he might spend
some time in confinement: "I shall abide in prison until we can pay," he
informed his wife, noting, "I shall be in good company there, for methinks a great many others [merchants] will have to go there, too."[12] Poor
prisoners, on the other hand, needed to work in order to survive, but
employment was rarely an option.[13] As one indigent inmate remarked,
although not a merchant, at least he was fortunate enough to have merchants as his friends. He, too, knew that the premises of imprisonment
were skewed in favor of the propertied and their protégés.[14]

Still, poor prisoners could expect to get some aid: individual and
institutional, direct and indirect.[15] The Florentine confraternity of
Orsanmichele not only supplied food and financed the release of prisoners, but also offered material support to their families. In 1324, for
example, the wife of an inmate called Dino received twenty soldi in
order to help her make ends meet; and in 1351, Gemma, a widow, obtained 10 lire in charitable aid while one of her sons was incarcerated.[16]
In 1395, Francesco Datini's wife gave 1 lira directly to an inmate's
mother.[17] Venetian magistrates addressed the problem of impoverished
inmates (and crowding) by offering flexible terms of release to insol-
vent state debtors. Avancio, the baker from San Gemigniano mentioned
in the previous chapter, was able to negotiate the repayment of his 107-
lire fine in annual installments of 10 lire.[18] Yet even this flexibility on
the part of the Great Council was limited to professionals who could
provide pledges and who showed promise of a steady income. And in
any case, such negotiations commenced only after several months of
incarceration had elapsed, and never guaranteed release.[19]

For the nonprofessional poor and those who lacked powerful patrons, the consequences of arrest could be dire: the family of Antonio
Frumeta, a decorated soldier, was financially ruined within a year; and
Marco Iusto, a former Venetian podesta, suffered the death of his wife
and all of their impoverished sons and daughters during his five-year
incarceration.[20] Druda, the wife of a veteran Bolognese inmate, fared
somewhat better, since she was granted permission to sell some of her
husband's property to meet the costs of his imprisonment and trial.[21]
But even she had to rely on the commune's goodwill.

As a gateway to trouble of all sorts, then, arrest was not to be taken
lightly. Understandably, some did their best to avoid it, primarily by fleeing and negotiating their penalty from abroad, but also through devising
other ingenious solutions. In 1353, for instance, the Venetian nobleman
Mafeo Gabriele embarked on a self-imposed four-year exile, "fearing
prison more than death";[22] and a local young man named Marco was
apparently so terrified that he pleaded to convert his six-month prison

sentence into serving on a galley, "or wherever it would please the lord doge," for three years![23]

But joining the fleet (or the army, as in Arras)[24] was not always feasible, and flight required money, connections, and some hope of survival outside one's city. Contumacy, moreover, could be regarded as an admission of guilt, and anyone avoiding arrest in this way risked a higher fine, a longer sentence of incarceration, and the confiscation of his or her property. Absconding also compromised the security of one's family, and could occasion the incarceration of one's guarantors.[25] Fleeing, in short, was self-selecting in the case of an impending incarceration, a last resort that was open to a privileged few.[26] Another potential solution for avoiding arrest, namely, physical resistance, was as uncommon, it seems, as it was pointless in the centralized city-state.[27]

FIRST NIGHTS

One of the novelle of Franco Sacchetti (d. ca. 1400) relates the purportedly true story of a young judge from the Florentine merchant court who, unable to pay a certain fine, was imprisoned at Le Stinche. The bright, handsome young man (*assai giovane e pulito e chiaro*) was greeted by a veteran inmate, Massaleo degli Albizzi, facetiously described as "a new man with many new indulgences" (*uno nuovo uomo e con molte nuove piacevolezze*). Massaleo looked after the newcomer, invited him to share his dinner, and, seeing that his protégé had yet to arrange for a bed, offered to make room in his own—a proposal that the judge, rather unwisely, accepted. During his first night in prison, the "fish" was torn from his sleep by Massaleo's intimate stroking:

> But, what are you doing to it?!
> Forgive me, I thought it was mine!

The incident became the cause of much laughter, and the story concludes as the young judge, having forgiven his friend's "innocent mistake," finds a new bed to occupy.[28]

Behind the tale's homoerotic humor lie the emotional distress and the unnerving realities of prison life: a new place, with new social rules. The judge's ordeal is reminiscent of a common initiation rite, still prevalent in prisons today.[29] Its purpose was simple and its timing precise. As Sacchetti put it, in molesting his guest Massaleo was moved "more by indulgence than by vice" (*piú per piacevolezza che per vizio*). Perhaps, then, the veteran inmate was testing the newcomer in order to impose status divisions (patron/protégé) and allocate sexual roles (superordinate/subordinate, active/passive). Either way, as prison observers and inmates today would agree, the judge's response was crucial in shaping his prison career. If he had allowed himself to be terrorized into homosexual intercourse, he would have been branded as weak—by all accounts a ruinous tag in prison. And regardless of his status outside the walls, any claim he might have had to authority would have likely vanished.[30] In his instinctive naïveté, the judge seems to have avoided a miserable existence by a hair's breadth.

However effective, the response came at a price. The tale's conclusion reveals, casually but unmistakably, a rather tragic aftermath. The protagonist is described as henceforth "a possessed man" (*un uomo invasato*)—an expression underscoring a drastic mental deterioration; and the usage of the past perfect tense in the story's final sentence suggests that he remained in bed for the duration of his stay: "And in that [bed], while he remained in prison, he slept" (*e in quello [letto], mentre che stette in prigione, si dormì*). Such a reaction is attested elsewhere, at least as a literary trope: in another Italian tale set in 1410, the imprisoned protagonist is described as "dozy on account of the melancholy and discomfort [or embarrassment] of being in prison" (*sonnacchioso per la malinconia e del disagio dello stare in prigione*).[31] Mild depression and other forms of emotional withdrawal such as constant sleeping are recognized today as characteristic, if reversible, behaviors of newly arrived inmates, and this may have been the import of the above descriptions.[32] In any case, the tales capture key dimensions of the encounter with prison life: mental solitude and social disconnection among inmates whom scholars have variously described as "little islands in a dead sea" or "atoms interacting in confusion."[33]

But how typical could the judge's ordeal have been? A further incident presents a scenario that is, ostensibly, quite different. According to the chronicler Simone Filipepi, in 1486 a confessed thief and sodomite called Pacchierotto, "one of the most shameful men of Florence" (*uno de'più vituperosi huomini di Fiorenza*), was sentenced to public humiliation and perpetual imprisonment. Wearing a large miter of infamy, he was whipped and led around the city until he reached Le Stinche. Entering the compound, Pacchierotto was received by "the sodomites, the thieves, and the blasphemers, who were all awaiting him joyfully."

> Upon arrival, they made him their new *capitano*, joyously singing together for some entertainment. Since he was so well esteemed by the group, they sat him at the head of the table with another miter, bigger than the first. Poor Pacchierotto was weeping because of his shame and the pain of the flogging. But seeing among those ribalds some who had their foreheads branded, some without a nose or ears, some with only one arm, and others who were worse off than he, he was somewhat consoled. And thus he remained quite honorably in that place for several years.[34]

Unlike Sacchetti's delicate judge, Pacchierotto took Le Stinche by the throat. The shame of the outside world soon gave way to new honors as the thieving sodomite reclined at the head of a festive table, was "crowned" with an enormous new miter, and was cheered by his cronies. Yet the warm reception he won was not merely entertainment, a perverse display of a personality cult, or even a ritual "rejection of rejecters."[35] However mockingly Filipepi tried to render the scene, the celebration, much like Massaleo's sexual affront, sought to reinscribe status roles within the prison.[36] An arch-deviant such as Pacchierotto (purposely imaged as Savonarola's antithesis) was made a leader, a *capitano* of dissidents, though without displaying much agency on his part, as the recurrent use of the passive voice suggests. Still, his power in the subverted world of the prison was not entirely divorced from external, normative values. For the new leader, though beaten and humiliated, drew much of his confidence from being physically intact. Thus, in their different ways, both the young judge and Pacchierotto retained something of their identities at the prison gate. This continuity may have been the key to the former's disgrace and to the latter's success.

The above accounts of prison social dynamics in the making convey complementary experiences. It is likely, however, that the judge's ordeal was more common than Pacchierotto's festive reception, not only because there is less room "at the top," but also because most men entered prison as debtors and minor offenders rather than as seasoned criminals. Yet both cases confirm that the constant trickle of convicts into prison served as a daily reminder of external realities. This human ebb and flow, along with the presence of a long-standing inmate community, supported both imported and indigenous aspects of prison culture.[37] Human traffic, moreover, ensured that the prison was not a social or cultural threshold, although some of its internal dynamics, as we shall see, were geared toward subverting external structures.

FAMILIAR ORDER: THE WARDS

Whether purpose-built or appropriated piecemeal, municipal prisons were arranged to reflect external normative classifications and assist in controlling a diverse inmate population. In Siena, a resolution from 5 February 1297 called for the designation of separate spaces for condemned malefactors, debtors, women (for whatever cause), and persons about to stand trial, "except for the noblemen of the city or *contado* and the good men of the city," for whom the podesta was encouraged to find more suitable accommodations, where they might be detained after paying a surety.[38] In one form or another, such

divisions were common throughout Italy and beyond.[39] Another basic
distinction (and its concomitant physical division) was made between
men and women, whose separation reduced the threat of heterosexual
misconduct and violence. Last, the simple grouping of inmates into
discrete spaces—for instance, according to crime, socioeconomic status,
or health—reduced friction, prevented outbreaks of mass violence, and
helped reduce the spread of disease. Certain felons were even placed in
solitary confinement if they were deemed particularly violent, potentially subversive, or seriously ill.

All this may seem banal, even obsolete, from the perspective of modern security and medicine, with their preference for individual cells.[40]
Yet the establishment of wards marked another significant departure
from previous practices, be it the solitude of feudal dungeons and aristocratic towers, or the mass incarceration of war captives.[41] Underlying
this development was the notion that violence—between officials and
inmates, as well as among the latter—was undesirable, as were rampant
diseases. Thus, if prison wards reflected some fear of losing control over
the inmates, they also disclose a preference for maintaining culprits
alive, safe, and in reasonable health—a tendency approvingly noted by
contemporary chroniclers.[42]

Dignity and security, however, were not the only motivations for
building wards. It was no less important, at least in principle, to distinguish among categories of offenders. The men who petitioned to construct a new prison in Siena in 1327 called for a facility "in which there
would be distinct places for holding perpetrators of major offenses, for
those of minor offenses, and for those held for debt."[43] A similar distribution of wards either existed or was aspired to throughout Italy and
beyond.[44] Separation of the sexes was usually instituted earlier and was
therefore more common, as was that between laymen and clerics, wherever the episcopal palace lacked an adequate facility.[45] Such conclusive
evidence for a variety of divisions within medieval prisons challenges
at least one scholar's assertion that men, women, and children were
separated for the first time in nineteenth-century facilities.[46]

Segregation according to offense was only loosely maintained,
however. Given that space was limited and that the inmate community
was in constant flux, a degree of improvisation was to be expected, to
which the wardens and guards' corruptibility could have lent a help-
ing hand.[47] *Ad personam* arrangements are recorded, and the sparsely
populated women's wards could periodically be altered to accommodate other inmates.[48] A further obstacle to maintaining rigid legal
distinctions was the category of debt. As demonstrated in chapter 2,
"debt" served as a catchall title for a wide variety of offenses, from
gambling, to fraud, to violent assault. Thus, congregating all debtors in

one ward only seemingly implemented the magistrates' policy while in fact undermining it. The prevalent division among Venetian inmates, for instance, was that between convicts (including debtors) and those under interrogation, held in the palace's lower and upper prisons, respectively. Yet even here the distinction was never clear-cut, despite the efforts of the judges at the court of appeals, who demanded in 1309 that sentences specify a miscreant's place of incarceration, where he or she was to serve the full sentence.[49]

Notwithstanding legislative efforts, then, wealth, status, and connections, rather than the gravity of an offense, were more consequential to one's placement in prison.[50] Anyone who could afford it paid to ameliorate his conditions, whether formally through agevolatura (when this was available), by reaching an ad hominem agreement with the government, or through an informal arrangement with the prison staff.

Wealth and social status had little effect on two categories of prisoners. As a rule, and not only in theory, women could not better their conditions; they were all held in a single ward, a fact that probably reflects their numerical inferiority rather than official prejudice.[51] The isolation of female inmates as a group left them more prone to abuse. In 1363, Luchetto, a Bolognese prison employee (familiare), victimized a female inmate called Madalena, threatening that, unless she had sex with him, she would suffer greatly and never be released. Luchetto's coercion was discovered, however, and soon he joined the inmates' rank and file.[52] But such incidents, in Bologna and elsewhere, would continue. In 1366, Niccolò Bertolucci, a local guard, entered the women's ward with a number of his associates, seeking sexual gratification. He threatened two inmates, Garda and Constantia, with placement in a section of the prison called "the oven" (lo forno; perhaps a torture chamber, or else an empty threat) unless they agreed to have sex with him. Constantia, the inmate who explicitly rejected Niccolò, was subsequently raped, while Garda was taken to some upper chamber.[53] The following year, nine Florentine inmates were fined five lire each for approaching Le Stinche's women's ward "in order to chat" (ad parlandum).[54]

Understandably, then, magistrates were reluctant to establish wards for female offenders in their new communal prisons. As noted in chapter 1, such facilities were founded in Bologna in 1328 and in Venice only in the 1360s. Prior to that, women in both cities were sent to monasteries. But even once established, these wards remained highly segregated: in Florence female culprits were locked behind three different locks whose keys were distributed among several functionaries;[55] and in Bologna an entirely separate staff supervised the women's ward at least for the first decade of its existence.[56] In fine, independent women's wards developed much earlier than is usually supposed, even if their raison d'être, eliminating the abuse of female inmates, proved to be only a partial success.[57]

The other group of prisoners assigned specific quarters were the infirm and, less frequently, the insane. To be sure, sickrooms were later additions to most medieval prisons. Well into the 1350s there was no such facility even at the elaborate Le Stinche, and a physician was the latest addition to the permanent staff there.[58] In late 1320s Venice, a surgeon named Ricobaldo used to treat the inmates free of charge despite his own poverty,[59] although sick prisoners could be temporarily or permanently released, as would those deemed mentally unstable.[60] Usually, however, Venetian invalids moved to more comfortable cells with the proviso that time spent under ameliorated conditions would not count toward the completion of their sentences.[61] Thus, by around 1400, sick inmates in Venice were more likely to remain in custody than delay their sentence or recover outside, even if that meant that they had to be succored by their families.[62] The Bolognese prison administration was even less prepared to deal with infirmity. When Uguicio di Martini Bernacino fell ill in March, 1326, he was allowed to seek a cure outside the prison, but not before leaving his son, Cabriogino, in his stead.[63] More than twenty years later, there was still no medical facility or staff on the premises.[64] In Siena, a hospital ward was founded around 1340, apparently in response to the death of twenty-two inmates within two months, an exceptionally high death-toll by any account.[65] And although a medical professional is absent from the prison's payroll in later years, the creation of a prison infirmary was in line with regional developments at that time.

The distribution of inmates among wards accommodated two systems of classification—legal and socioeconomic—but was skewed toward the latter. Maintaining external social divisions such as gender, health, status, and patronage undermined the creation of an inmate community based on a criminal hierarchy. Thus, founding wards was more than a security measure—it safeguarded a social worldview precisely where it was most vulnerable. If urban space was a scripted meeting point for all and sundry,[66] the municipal prison afforded a potentially unmasked encounter for social unequals. Social memory was the Achilles heel of a purportedly egalitarian space such as the prison: no wonder that it was particularly important here to keep clerics away from prostitutes, poor offenders from merchant debtors, and the sick and insane from everyone else.

The concern for order and hierarchy was reinforced not only via static holding units, but also through movement within the compound. The personnel were veritable agents of movement with (theoretically) unlimited freedom both to wander and to shift inmates around; the

agevolati, or privileged inmates, gained some spatial liberty by vir-
tue of their status, wealth, or patronage; the poor and run-of-the-mill
prisoners were mostly restricted to their wards, but even they had
greater liberty than the women, the sick, and, where relevant, the insane. Ironically, and as modern prison studies frequently confirm, staff
members were themselves prisoners of sorts. For despite their relative
mobility within the walls, they too were free to roam only certain areas
of the compound, which they could not leave at will.

The social order that the wards embodied was frequently undermined, be it through charitable intervention or financial necessities.
Occasionally, as in Siena, the wardens had to maintain a certain number
of poor prisoners among the agevolati;[67] and while health and gender
remained firm categories of inmate classification, agevolatura status lost
much of its original prestige over time. It was suggested in chapter 2 that
agevolatura rates (and prison fees in general) were deflated throughout
the later fourteenth century in an attempt to maximize the prison's revenues; and that what had prompted these adjustments was the general
impoverishment of the inmate population. From a different perspective,
however, reducing the fees also broadened the socioeconomic basis of
the prison's privileged group. Thus, the impetus of these adjustments
may have been both the preservation of social order as well as economic
viability. By allowing external hierarchies, however diluted, to remain
grafted onto the prison's physical layout, urban magistrates avoided a
leveled playing field and what otherwise might have been perceived as
an inmate population that could be dangerously egalitarian.

DAILY LIFE: ORDER AND DISSIDENCE

One of the startling differences between liberty and imprisonment
today is the potential strictness of the latter's routine—an environment
where "power is articulated directly onto time."[68] This is especially true
for those who, prior to their incarceration, led an uninhibited or even
abandoned criminal lifestyle, and for whom the regimentation of time is
often the source of great distress.[69] Nothing, however, could have been
more foreign to medieval prison inmates than a formal daily schedule;
there simply was none.[70]

Although both a rigid timetable and its total absence can create
monotony, sheer boredom was a central aspect of medieval prison life.
Prisoners seldom worked, and diversions were scarce: visits were limited, reading material hard to come by, space for recreational activities
mostly unavailable, alcohol prohibited (outside of Venice), and prostitutes rare. Financial and legal affairs could occupy some of a prisoner's

time, but these were often over within several weeks, and seldom guaranteed even an occasional leave.[71] Begging outside the walls was only intermittently allowed even before the practice was gradually abandoned in favor of employing penitential friars.[72] There were, of course, the daily masses and bread distributions, the weekly sermons and the supervisory committee's visits, and the city's liturgical cycle, which the inmates were well positioned to follow, however vicariously, during solemn oblations on major feasts or victories. All these were something to look forward to while counting the days.

Prison life was a struggle. The few that could, read and wrote.[73] At Le Stinche, literate inmates could occasionally earn some money by copying manuscripts.[74] Others left invaluable personal impressions of their experiences. Ser Jacopo del Pecora of Montepulciano, imprisoned at Le Stinche for more than fifteen years, composed letters and poetry in terza rima.[75] While incarcerated in the Sienese prisons, the Florentine burlesque poet Burchiello (1404–49) wrote: "I have no water except for the roof drops, / Nor the sun if it is not checkered. / I can't have bread unless of affliction; / If I was ever happy, let evil kill me."[76] Dino di Tura, who languished for several months at Le Stinche in 1343, wryly declared that "the prison is the best place in the world … its doors are open to anyone."[77] And Adoardus de Assisi, vicar to the papal legate in Bologna, where he was imprisoned in 1362, describes a fate worse than death: "Since Fortune so / Cruelly cast me down, / I pray to you, / Death, earnestly, / To end these sorry tears."[78]

Inmates also passed their time by decorating the cells with graffiti. They carved day-charts, lamented their fate, composed prayers, recorded deaths, and occasionally drew objects such as buildings, ships, and human figures.[79] Other prisoners blasphemed and sang dirty songs,[80] struck up illicit conversations with female inmates,[81] conspired to escape, or plotted revenge against personal enemies or the government.[82] Those who were fortunate enough to be incarcerated in Venice could purchase duty-free wine (possibly due to the damp weather), but elsewhere drinking was forbidden.[83] Some inmates engaged—and at times forced others to engage—in homosexual or heterosexual intercourse.[84] But by far the most popular pastime seems to have been gambling, an activity formally forbidden within the prison (and often scorned outside) for its perceived blasphemous nature and its potential for debt and violence.[85]

Violence, however, had an independent existence, irreducible to a by-product of gambling. Alarmed by repeated acts of aggression at Le Stinche, the Florentine magistrates ordered in 1355 that any inmate who injured another must be summarily tried by the podesta and pay the condemnation within eight days, or else have an arm amputated.[86] Yet

Fig. 3.2. Inmate graffiti from the Pozzi, Venice, depicting St. Mark's Tower and an invocation (undated).

even if the regulation was enforced, its deterring power was weak. For inmates routinely turned on one another, and rape, brawling, and stabbing were common: Naso di Baldo of San Felice confessed to a sexual assault;[87] Cataldo di Baroco was placed in solitary confinement for one month, "on bread and water," for beating a fellow inmate;[88] a day after Biagio di Filippo struck Ubicinio di Gentile "with an empty hand," the latter retaliated by stabbing Biagio with a knife;[89] and so it goes.[90] These particular incidents left no casualties, but others did.[91] It is against this background that we can perhaps begin to understand the fear of Marco, the young Venetian mentioned above, who would languish three years behind oars rather than spend six months behind bars.

Interpretations of modern inmate violence—physical, sexual, verbal, and emotional—abound.[92] And whether seen as a sinister aspect of an indigenous culture or as yet another arena for ensuing struggles outside the prison walls, such activity is commonly agreed to be endemic.[93] Medieval documents lack much of the circumstantial data that would facilitate a responsible investigation of prison violence, at least by modern sociological criteria. The succinct descriptions of such incidents and the obscured biographies of run-of-the-mill inmates inhibit geographical or socioeconomic profiling of either victims or aggressors. Age, for instance, commonly perceived today as a mitigating factor in aggressive behavior,[94] is rarely reported in the available documentation for the Middle Ages. The same paucity of information likewise prevents any meaningful estimate of the relation between violent behavior and the length of an inmate's sentence, the time elapsed from his arrest, or his (potential) proximity to release.

One pattern that does emerge, however, is that violence concentrated almost exclusively within the inmate community. Only on rare occasions, such as during mass riots (usually instigated in the context of external political turmoil) did prisoners assault staff. On 20 August 1322, the Bolognese prison guards lost control over some armed inmates, who forcefully broke the prison gate; and in the upheaval precipitating the expulsion of the Duke of Athens from Florence in 1343, inmates trashed Le Stinche and, shrewdly, destroyed its archive. In neither these nor later cases, however, were the personnel severely injured.[95] To be sure, whether prisoners perceived themselves to be locked in a perennial struggle with their captors is an entirely different matter. It seems, for instance, that animosity between prison inmates and staff today could hardly be overstated, yet seldom does it escalate into open physical conflict. This, in turn, has to do with the prison's highly controlled environment and the potential repercussions—personal and collective—of such acts. Yet even in the relatively loose environment of medieval prisons, with their open wards and a low guard/inmate ratio, the former were hardly ever hurt.

We have already encountered an important function of prison violence, namely, the creation or affirmation of status roles. In the accounts of Sacchetti and Filipepi examined above, status and sexual roles were created through shaming or molestation. But other methods such as verbal threats or physical assaults could be equally effective. In this sense, medieval inmates and men at large shared similar cultural values; physical brutality permeated Italian urban society, with its proclivity to violence and vendetta.[96] Thus, as in the free world, violence in prisons was a tool for both enforcing and contesting public order.[97] Indeed, as a major aspect of inmate culture, aggression among inmates was integral to the daily struggle against officialdom.[98] And along with drinking, escape, and gambling, violence can be seen as an attempt to emerge from anonymity and "beat the system,"[99] an endeavor that, ever since the foundation of communal prisons, continued to evolve. If, for instance, in 1349 the supervisors of Le Stinche were supposed to investigate gambling and drinking as typical violations among inmates, by 1366 the list of potential infractions, as related in the supervisors' charter, expanded to include swearing and blasphemy, prostitution (both among inmates and by means of importing prostitutes), entry into the women's ward, sodomy, illicit contacts with the outside world, and general disregard for prison regulations, including physical assault.[100] The pattern of dissident behavior in prison was one of continuous expansion and adaptation.

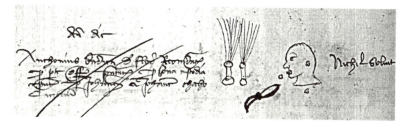

Fig. 3.3. Flogging and dismemberment of a Bolognese inmate. To the right of the initial entry, and where the details of an inmate's release or punishment were normally recorded, the scribe drew two whips, a knife, and the inmate's cut-out tongue and left ear. The inscription (and presumed justification) at the far right reads, "Nichil solvit": paid nothing. Archivio di Stato di Bologna, *Uffici a Competenza Specifica*, Soprastante alle Prigioni b. 1, Reg. 6, fol. 34r (October 1402). (By kind permission of the Archivio di Stato di Bologna.)

But if the charter of Le Stinche's supervisors serves as a barometer of inmate dissidence, the mercury's *rate* of decline remained slow throughout our period: no storm was in sight. Indeed, the annals of the tumultuous fourteenth century contain not a single instance in which a government had to repress an inmate riot that was independent of external political unrest. Considering prisons' small staffs and relatively lax security, wardens were fairly successful in reducing the risk of concerted inmate violence. To do so they employed two methods. The first was to preclude personnel from executing corporal punishments or from being involved in torture, as was done in Florence, Siena, and elsewhere.[101] But such a policy was not everywhere applied: Venetian upper prison guards participated in torture sessions, and their Bolognese counterparts could augment their salaries by flogging inmates and performing dismemberments and even executions.[102] A rare burst of "creativity" recorded in a Bolognese prison register (fig. 3.3) perhaps bears witness to the staff's dual capacity. But a second and arguably more efficient method to avoid incurring the inmates' wrath was to allow their lives to be sufficiently tolerable. And what partly rendered the experience tolerable was the maintenance of ties with the outside world.

THE WORLD OUTSIDE

Passing through Venice en route to the Holy Land in 1484, Felix Fabri, a wandering German friar, remarked on the locals' sense of compassion: "Not only do they exhibit piety toward those who merit it, but also toward those who deserve the harshest discipline." What had occasioned the observation was the pilgrim's encounter with the local prisons:

> The malefactors' prisons, located under the palace's promenade, have a view of the public square, and are illuminated by open windows that are blocked by iron bars. Through these windows the inmates can look out, stretch their hands, and converse with the nearby crowd. And if they are poor, they can ask passersby for alms.

"One of the many cruelties of the Germans," the author reflected on his native land, "is that the malefactors' prisons are inhuman, frightening, and dark; located in the depths of towers, humid, cold, and often crawling with snakes and toads; far apart from any humans."[103] Medieval German prisons remain a major scholarly lacuna, but whether Fabri's characterization was real or imagined, from a broader, regional perspective it was precisely this type of prison that was gradually relinquishing its place.

To be sure, even this famous account of Venice's prisons is idealized in more than one respect, influenced as it was by Fabri's reformist ideals and the audience he had in mind.[104] Nevertheless, and despite his minor temporal remove, Fabri observed the same compound and essentially the same regime of the period under investigation. More importantly, his description underscores two prevalent features of medieval prison life: visibility and accessibility. As we have seen, urban prisons were both conspicuous and physically central, in keeping with a concerted effort to integrate them into a new public sphere and expedite the work of the courts. But, perhaps in unintended ways, the prison's location deeply affected the inmates' welfare.

For prisons were not fortified islands, impermeable to the stream of medieval urban life. Political, religious, legal, and commercial activities never engulfed or washed over them without leaving sediment and carrying residue. Apart from the myriad public officials, clergymen, friars, confraternity members, lawyers, notaries, businessmen, creditors, victims, service givers, prostitutes, and family members who encountered the inmates on a daily basis, the facility's central location guaranteed its constant exposure to anyone working in or passing through a city's center. The inmates' cries, their outstretched hands, even their scent, were strongly present.[105] And, as the next section illustrates, prisoner oblations on major feasts gave palpable and symbolic expression to their position in the civic hierarchy. Even in the hectic routine of urban life, prison inmates were hard to ignore: the parishioners of San Simone resided across from Le Stinche's walls;[106] in Bologna, fifteen artisans and merchants plied their trades in shops hard by the lower prison.[107] A high mortality rate among Sienese inmates and the squalor of the existing facilities moved several citizens to petition for a new prison;[108] and, as described in the prologue, a similar threat of mass death at Le Stinche, during the 1333 flood, prompted the government's intervention. The visibility of prisoners was not limited to Italy. In 1395, a certain Gaillart took pity on a desolate woman thrown into a chamber at the king's prison at Le Puy, France, on the charge of murder. After pleading unsuccessfully with Rossignol, the jailer, Gaillart, accompanied by a group of friends, stormed the place, dragged Rossignol outside and severely beat him.[109] The public eye was watchful.

Visibility, moreover, was accompanied by accessibility. Soon after his arrival to prison, Il Grasso, the "framed" protagonist of a 1410 tale, received a flask of wine, some bread, and other food items sent by his friends outside. He was also able to communicate freely and frequently through the prison windows.[110] Though imaginary, the story faithfully conveys how basic arrangements of prison life relied on external intervention. If there was a black market in prison, nowhere does it emerge from the available sources. There seem to have been no formal restrictions on personal items (candles, bedding, writing materials, etc.), although searches for and confiscations of weapons and potential escape aids did occur (see below).

Where there was no kitchen, as in Florence and Venice, families, charitable individuals, and confraternity officials routinely fed the inmates.[111] In Bologna, where meals could be purchased, poor prisoners often could not afford them, and had to rely on a friar funded by the commune for their daily bread.[112] Family members and other individuals could offer medical aid, at least prior to the foundation of sickrooms. In Florence, arguably the most self-sufficient of Italian prisons, the chaplain held mass at the internal chapel, but elsewhere communion and confession depended on visiting friars and priests.[113] The inmates and staff's reliance on a constant interaction with the outside world meant that access to prisoners was monitored but not restricted; only under exceptional circumstances did inmates resort to pleading for visitation rights.[114]

Among the many pains of present-day imprisonment, severing ties with the outside world is considered not only the harshest, but also the most deleterious, for both the prisoner and his or her family. Conversely, social psychologists of the modern prison have emphasized time and again the direct relation between the availability of outside contact and the inmates' reduced recourse to violence and violation of the prison's behavioral code.[115] On average, convicts today are eligible for one monthly visit that lasts thirty minutes.[116] That is, in the span of one year, a prisoner can see his spouse and children for a total of six hours— provided, of course, that he maintains his visiting privileges and that his family can afford the sometimes long and costly trip. Accordingly,

a convict's main (and often sole) representative of the free world today
is the guard, who in a sense is no less a prisoner. The outcome, it is
argued, is often a polarized and antagonistic view of society, a view
that for many can become an obstacle for reintegration and a catalyst
for antisocial behavior in prison.[117] Not surprisingly, prison reformers
often reiterate the need to liberalize visitation procedures and increase
the inmates' exposure to members of society at large, including, in the
case of male convicts, women.[118]

Not all modern studies conclude in favor of convicts' maintenance
of intimate ties or liberalizing their access to free society.[119] Yet, if not
a panacea for recidivism, there is a growing consensus that *structured*
engagement with the outside world is likely to reduce the pains of
imprisonment and facilitate a smoother transition into life at large.[120]
As we have seen, the semi-inclusive nature of medieval incarceration
obviated total social seclusion. And while the permeable walls of these
institutions did not necessarily reduce violence within and crime outside, they enabled prisoners to maintain strong daily ties with their
families, friends, spiritual guides, and professional associates. There
were, of course, certain negative and even dangerous ramifications to
such access, such as the smuggling of weapons, the trafficking of prostitutes, and potential threats to convicts' antagonists on the outside.
Furthermore, prison breakouts that were predicated on external assistance were more frequent than independent escapes (see below). And
it is also worth considering that an inmate's proximity and access to his
family and friends may have exacerbated, rather than diminished, the
emotional stress of separation.

The Journey's End: Death, Escape, Release

There may be fifty ways to leave your lover, but there were only five
to leave a medieval prison: in a solemn procession, in broad daylight,
under the cover of night, with a help of a friend, or in the coroner's cart;
in other words, through amnesty, parole or any formal termination of
a sentence, in an unaided escape or assisted breakout, and upon death,
whatever its cause. By and large, most prisoners in this period left the
prison behind after paying their imposed fine or debt, or once their
original or modified sentences were completed.

Judging by the extant registers of Le Stinche from the second half of
the fourteenth century, between 38 and 53 percent of all new inmates
were released within half a year. Of those whose incarceration crossed
into the next administrative term, between 70 and 82 percent were set
free within the following six months.[121]

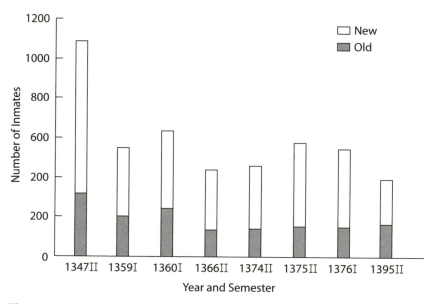

Fig. 3.4. Inmate turnover at Le Stinche. Based on Archivio di Stato di Firenze, *Soprastanti alle Stinche*, Carcerati 82–85, 88–91.

Death rates were low among the Italian urban prisons. And were it not for famine, plagues, and political altercations—and these were rampant in the fourteenth century—the number of inmates who died incarcerated would have been lower still. The figure of sixty casualties within two years cited in 1327 by the petitioners for a new prison in Siena is exceptionally high, as is the reported loss of twenty-two inmates there during January and February 1340.[122] By contrast, between 1332 and 1387 only seven prisoners are reported to have died at Venice;[123] the first wave of the Black Death struck down the relatively low figure of twenty-five inmates at Le Stinche, in contrast to Villani's claim that the daily death toll there was two or three; and during a less eventful semester, the prison's notary reported a total of three deaths.[124] Significantly, there is no indication that any of these incidents were the result of a suicide or self-injury. And although such incidents were periodically reported elsewhere, they never approached their startling current rates of between two and sixteen (!) times higher than that in free society, constituting present-day inmates' primary "cause" of death.[125] But if deaths were uncommon, escapes were surprisingly rare. The following case, recorded in fourteenth-century Siena, illustrates some of the complications involved.

The grounds for Chiaretto Fianno's arrest are unknown.[126] Whatever the charges, the conditions of his incarceration were relatively favorable, for he was free to wander within the prison. The compound itself was divided into separate wards where conditions differed: some inmates were immobilized, others, like Chiaretto, belonged to a privileged group whose benefits included better access to the outside world. By contrast, his fellow inmates, Goro di Giacomo and Domenico di Ghiro, were chained down. This renders somewhat puzzling their precise knowledge of when one of their sisters and one of their fathers were to drop off two chisels, a necessary first step for their escape.[127] Perhaps word got through with a new inmate, perhaps arrangements were made when they last saw one another, perhaps a prison guard was bribed to run an illicit errand.[128] In any case, the information remained useless without access to the window through which the chisels were to be delivered. Goro and Domenico decided to contact Chiaretto.

Once again, their choice of courier and method of solicitation remain a mystery. They may have paid him (though this is never mentioned in the records), they may have appealed to his non-Sienese affinities (which they shared),[129] or they may have offered to include him in their plan. Speculations aside, Goro and Domenico convinced Chiaretto to perform a rather crucial service.

Chiaretto obtained the chisels, but it was not long before the incriminating possessions were discovered. In fact, Chiaretto never had the chance to pass them on. Caught during the inspection rounds of Giacomo d'Ambroggio, the vigilant prison warden, Chiaretto was fined the substantial sum of one thousand lire, payable within ten days. The plan was foiled, and although we do not know what became of Goro and Domenico, Chiaretto continued to languish in prison. By the time the General Council reviewed his appeal for charitable release, he had already been eleven months and six days behind bars, not enough time— in the Council's opinion—to secure his pardon. The request was denied.

Francesco Berni, a later Florentine poet, would have us believe that the medieval prison was literally a "factory" of escapes: "There you can hear the noise of hammers, / Of picks, and of beams [working] to send / Free anyone hither and thither."[130] The description is apt, considering that prison walls were rarely strong, high, or particularly well guarded. Moreover, access to the outside world was frequent, and the personnel were notoriously corruptible: the threat of an enormous fine for aiding escape often proved to be an insufficient deterrent for these modestly paid officials.[131] Given all this, it is not surprising that men like Goro and Domenico attempted to flee, but that they did it so rarely.

In 1291, during a shortage of food at the Sienese prison, inmates were allowed to beg around the city, "based on the belief that escape might condemn them to even greater hunger."[132] Indeed, the relatively low rate of escapes was due substantially to the inmate's options once outside. For a successful escape only begins by leaving the prison; how to survive beyond its walls is a different challenge altogether. The anonymity of the modern metropolis and the availability of transportation were not characteristic of medieval urban centers. A convict on the run had to remain in hiding—an impossible feat given the scale of medieval cities—or else flee—a choice that was impractical for men without considerable means. Escape (and extended contumacy, for that matter) meant a significant change in one's life, and few were willing to make this sacrifice given the dangers it entailed: between 1316 and 1393 merely thirteen successful and botched escapes were recorded at Venice, that is, roughly one event every six years; the Bolognese criminal-court records reveal a similar infrequency; and an even lower rate is recorded for Arras, where no incidents were reported during the entire first half of the fourteenth century.[133] Berni's verses, in short, were an exercise in wishful thinking: the prison's invisible walls were a more powerful deterrent than its physical ones.[134]

That said, prisoners originating from the city's hinterland and residents of other cities and regions probably stood a better chance of regaining their liberty. Goro and Domenico not only had a place to return to, but also enjoyed "logistical" support from their kin. It was perhaps naive of them to ignore the commune's ability to reach into its own *contado*, but the area outside the city walls was more congenial to a semiclandestine life, at least for a while. Citizens of other cities could be almost certain of a better fate if and when they reached their homes, since there was a very slim chance that their own governments would hand them back. At worst, they could be tried and perhaps even reincarcerated among their own people. It is no coincidence therefore that of the three attempted escapes recorded for Bologna between 1355 and 1364, the first was by a Florentine and the second by a resident of the city's hinterland. The third attempt was organized by a group of inmates, of which at least seven men (of nine) were not residents of the city.[135]

A final method of release was to offer prisoners at the altar of a major church during special feasts. On Christmas Day, 1337, for instance, Sienese citizens and visitors gathered at the local cathedral could observe a solemn procession approaching its final stage. In their highly ordered sequence, the group advancing up the hill represented the city's idealized hierarchy, from its highest officers to the members of its guilds and parishes. Closing the procession that day were a number of prisoners in white garb.

The group entered the cathedral and passed in front of the altar, holding candles in their hands. Among them was Tuccio Salvi of San Giovanni, who insulted one of the priors' sons, and was fined 105 lire. Failing payment, he remained incarcerated for two years. Also present was Pacino, a Florentine residing in San Antonio. Over a year before he offended Dota Giovanni of San Abbia with "injurious deeds and words," for which he was fined 50 lire. Unable or unwilling to pay the sum, he languished in prison thereafter. Then there was Vannuccio Renaldi of Cegnano in the Sienese *contado*, fined 75 lire for theft over one year previously and incarcerated ever since. Ginocco Maccioli of Casanuovola, also in the Sienese *contado*, had been fined 200 lire for assaulting Andrea Vanni and a further 30 lire for selling salt without a license. He, too, did not pay his condemnation, and had been in prison for two years. And there were eight others, each convicted and subsequently imprisoned upon failure to pay their fines: veteran and recent inmates, with original fines ranging from 2 to 600 lire, Sienese and foreigners, natives and immigrants, men and women—all stood solemnly at the altar that day, waiting to regain their freedom.[136]

They were released as an act of charity and thanksgiving that had by then become routine. Three times a year—on Christmas, Easter, and the Feast of the Assumption (the Virgin was Siena's patron saint)—a committee would select a number of inmates who met the basic criteria for oblation, usually a minimum stay of six months and, in case a private debt was involved, the creditor's consent. The lists were then presented at the General Council, debated, modified, and finally approved. Of the sixteen inmates eligible for release that Christmas, only twelve were released.

Offering prisoners was a fairly common rite well beyond Tuscany.[137] (In Venice the practice was occasional rather than routine, and was usually prompted by an important victory or a military upset.)[138] In most cases, oblation was a highly regulated measure: minimum-stay requirements and maximum debts or fines, both of which varied from town to town and between periods, were strictly applied, and the accuser's consent (or that of his or her family) had to be obtained. In any case, many inmates owed their freedom to solemn oblations: in 1328, at least seventeen men and one woman left the Bolognese prison this way; in 1332 the number of oblates rose to sixty-nine.[139] In Siena, fifty-four inmates, including nine women, were offered throughout 1324, twenty-seven (among whom four were women) in 1328, sixty (fifteen women) in 1329, fifty-two (twelve women) in 1337, and thirty-three (five women) in 1361.[140] And a decade before the foundation of Le Stinche, Florentine magistrates could already liberate between twenty-five and fifty prisoners during each of the three major feasts, although the actual figures were somewhat lower because of a recurring shortage of inmates who could meet the relevant criteria.[141] In principle, however, the average annual number of oblates presented at St. John's Baptistery could make up a full quarter of the released inmates.[142]

Oblation was a concluding act in an unfolding legal drama. These solemnities ended a convict's passage through the prison by way of a ritual return to free society. As such, releases reflected the idealized purpose of incarceration. The available descriptions of the rite evoke an image of the offered inmates as purified citizens: humble, dressed in white, and bearing a candle—the symbol of Christ—they advanced at the procession's rear, and proceeded to the altar, where they were ritually "sacrificed" on behalf of the commune. The event contrasted sharply and aptly with the defamatory and often violent processions of culprits, events that often commenced and sometimes ended at the prison gates.[143] The ritual cycle thus completed frames the liturgical and symbolic roles of incarceration in the economy of civic justice.

The notion that imprisonment is a transformative experience was far from new in the late Middle Ages. As we shall see in the next chapter, the nexus of incarceration and spiritual purgation already pervades early Christian martyrology and exercised a strong influence on centuries of monastic spirituality. Moreover, perpetrators of major crimes were commonly "imprisoned" in local chapels in preparation for their public penance during the Easter liturgy.[144] The focus on the socially rehabilitative role of the local prison comes into sharper relief in a unique procedure developed in Florence. On numerous occasions, convicted citizens who were not yet or no longer incarcerated, and who had pacified their accusers, were granted a "nonsolemn absolution" by the priors. The pertinent provisions stipulated that the offender was to go into one of the prisons (Le Stinche, the Volognana, and, for a brief period, the Magnati Prison) and have his or her name entered in the prison register. There was no minimum-stay requirement at the prison, but every such provision specified that the culprit had to be physically present "within the enclosure or the walls surrounding those prisons" (*in claustro seu intra muros circondantes ipsos carceres*), whence he or she was to proceed independently to St. John's.[145] How to interpret this abbreviated incarceration? An element of deterrence seems to have been involved in the offender's exposure to the prison. But retaining both the prison and the altar as pivots in the process implies the impossibility of forgiveness without token suffering, of reintegration without symbolic exclusion, of absolution without incarceration.

Both solemn and nonsolemn oblations were scripted, ritualized acts. As such, they served as a clarifying lens: oblations were idealized scenarios that drew force from their incongruity, not compatibility, with reality.[146] Since the procession's order reflected the city's ideal social contract, the staged composure of the offered inmates portrayed their desired penitence but at the same time hinted at their negative character, as perceived by free society.[147] This suggests that contemporaries were aware of the prison's social realities, including its shortcomings in curbing deviance, let alone in effecting remorse or spiritual purification. In fine, inmate oblations were premised on an open secret about the experience and function of the prison.

CONCLUSIONS

> Before the days of Howard and Bentham and the Philadelphia Quakers, nobody, for some odd reason, seems ever to have thought of making prisons orderly and efficient. … [T]here existed, not a world of men and women, not even a world of beasts, but a chaos, a pandemonium.[148]

In light of their material conditions and the treatment that inmates received there, medieval prisons were wont to be unpleasant places. All things considered, however, their current stereotype as "hellholes" or, as Huxley suggests, a Hobbesian "natural state" is undeserved. By coeval living standards prisons were far from intolerable. Urban inns, for instance, were notoriously crowded, filthy, and often dangerous;[149] and low-income *family* accommodations could consist of a cramped, wooden single room.[150] Before the onset of the plague cycle in 1348, western European cities were densely populated, and public hygiene fell well short of stringent bylaws.[151] In contrast, local magistrates routinely purged their prisons to reduce crowding, and under normal conditions death rates among inmates, whether from disease, violence, or suicide, were low, and escape attempts rare. A host of functionaries, family members, service-givers, and charitable individuals frequented the prisons, and brought a measure of solace to the prisoners' lives. Even the poorest inmate received some food, had access to legal and spiritual counsel, and was sooner or later released. Unlike today, the major danger that a medieval prisoner faced was a spiraling debt, not physical survival in an ultraviolent cage.

Urban prisons were far from being dumping grounds for dissidents. This is nowhere more evident than in the physical and administrative modification of these facilities throughout the late thirteenth and fourteenth centuries. As we have seen, prisons did not simply expand along with the growing rates of incarceration, but were rethought. Founding chapels and infirmaries, investing in staff accommodations, and digging fountains within these compounds all reflect widespread recognition of and adaptation to long-term imprisonment. Hiring friars and public advocates likewise responded to a major presence of impoverished inmates, whose length of incarceration was often beyond their control. The quest for efficiency entailed the assembly of all captives, including the often-segregated female, infirm, and insane miscreants, into one central space. And the division of this space into wards was geared toward preserving social classifications that were threatened by centralization. All this required attention and forethought, not neglect.

While contesting these facilities' image as earthly infernos, this chapter also questioned their understanding as liminal spaces. Apart from prisons' central location and accessibility, the grafting of normative divisions and external hierarchies onto their internal design strongly suggests an experience that was unlike wavering "between two worlds," or of being "neither here nor there ... betwixt and between the positions arrayed by law, custom, convention and ceremonial."[152] Moreover, as stressed throughout this chapter, an inmate's social ties with the outside world were altered but not severed, as they would have been in an ideal liminal condition. Most male prisoners, for example, could maintain their extramural status by situating themselves in an appropriate ward, through arranging for suitable services, and by relying on existing patronage ties. And, in fact, egalitarianism—a key characteristic of liminality—posed a serious threat to the smooth running of prisons, whose administrators were invested in safeguarding social divisions, not only for the sake of profit, but also, and perhaps primarily, in order to defend social order at its most vulnerable.

Medieval prisons operated as spatial and temporal extensions of urban life, connecting free society back to itself. And unlike their modern heirs, these facilities were not sealed corridors. To be sure, the inmates' and administrators' reliance on external support was only partly ideological, and mostly practical. There were obvious economic and administrative benefits to prisoners' daily interaction with free society, but disadvantages were plentiful. However, to judge by the patterns of prison violence, escape, and suicide rates, it seems that semi-inclusion compensated for the dangers attendant upon accessibility. But whether or not the prison engendered a sense of guilt or remorse among its residents, or, moreover, if it was perceived as an apt retribution for a culprit's offenses, is still to be determined. It is to these questions that we now turn.

Chapter Four

THE PRISON AS PLACE AND METAPHOR

IN HIS COLLECTION OF proverbial wisdom, *Libro di buoni costumi* (ca. 1360), Paolo da Certaldo lists release from prison as one of the five greatest joys, and incarceration among the five gravest sorrows, a man can experience.[1] To da Certaldo, the notion that the very same place may lead equally to exhilaration or despair was reminiscent of the doctrine of Purgatory:

> Imagine that you are in prison, abandoned by relatives and friends, with no one ever coming to see you; and someone whom you do not know comes to visit you, and takes you out of prison. What would you make of it? It is the same concerning the abandoned souls [in Purgatory], and he who prays or has prayers said for them.[2]

Juxtaposing prison and Purgatory explains the latter's economy in terms of the former's experience. By the same token, alluding to the afterlife offers a commentary on prison life: a prisoner who lacks external support, that is, whose outside contacts have failed him, is likely damned; conversely, if one can secure external aid, he might obtain interim relief and perhaps even regain his freedom.

Beyond acknowledging the importance of maintaining ties between inmates and free society, da Certaldo's observation communicates a special bond between prison and Purgatory, or more broadly speaking, between incarceration and purgation. The link had an ancient pedigree. For the previous millennium, literary conventions of portraying the prison experience gravitated around a set of metaphors that aligned suffering in captivity with intellectual and spiritual growth. Such instances appear in a number of biblical narratives and in many early Christian texts, although perhaps the most famous exemplar is Boethius's *On the Consolation of Philosophy*, composed in the early sixth century.[3] Since this body of literature often served as a point of reference and departure for medieval observers of the prison, and thus helped shape their horizons of expectations, the first part of this chapter describes how the association between imprisonment and spiritual purification originally developed, and in what contexts it was employed prior to the fourteenth century.[4]

But while the prison/Purgatory nexus remained influential both before and after the formulation of a doctrine of Purgatory by the

Fourth Lateran Council in 1215, it did not go unchallenged. As the second section of this chapter argues, the first literary departure from this association occurred during the early Middle Ages and is linked to the topos of jail-breaking saints. Following this excursus, the third and final sections demonstrate how later authors, particularly from the fourteenth century on, expounded new interpretations of the prison as a place in ways that broke with earlier conventions, for instance by portraying it as an earthly Hell, or by describing prison life without referencing a Christian hereafter. These writers' focus on the edifice of the prison can be seen as part of the reemergence of the city and its architectural constituents as a major artistic subject.[5] But the composition of both "infernalized" and "secularized" descriptions of the prison also coincided with the institution's spread, a process delineated in the previous chapters.

However interpreted, celebrated, or mocked, municipal prisons emerge from a variety of late-medieval representations as permanent components of urban space. Visible and accessible, prisons and their inmates became part of a civic discourse: the prison was listed among the city's public buildings, and its prisoners were numbered among the citizenry.

EARLY IMAGINARIES: MARTYRDOM, MONASTICISM, AND PURGATION

The literary history of medieval prisons begins with the Bible yet widely draws on late-Roman penal practices. Interpreting the prison as a place and imprisonment as an experience was part of the Judeo-Christian tradition, whose scriptures abound with prisoners and prison scenes: from Joseph's captivity, to the incarcerations of the prophets Hanani, Michaiah, and Jeremiah, to the prison execution of John the Baptist and the appearance of angels before the jailed apostles.[6] Each of these instances portrays imprisonment as unjust. Bolstering a similar antagonism, reported abuses in Roman provincial jails furthered the notion that prisons were prone to become places of punishment in practice, despite theoretical prohibitions.[7] Not surprisingly, contemporary jurists professed a particular grudge against punitive incarceration: two oft-quoted legal dicta dubbed imprisonment as "dismal to the innocent, but not harsh enough for the guilty," and as a measure "meant for the custody of men, not for their punishment."[8]

Largely as a response to their persecution under the Romans, early Christian apologists developed a basic imaginary of the prison. Martyrological narratives set in and around Roman jails introduced a literary "sweet inversion" of despair into hope, of physical suffering into spiritual empowerment, and of secular coercion into divine grace. In this way, theodicy helped disseminate incarceration as a leitmotif of Christian spirituality, first among ascetics and later in monastic circles. As we shall see, self-imposed incarceration became a common metaphor for the angelic life and soon assumed purgatorial qualities. With one exception, which will be discussed below, the tie between prisons and purgation (and later, Purgatory) went on uninterrupted for more than a millennium.

The martyrological literature conveying the experiences of Christian confessors presents the prison as a place of personal trial and eschatological triumph, and incarceration as a process of spiritual growth, potentially culminating in revelation.[9] Thus, rather than precipitating apostasy, the harsh conditions of the Roman jail accelerated religious perfection: a classic "sweet inversion." In the emphatic words that Prudentius (348–405?) attributed to Fructuosus, the martyred bishop of Tarragona (d. 259),

> Prison to the Christian faithful is the path of glory,
> Prison propels to the heavens' summit,
> Prison unites God with the blessed.[10]

As a new locus of holiness, the prison attracted substantial attention from early Christians, whether laymen or clergy. The efforts of pious individuals and local bishops soon crystallized into a work of mercy (*opus caritatis*) grounded in Christ's praise, "I was in prison, and you came to visit me" (Matt. 25:36).[11] Aid to prisoners took on a range of forms, from providing food and solace, to negotiating the inmates' conditions, to intercession through prayer.[12] On their part, imprisoned confessors helped direct their free brethren by encouraging devotion and even by drafting civic petitions, sometimes to the dismay of the local clergy.[13] As the persecutions waxed and finally waned, charity toward prisoners emerged as a highly public aspect of Christian piety, occasionally cutting across religious divisions.[14] Assisting non-Christian culprits, in turn, altered this particular form of charity from a predominantly religious statement to a subversive political act. For by emphasizing the illegitimacy of incarceration, early Christians expanded their plea for religious tolerance into a critique of Roman penal practices. Either way, the outcry against incarceration reinforced the prison's image as a cruel and unjust place, and by implication as an experience pregnant with spiritual potential.

The emergence of the Roman prison as a *Sonderwelt*, "a special place" straddling heaven and earth, where miracles multiplied and confessors received a unique spiritual baptism, developed into a

Fig. 4.1. St. Felicitas flanked by her sons and jailers. Outline of an apse mural at the Chapel of St. Felicitas, Rome (sixth\seventh century), reproduced from Giovanni Battista de Rossi, "Scoperta d'una cripta storica," figs.11–12.

key paradigm of Christian perfection. Early ideologues of Christian asceticism routinely employed the language of incarceration to describe a desirable and beneficial state. In the words of Tertullian (140–230): "The prison serves the Christian as the desert [served] the prophet.... Let us take away the name 'prison' and call it 'retirement.' Even if the body is confined, even if the flesh is detained, everything is open to the spirit."[15]

By comparing the prison with the desert, Tertullian linked Christian asceticism with the formative experiences of the Israelites and Christ's spiritual training. It was a potent union, for self-abnegation offered another path to Christian perfection, a path that augmented and eventually replaced the example of the persecuted martyrs.[16] In order to create continuity and commutability between "red" and "white" martyrdom, that is, between violent death for one's faith and the penitential life,[17] Tertullian and others turned the confessors' experiences in prison into a metaphor for self-imposed torment. The metaphor subsequently found its way into monastic spirituality, which spawned a distinct new strand of carceral language. Thus, according to the Desert Mother Syncletica (d. ca. 400),

> In the world, if we commit an offence, even an involuntary one, we are thrown into prison; let us likewise cast ourselves into prison because of our sins, so that voluntary remembrance may anticipate the punishment that is to come.[18]

This passage, and many others like it, established the ideal monastic life as a prefiguration of a Christian hereafter. The analogy is particularly apt considering that it was attributed to a woman who lived with her sister in an abandoned tomb. Ostensibly, Syncletica sought to create a seamless transition between this life and the next, but the scene of her trials also suggests that adapting to the conditions of a wretched inmate may offer the possibility of redemption from worldly sins. Other authors were more explicit: "In my fear of hell," wrote St. Jerome (331–420) to Eustochium from his hermitage, "I have consigned myself to this prison, where my only companions were scorpions and wild beasts."[19] In the Egyptian wilderness, Abba Ammonas (b. ca. 350) instructed a brother to adopt a frame of mind "like those of the evildoers who are in prison," and whose precarious state he likened to standing at the threshold of the apocalypse: "For they are always asking when the magistrate will come, awaiting him in anxiety."[20] And the sordid state of the fourth-century hermit Abba Bessarion was likewise marked by the passiveness of a prison inmate: "he lived in patience," wrote an anonymous biographer, "like a prisoner who is led everywhere, always suffering cold and nakedness, scorched by the sun."[21] And so it goes.[22]

The carceral language of early monastic spirituality was pervasive and enduring.[23] Its influence, moreover, far exceeded caves and convents, since the regular life, the beacon of Christian perfection, also served as a model for lay penitence throughout the Middle Ages, and monasteries occasionally functioned as loci of secular punishment.[24] With the proliferation of rural and especially urban anchorites, whose cells were embedded within parish churches across Europe, the association of self-imposed incarceration and personal salvation was further reinforced.[25] Another distinct reification of purgatorial enclosure is attested in several Umbrian towns, which saw the foundation of groups of individual cells occupied by lay penitents and located near (but not in) local convents. These enclosed men and women, organized into confraternities and commonly referred to as *incarcerati*, *cellari*, or *murati* ("imprisoned," "celled-in," or "walled-in"), sought to purge their sins by living exclusively on alms and food donated by passersby, and supposedly never left their cells.[26] This was yet another way in which the prison made its urban mark.

EXCURSUS: JAIL-BREAKING SAINTS

The prison's martyrological pedigree fit uncomfortably with the use of incarceration by secular lords and the clergy's involvement in the administration of prisons in the post-Constantinian era. Once the Roman Empire legitimized Christianity and finally adopted it as the state religion, bishops and deacons assumed paralegal responsibilities over monitoring prison conditions, albeit this time as imperial officials.[27]

Further, they began establishing their own facilities to detain erring clergy and monks, citing a commitment to bloodless penalties.[28] In 539, Paul, bishop of Gerasa (in present-day Jordan), even founded a civic prison, dubbing it a "holy building ... on account of its utility."[29]

Initially, the collusion between ecclesiastics and secular lords over a measure that formerly epitomized Christian suffering failed to strike contemporary observers as ironic. They may have interpreted the clergy's involvement in the administration of prisons as the lesser of two evils, or perhaps as a political and moral triumph. Alternatively, it may be the case that the reduced scale of incarceration, once mass religious persecutions ended, was easy to ignore.[30] Gradually, however, with the withdrawal of the Roman Empire from its western provinces and the political fragmentation that ensued, the use of imprisonment for laymen and the church's complicity in its implementation came under criticism. It was in this context that a hagiography of jail-breaking saints developed, particularly in western Europe.[31] According to Gregory of Tours (d. 594), during the funeral of St. Germanus, bishop of Paris, "Certain prisoners called upon him [Germanus] as his body was being carried by in the street: the corpse became heavy but, when the prisoners were released, it was lifted up again with ease." Whenever he could obtain gold or silver, Eparchius, the venerated recluse of Périgueux, "would spend it in supplying the needs of the poor or in freeing people from prison ... and many a time he persuaded judges to pardon the accused, more by the power of sweet reasonableness than by violent pleading." Other tales relate direct divine action:

> One night in the gaol at Clermont-Ferrand the chains holding the prisoners came undone by the intervention of God, the gates of the lock-up were unfastened, and they all rushed out to seek sanctuary in a church. Count Eulalius had them loaded with fresh chains, but no sooner had these been placed in position than they snapped asunder like brittle glass.[32]

While scholars strongly disagree over the social and political motivations underpinning the literature of jail-breaking saints, the topos clearly foreshadows later developments in its abandonment of the prison compound as necessarily a locus of holiness. The inmate's innocence or guilt was immaterial to patrons such as St. Leonard and a number of bishops and other miracle-workers who focused on chastising jailers and their collaborators.[33] Unlike their angelic biblical predecessors,[34] these saints broke Christians out of prison in defiance of the prevailing, if unstable, political order, and as a critique of its corruption. Whether or not such narratives also challenged the clergy's complicity in secular justice, it was certainly the first major instance in the long literary history of the prison where incarceration was utilized as a way to promote the general exercise of mercy, rather than to underscore the innocence (let alone holiness) of prisoners.

In the final account, however, jail-breaking hagiography remained a marginal strand throughout the following centuries. In his late-medieval incarnation, St. Leonard, an erstwhile patron of inmates, reemerged as a guardian of hospitals, and became an important cultic figure in regions where incarceration was not particularly developed, such as Bavaria.[35] By contrast, the proliferation of urban prisons across Europe never yielded a specific cult of jail-*breaking* holy men, although various saints, including St. Louis (Louis IX) and St. Francis of Assisi, did become associated with releasing prisoners and captives.[36] On the other hand, the expectation of a cultic figure directly responding to the proliferation of municipal prisons is perhaps unwarranted. As the next section stresses, the appearance of prisons in cities presented new challenges for interpreting incarceration as a religious experience rather than offering a convenient place in which contesting narratives might easily come to rest. Although rescuing prisoners or alleviating their conditions were goals shared by urban magistrates, confraternities, local bishops, and friars, their respective ideologies may have been quite different. It is small wonder that the only concerted appeal by or on behalf of Christian prisoners in this period was made in the context of crusading, and concerned war captives, who were more easily construed as prisoners of faith than criminal offenders could ever be.[37]

FROM PURGATION TO PURGATORY: GOD'S GREAT PRISON

Despite the presence of a hagiography of jail-breaking saints, the association between imprisonment and purgation remained a staple nexus of monastic literature throughout the Middle Ages. By the early thirteenth century this link received further reinforcement by way of doctrinal developments regarding the economy of personal salvation. In the Fourth Lateran Council (1215), Purgatory, originally an ambiguous aspect of the Christian afterlife, achieved a coherent logic and status. According to Jacques Le Goff, Lateran IV sanctioned a shift, already attestable in the mid–twelfth century, from purgation as an action to the "birth" of Purgatory as a distinct space in netherworldly geography, possessing a defined role in the economy of salvation.[38] The subsequent attention to Purgatory, whether in art, theology, or literature, served at least inadvertently as a vehicle for the transmission of carceral language from the monastic to the secular world.

Views of Purgatory were both common and diverse, as Le Goff demonstrates. But given the long-term association between the monastic life and purgation, it is hardly surprising that monks or monklike figures appear as guardians of and guides to Purgatory in the context of a revitalized interest in the hereafter.[39] The pertinent literature elaborated on the ancient metaphor of imprisonment as an act of purgation, and for the first time cast God in the ambiguous role of a potentially benevolent jailer. In 1272–73, at the Parisian Beguinage of Sainte-Catherine, a number of preachers (mostly mendicants) exhorted their audience to pray for the tormented souls in Purgatory. The intercession, one friar explained, was intended "so that God will release his prisoners from the prison of Purgatory." In a later sermon the same preacher stressed that the living are not to exert themselves for the sake of the afflicted souls in Hell, "but for those who are in the Lord's prison [Purgatory], and who cry and bawl at us, so we may liberate them through our alms, fasts, and prayers."[40] Le Goff may have overgeneralized from the above sermons in concluding that the view of Purgatory as God's prison was one of its major aspects. Yet praying to expunge souls from Purgatory certainly evokes the ancient tradition of interceding on behalf of the persecuted confessors.[41] Thus, thirteenth-century developments in the conception of Purgatory helped disseminate even further a long-standing link between incarceration and purgation, a link that Paolo da Certaldo and others were soon to employ.

To recap: Christian martyrological narratives commonly imaged the Roman prison as a place of spiritual growth and purgation. Later apologists embraced this "sweet inversion" to promote nascent ascetic practices. With the reduction of persecutions and the near-disappearance of "red" martyrs from the Christian purview,[42] numerous writers adopted the language of incarceration to convey the mystical experience of the monastic life ("white" martyrdom), thereby forging an enduring bond between the purgatorial life par excellence and abject imprisonment. With the spatialization of Purgatory from the late twelfth century on, various authors harkened back to this association by fashioning Purgatory as God's great prison.

THIS WORLD AND THE NEXT: THE URBAN PRISON

To turn our attention from theological imagination to the civic world is to discover that the literary history of the prison/purgation nexus had come full circle by the late Middle Ages. If the shift from the prison as place to the prison as metaphor is evident by Late Antiquity, the creation of urban prisons from the mid–thirteenth century onward reacquainted contemporaries with a concrete, indeed unavoidable, edifice. After a long prisonless lull, during which the "sweetly inverted" prison served almost exclusively as a model for the angelic life, how were urban residents equipped to interpret this old-new institution, recently realized anew and then packed with debtors and convicted criminals rather than innocent victims of arbitrary injustice or aspiring holy men? Put differently, when Purgatory was imagined in the thirteenth century, the prison was one of its obvious models; but if Purgatory was God's great prison, could the urban prison become an earthly Purgatory?

In order to console Egidius, the legendary founder of Padua, an angel took him on a virtual tour of the city's "future" landscape. No city will be "better and nobler, far and wide," he promised the defeated king, celebrating Padua's fourteenth-century flourish: gated walls, bustling markets, and magnificent public edifices. Passing through the podesta's palace, the heavenly guide paused to indicate with pride "a terrible, fetid place, called Basta, where men will be placed who owe money to others, and almost all the criminals." It was not the only prison space Padua could boast of:

> One of the palaces to the west will be called the New Prison, and it will be very strong. This palace will be divided into three parts. The first will contain men who owe money to others or to the commune of Padua for fines or taxes. And this part can be likened to Limbo. In the second will be those who have committed crimes, and this can be equated to Purgatory. In the third will be placed homicides, thieves, plunderers, and other criminals, after their offenses are made known to the podesta. And this third, dark part, where no light will ever penetrate, you could truly compare to Hell.[43]

The angelic-vision narrative, composed by Giovanni da Nono around 1318, combines several interpretations of the prison as place. By raising a triple bridge (Limbo, Purgatory, Hell) to connect Padua's New Prison and the afterlife, the author describes three distinct regimes applied to its inmates: one for debtors, one for minor offenders, one for major criminals. To be sure, the accuracy of da Nono's account is questionable: as stressed in the previous chapter, a neat grafting of legal categories onto the physical edifice was unlikely, however desirable. Moreover, the parallels he draws between certain violations and specific regions of the hereafter offer only a pseudohierarchy of crimes and punishments. To follow the author's logic, each "ward" was distinguished by the harshness of its regime and the length of one's stay there: Limbo (debtors) is light but permanent, Purgatory (minor offenders) is harsh but temporary, and Hell (major criminals) is both harsh and perpetual.

The gradation is somewhat puzzling even without positing da Nono's familiarity with Dante's *Comedy*, fragments of which began circulating as early as 1314. For doctrinally, Limbo is a terminal state over which its denizens exercise no control whatsoever. Surely this was

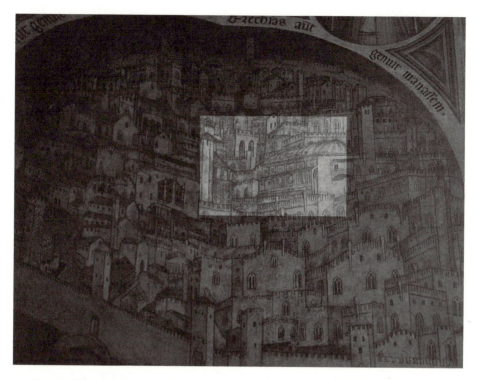

Fig. 4.2. View of fourteenth-century Padua. The highlighted area encloses the communal palace (*right*) and the prison as its left continuation. (Chapel of San Luca at the Basilica del Santo, Padua.)

not the rationale of a debtors prison or of coercive incarceration in general? Next, the perpetual agony inflicted upon major offenders seems more like an allusion to the latter's punishment in the afterlife, that is, in real Hell, than a description of their present plight. And in fact, da Nono's phrasing (*postquam potestati de illorum delictis erit manifestum*) suggests that, technically, these men are still under custodial arrest, since they have not yet been sentenced. If so, the miscreants' suffering can perhaps be attributed to a fear of eternal damnation, rather than specifically to a deprivation of freedom and its attendant pains. The most coherent aspect of the account is the comparison between imprisonment and Purgatory: only here are culprits suffering punishments broadly tailored to their own crimes.

The apparent fuzziness of the text can be resolved by establishing the author's goals and audience. *Laudes civitatum* (praises of cities), a genre to which da Nono's account pertains, had no qualms about appropriating the vocabulary of divine justice to celebrate the achievements of an existing regime, be it military, architectural, diplomatic, financial, or administrative. After all, it was a literary commonplace that "cities were made to resemble Paradise."[44] And since the justness of divine retribution was unquestionable, any secular system that sought to imitate it had to be praiseworthy—and if an angel can deliver the encomium, so much the better. Accordingly, in this highly idealized account, the municipal prison embodies Paduan justice as a whole and in a manner that emphasizes its attributes as a perfect civic model.

Despite its idiosyncrasy, da Nono's text offers a convenient vantage point for examining the use of netherworldly allusions in descriptions of late-medieval urban prisons. Given the long-standing association between incarceration and purgation, Purgatory, which by the thirteenth century had achieved a coherent logic and status, served as an obvious model for earthly justice. Yet as the above text illustrates, interpretations of the prison as place did not rely exclusively on Purgatory, but also drew on infernal imagery. The difference between the two realms cannot be overstated. As a recent American translator of Dante's *Comedy* notes, there is a modern tendency to forget that Purgatory is essentially a *good* place to be in.[45] It is also by definition a temporary condition, which, as Paolo da Certaldo reminded his readers, can be further abbreviated through the prayers of the living.

Two widely different statements attest to the implications of imagining the prison as an earthly Purgatory. Lamenting his fate in the Sienese prisons, the burlesque poet Burchiello (1404–49) sought to kindle his readers' pity, so they "may offer prayers to the almighty *Creator*/To restore our freedom soon."[46] And in a letter from 1395 to a potential benefactor, a veteran inmate at Le Stinche described himself as "living in misery, perhaps purging the sin of many."[47] Both Burchiello's ironic allusion to the urban officials as interventionist gods and the inmate's genuine plea for support relied on the notion (or rather, recognition) that release depends above all on other men's actions.

In contrast, neither intercession nor purgation was available to the residents of Hell. Thus, to liken the prison to Hell is to make a radically different statement about the nature and goals of incarceration. Yet it is precisely such statements that begin to gain ground in the fourteenth century. Place-names testify to this budding approach: as in Padua, so in Verona, one of the prison wards was called "the Inferno"; the Flint Tower, at the Tower of London, was fondly nicknamed "Lytle Hell"; and by 1310 "Helle" was also the name of the king's debtors prison at Westminster.[48] The most elaborate and explicit use of infernal imagery is to be found in Zuanni Manenti's Dantesque journey through the Venetian justice system, the *Specchio de la Giustitia* (1541). The otherwise

unknown author dedicates a third of the poem to an exploration of the
local prisons, under the title "Inferno del mondo":

> I am going to the dark prisons
> To see the unhappy malefactors
> Who suffer harsh pains for their vices.
> I am going to the place of fetors,
> Among the tormented, and the foul Inferno,
> Where men suffer pains and great tortures.
> It is so bitter that eternal [Hell] is hardly more so;
> And such, that entering with my escort,
> I said to him, Alas! for I see no light.[49]

Despite their temporal remove, Manenti's poem and da Nono's
propaganda share not only a major goal, namely, praising a local justice
system, but also develop similar themes when describing their respective prisons. For in Venice, too, the cells are dark, gloomy, foul, and
filled with tormented voices and bitter weeping. As the narrator puts it,
the wards "resounded so/From the voices of the afflicted and sufferers/
Whose swearing makes my head ring."[50] There is likewise a variety of
inmates: debtors and thieves, but also violent criminals. Yet the prison's
internal organization discloses no underlying categorization or hierarchy. Perhaps, unlike Dante, Manenti believed that Hell entailed a fairly
uniform experience. But he may have also been evoking the reigning
administrative confusion.

The foregoing examples illustrate a new association between Hell and
the prison, a link that survived well into our times. A famous exemplar
of this trope is found in *The Devil's Thoughts* by Samuel Taylor Coleridge
(1772–1834), who added these verses to a growing anthology:

> As he went through Cold-Bath Fields he saw
> A solitary cell,
> And the Devil was pleased, for it gave him a hint
> For improving his prisons in Hell.[51]

Like many before him, Coleridge coupled the monastic cell and the
prison. But by rendering them as a joint model for infernal torture, he
eliminated their erstwhile purgatorial attributes. Much in the same
vein, Oscar Wilde (1845–1900), himself imprisoned for homosexuality, depicted his fellow inmates as "the devil's own brigade," dwelling
"each in his separate hell":

> With bars they blur the gracious moon,
> And blind the goodly sun:
> And they do well to hide their hell

> For in it things are done
> That Son of God, nor son of man,
> Ever should look upon.[52]

Over the past two centuries prison reformers, scholars, journalists, and public intellectuals have made ample use of infernal allusions when describing modern and especially medieval facilities. Yet many of these observers share the misunderstanding that while medieval prisons were wont to be earthly Hells, similar attributions to modern penitentiaries would only serve to underscore an alarming aberration.[53] For ideally the modern prison should be a rehabilitative institution, and therefore resemble Purgatory, and certainly not Hell. Accordingly, with the twin models of Purgatory and the monastery in mind, the founders of Pennsylvania's Eastern Penitentiary encouraged inmates in 1844 to cherish their cells as "the beautiful gate of the Temple [cf. Acts 3:10] leading to a happy life and, by a peaceful end, to Heaven."[54] However, with what has been dubbed the "incarceration binge" of the last four decades, the link between Hell and the modern prison has been reforged, occasionally through scholars' pseudomedieval allusions: "For many persons entering prison, the inscription on the gate of Dante's inferno—'Abandon all hope, ye who enter here'—is becoming increasingly appropriate."[55] Norman Mailer would agree: "Hell was now clear to behold. It was Maximum Security in a large penitentiary."[56] And an anonymous U.S. inmate conveyed a similar sentiment in the following graffito:

> To the builders of this nitemare though you may never get to read these words. I pity you; for the cruelity of your minds have designed this hell: if men's buildings are a reflection of what they are, this one protraits the ugliness of all humanity. If only you had some compassion.[57]

The identification of prisons with an earthly Hell was probably a late-medieval innovation, one that survived the birth of modern penology as well as centuries of prison reform. Yet although references to Hell, Purgatory, or both continued to play a major role in medieval descriptions of prisons, some authors chose to break from this tradition altogether. Several late-medieval poems avoid referring to the hereafter or otherwise mock the alleged spiritual benefits (or afflictions) of incarceration. "Having turned it round and round/In my mind," declared the Florentine satirist Dino di Tura (d. 1373), "I have conclusively concluded,/That the prison is the best place in the world."

> In August one lives here like a prince,
> For it is never cold in that season,
> Since the wind from the north keeps away:
> It never rains late, or, for that matter, on time,

> [Even] if you remain for a thousand weeks;
> If you wish to see it, you still have time:
> If you hunger, there is bread for a lifetime;
> Thirsty? Here there is drink;
> If one enters today and dies, he's out tomorrow.[58]

A stint at Le Stinche in 1343–44 taught Dino di Tura a thing or two about prison life. In this untitled satire he goes on to report the embezzlement of alms by the warden and the prison's oppressive conditions: cold, hunger, darkness, and general neglect. The suffering he portrays, however, bears no relation to penance, nor is it couched in infernal or purgatorial terms. A glimpse of Hell emerges from the description of Babione, the corrupt warden, who "ambulates bare, or with ragged garb ... Bearing God on his neck, and the Devil in his heart." But even this allusion is geared toward underscoring the warden's hypocrisy, not imaging the prison as an earthly Hell. Di Tura's prison, in other words, appears to be a very worldly place, with an attendant "brotherly love" among the inmates:

> How is it going? I ask a chained man.
> He responds: You should be here!
> That is, life seemed good to him.
> He wished us—or better yet, me—to have
> That great joy;
> He would rather have placed me in his shoes.

Francesco Berni (1497/8–1535), another Florentine satirist, composed a poem, *In Praise of Debt,* whose main subject was no other than Le Stinche. Although somewhat later, it still echoes many of di Tura's observations and employs some of his techniques, for instance, the use of a mocking overture:

> O glorious Stinche of Florence;
> Celestial place, divine place,
> Worthy of a hundred thousand reverences ...
> There is nothing better than staying behind a wall,
> Comfortably at rest, sleeping with eyes shut,
> Safe in body and soul.[59]

Referring to the prison's "divine" character accentuates the author's dystopian view of it, as does his ironic assertion of comfort and tranquility. Berni also moves freely between irony and sarcasm when describing the inmates' conditions:

> You hold men there like hens in a coop;
> You give them their dishes in public,

> Just as is done with lions.
> Being there, one finally reaches
> That state which Aristotle described:
> Sensation ceases, and only the mind works.[60]

These verses juxtapose the inmates' animal-like conditions with the state of "supreme cognition" that allegedly follows from them. No wonder that the prisoners' main "industry," according to Berni, consisted of preparing escapes:

> There you can hear the noise of hammers,
> Of picks, and of beams [working] to send
> Free anyone hither and thither.[61]

The image of inmates laboring to execute an escape is not only a literal undermining of the institution, but also exposes the social conundrum of prison life: if Dino di Tura was cynical about "brotherly love," Berni reveals the inherent paradox of cooperation among prisoners, namely, that they join forces only in order to disperse. In sum, Berni's repeated nods to the real pains of imprisonment, much like di Tura's, are devoid of penitential content or pious netherworldly allusions. Le Stinche had a very earthly reality, lacking ulterior benefits.

The two poems speak with an inmate's voice, a useful strategy to convey the authors' antagonism to prison life. But how to account for their employment of a satirical rather than tragic or pathetic mode, and how if at all is this choice related to their avoidance from netherworldly imagery in describing their plight? A tentative explanation is that the authors feared that by alluding to the hereafter with pathos they would dilute their critique of the prison's administration and, by extension, of the local regime. Such logic is not entirely an inference *ex silentio*, for it is precisely by comparing the inmates' state to the tormented souls in Purgatory, or to those of the damned in Hell, that both da Nono and Manenti, in their idealized accounts, celebrated their cities' justice systems. By the same token, confirming that the magistrates are "giving them Hell," would run counter to the inmate-narrator's own political critique. Such goals are better met by satirizing the corruption of guards and the frequency of escapes, rather than dwelling on extrabodily suffering. In fine, by taking the path of irony, both di Tura and Berni consciously distanced themselves from the tragic mode and infernal imagery characteristic of prison descriptions in civic propaganda.

There were, however, other motivations to separate the prison from the afterlife. A lack of netherworldly allusions characterizes what is arguably the most famous description of medieval prison life, penned, significantly, by a religious reformer: the Dominican friar Felix Fabri, who visited Venice in 1484. And so he writes:

> The malefactors' prisons, located under the palace's promenade, have a view of the public square, illuminated by open windows that are blocked by iron bars. Through these windows the inmates can look out, stretch their hands, and converse with the nearby crowd. And if they are poor, they can ask for alms from passersby.
>
> In one prison I saw more than forty poor inmates walking around, crying for mercy. In another I saw imprisoned artisans seated at their workbenches and earning salaries despite their condition. In another cell I saw wealthy merchants playing dice and chess, their women standing outside the gates with their servants and slaves, talking to their husbands. In one private cell I saw a certain old Jew, incarcerated for debt, who had hanged himself ...
>
> [The guards] watched over many prisoners with much less caution, thereby offering many the opportunity to escape, especially when they notice that an inmate's adversary is unreasonably cruel ... To be sure, those who are imprisoned for grave offenses and who are likely to receive a death penalty are kept in stricter conditions, though they are tolerable.[62]

Fabri's view of the Venetian prisons differs widely from all the accounts we have encountered so far. Unlike Manenti's description of the very same compound, Fabri's depicts the inmates as rigidly (and probably unrealistically) classified into wards. In contrast to da Nono's portrayal of the Paduan prison, the Venetian culprits are grouped according to their socioeconomic status, not the gravity of their offenses. Indeed, the inmates' activities in prison are an extension of their extramural lives: the poor continue to beg, the artisans manufacture, the merchants idle, and the Jew lives separately. Compared to the poems of di Tura and Berni, Fabri's narrative reveals conditions that are generally good, or at any rate tolerable: the guards are considerate, and even the most wretched inmate has access to the outside world and can beg for alms. Most pertinent to our context, however, is the fact that the description is reminiscent of neither Hell nor Purgatory, a strategy that Fabri maintains even when decrying the dreadful state of prisons in his native land:

> One of the many cruelties of the Germans is that the malefactors' prisons are inhuman, frightening, and dark; located in the depths of towers, humid, cold, and often crawling with snakes and toads; far apart from any humans. Nor does anyone arrive to comfort those miserable souls, other than the cruelest torturers.[63]

Given that netherworldly connotations of imprisonment formed part of contemporary observers' horizons of expectations, Fabri's choice of keeping to a civic, secular register, was probably conscious, much like di Tura's and Berni's strategies. Here, too, the narrative approach was shaped to a large extent by the intended audience.[64] In contrast to da Nono's and Manenti's civic propaganda, Fabri, a dedicated religious reformer, focused on the Venetians' piety, hoping thereby to kindle charity among his own flock. The humane treatment of prisoners, both institutionally and by individuals, was a worthy goal, a goal that perhaps warranted an embellishment of the truth.

CONCLUSIONS

In the final account, the meaning of imprisonment was in the eye of its beholder, whether inmate, magistrate, jurist, religious reformer, or civic propagandist. From the fourteenth century on, there was no single unified understanding of incarceration, no reigning interpretation of what it is that prisoners actually or ideally undergo. True, civic ritual oblations could be explicit about the socially rehabilitative qualities of the prison experience, and some inmates contemplated the notion that their suffering was a cleansing experience. In this sense, the ancient association between incarceration and purgation continued to be influential, both before and after its bolstering by the doctrine of Purgatory.

At the same time, many denied the added spiritual value of their pains. This attitude was not limited to convicted culprits, as Felix Fabri's description of the Venetian prisons suggests. But while Fabri saw in the description of a benevolent prison regime an educational opportunity for promoting charity, authors like Dino di Tura and Francesco Berni took a more cynical view of prison life. To them, the prison represented an extension of civic society, since it bore little resemblance to the hereafter, just as urban magistrates exercised a very earthly justice: if the city was not an earthly Paradise, neither was its prison an earthly Hell.

Whatever their view, and despite the fragmentation of discourse around the description of incarceration, urban residents and visitors were by the fourteenth century preoccupied with local prisons more than ever before. How to account for this development? First and foremost, these facilities focused attention on themselves because they were new and ubiquitous. Yet other factors converged to bring prisons to contemporaries' notice: their central location, their accessibility, the sizable inmate turnover, the latter's maintenance of their social ties with the outside world, the symbolic importance of local justice systems, and a growing penchant, especially among Italians, for documenting their physical environment. And although interpretations varied, sometimes even widely, it seems that in its early days, the urban prison was not a place of shame, a black flower (to use Hawthorne's phrase) to be eradicated or simply camouflaged as a downtown hotel or office building. Rather, the prison became another public site for celebrating or protesting against the regime, for promoting charity, and for negotiating or challenging social order. That the prison has become a blind spot in today's appreciations of the medieval urban panorama reveals more about modern aspirations for a manicured backyard than about medieval realities.

CONCLUSION: "MARGINALIZING" INSTITUTIONS, INSTITUTING MARGINALITY

IN RECENT DECADES prisons have been eliminated from Western cityscapes. And although more pronounced in the Anglo-American world than elsewhere, this process is ubiquitous: Paris's only remaining penitentiary tellingly lies on its *Périphérique*, the old metropolitan border; Toulouse's huge octagonal prison was one of the last major inner-city penitentiaries to be demolished, in the summer of 2002.[1] Whether due to real-estate prices, the power of zoning boards, anxieties over urban communities' well-being, elites' ignorance about the relative immobility of the poor, or the desire of depressed rural communities for new sources of employment and income, city dwellers now encounter prisons and prisoners most commonly through the medium of their television screens.[2] It is no longer sufficient that prison walls keep convicts indoors and out of sight; it is the very walls that are rendered invisible under pressure by not-in-my-back-yard (NIMBY) lobbies. Over a decade ago, when Los Angeles policymakers decided to build a new prison in the downtown area, they made every effort to camouflage it among the slew of hotels and business centers, leaving tourists and bankers unknowingly ogling drug lords.[3]

Modern penologists and social theorists seem to agree that even if the West has created a monster in the shape of a prison system, abandoning it is not yet (or no longer) a viable option. But a broader historical perspective, such as was presented in the previous chapters, qualifies the premise of this statement, namely, that prisons were inherently monstrous creations. "What went wrong?" is a question to be discussed among experts of the late twentieth century, for whatever contemporary penal systems are experiencing, it is certainly *not* a return to some "medieval" past.

It is often assumed that the history of penology and that of the prison are one and the same. Two arguments refute this common view, however. First, the municipal prison was largely a late-thirteenth-century development, not a modern one. Second, the social and material conditions that characterized these institutions during the first major effort to routinize their activity were tolerable, especially thanks to their location and the inmates' access to the free world. So far, these arguments have been employed to modify the traditional chronology of the prison's history and challenge a prevalent (and somewhat self-contradictory) perception of premodern incarceration as both savagely cruel and not punitive. But what are their wider implications for the study of medieval urban society?

Let us begin by restating three central premises underlying a discussion of premodern prisons. First, the systematic employment of punitive incarceration is justly tied to the development of the modern prison, a "total" institution operating as a chief vehicle for implementing penology under the aegis of the modern state. Yet this particular development arrived some five hundred years into the history of the prison itself. For as a stable, supervised public institution, the prison appeared on the European landscape between the middle of the thirteenth and the close of the fourteenth century. As the first two chapters demonstrate, this period saw an unprecedented activity in and around such facilities: wards were built or appropriated, staffs were hired and regulated, supervisory committees were appointed, inmates classified, statutes drafted. If documentation separates history from prehistory, the prison was born well before 1400.

Second, punitive incarceration was familiar to medieval law and urban magistrates, even if this fact troubled contemporary jurists. Venice was probably exceptional in devising a formal calculus to convert fines into jail time, but the practice is attested elsewhere, as are individual statutes that prescribed imprisonment as a primary, additional, or substitute penalty for a wide range of offenses. But what has most obscured the practice of punitive incarceration in the late Middle Ages is the category of debt, and this on two accounts. First, as Richard Ireland has argued, it is fallacious to describe imprisonment for debt as "coercive," or merely so, since the measure entailed an inherent punitive element against a breach of faith.[4] Thus, insofar as most medieval inmates were debtors, they were being punished independently of having to appease their accusers, be it private creditors or the state. Beyond legal theory, and as was emphasized in chapter 2, "debt" is itself a misleading tag. A substantial number of inmates were incarcerated as public debtors for failing to pay a fine imposed for any number of offenses, from fraud to violent crimes. Often, especially in the case of poor convicts, the imposed fines were impossible to pay, thereby creating a situation that was only exacerbated by the incapacitation of a poor breadwinner. Incarceration, in other words, could often be an administrative measure gone sour—"hopeless" coercive imprisonment—or simply a sub-rosa punishment.

Third and last, the medieval prison's current image as a "hellhole," a view still shared and occasionally even perpetuated by medieval, let alone modern, historians, is simply untenable.[5] This, in turn, challenges a progressive or ameliorist understanding (even if in theory) of modern prisons and penology. As chapter 3 demonstrates, material conditions inside the prison, the creation of wards, and inmates' access to the outside world combined to render medieval captivity a tolerable if unpleasant experience. This observation, at least in the Italian case, is further supported by low death rates (whether from disease, violence, or self-injury), the infrequency of escapes, and the scarcity of inmate violence directed against personnel. Impressions of prison life, whether by inmates or external viewers, likewise underscore the relative tolerability of medieval incarceration. To be sure, the rise of urban prisons was accompanied by a fragmentation of a long-standing association between imprisonment and purgation, a nexus that was heir to Christian martyrological literature and monastic spirituality. Yet, as chapter 4 argues, the few documented instances whereby contemporaries referred to the prison as an earthly inferno were composed as civic propaganda, and served to celebrate a particular regime's capacity efficiently to execute secular justice. In contrast, authors who spent (or claim to have spent) time in prison, and visitors who observed such facilities from without, convey the impression that, for most medieval inmates, the prison was typically a more coercive version of life at large.

In documenting these developments, the present volume joins a number of local and regional studies that seek to illuminate the early history of the prison. These efforts, carried out mainly by legal and institutional historians, have lately initiated a shift, even among nonspecialists, from a view that punitive incarceration "did not exist or represented at best a negligible exception" prior to the nineteenth century,[6] to a growing recognition that punishment must be enumerated among the routine purposes of imprisonment in the late Middle Ages.[7] Among specialists, this consensus has been expressed most recently by Jean Dunbabin:

> If purpose-built self-standing prisons were still rare by 1300, rooms had long been set aside in castles and urban public buildings for the purpose of keeping captives, and the number of prisons was increasing rapidly. Once in existence, these were soon discovered to be useful for purposes other than custody, including punishment of those convicted and the detention of debtors.[8]

But if the legal and institutional aspects of medieval incarceration have by now been firmly established, their interpretation has only just begun. For regardless of their formal goals, medieval prisons served diverse functions, some stable, others changing, as is the case today.[9] Besides curbing deviants' impact on the outside world and rendering local justice administrations more efficient, prisons could, for instance, address contemporaries' desire for vengeance or retribution; incapacitate

offenders through ageing and malnutrition; establish, celebrate, or re-
generate official power (with particular emphasis on safeguarding the
economic interests of the propertied); and perhaps even foster a sense
of remorse and reaffirm normative values. Whatever the case may
be, in founding and especially maintaining prisons, medieval polities
passed a litmus test of power and stability.

At first blush, this observation seems to corroborate a key thesis
regarding the historical relationship among the formation of centralized polities, institution-building, and the so-called persecuting mentality of medieval society, all of which developed in western Europe
roughly at the same time. According to Joeseph R. Strayer, medieval
state-building was then in full thrust; Robert Bartlett argues that institutions such as mints, secular chanceries, and universities were becoming instrumental for the "Europeanization of Europe"; and R. I. Moore
famously asserts that by the late thirteenth century Western society had
manifestly closed its ranks.[10]

But prisons were not mere by-products of political centralization or
of a quest for social and religious homogeneity. That a regime chose to
develop a prison and to regiment it the way it did sheds light on the
kind of consolidation sought and on the factors that helped shape it.
What, then, were the mechanisms or mentalities driving this process,
beyond the circumstances that had enabled it, and regardless of the
functions that prisons eventually came to fulfill?

One approach to understanding the formation of institutions is in
terms of a response to social problems.[11] Social problems, however, lack
an objective existence; they come to be seen as such in a highly complex
process that begins with subjective identification, advances through
legitimation and formal recognition, and culminates with the development and implementation of a formal plan of action.[12] The successful or
partial completion of this process depends on numerous contingencies,
and progressing from one stage to the next entails a continuous negotiation of the problem's "nature" and the desired "remedy." Finally, applying the approved "solution," much like enforcing the law, involves
a further set of considerations and even obstacles that mold an institution's initial form.

Recognizing these complexities, recent historians of institutions have
sought to uncover the myriad factors attendant upon the development
of their respective subjects, with a particular emphasis on "total" institutions (a category first framed by Erving Goffman) such as hospitals, insane asylums, boarding schools, and prisons.[13] Rather than
assume that hospitals, for instance, inevitably grew out of the proliferation of medical knowledge and reflect a stronger sensitivity to human
suffering, scholars as diverse in their approaches as Gerald Grob, David

Rothman, and Michel Foucault have given due attention to the contexts in which governments and charitable groups created such facilities, to the goals they purportedly served, and to the functions they ultimately fulfilled.[14] Historians of premodern institutions in turn have faced the double challenge of explicating and predating the emergence of several allegedly modern institutions, from hospitals, to reformatories and brothels, to prisons, although in no case is there a convincing argument for the "totalness" of any of these facilities, with the obvious exception of monasteries.[15]

While the goals and functions of premodern, "proto-total" institutions varied greatly, there is a scholarly consensus regarding their proliferation particularly in urban centers, and to the role that they played in the reification of social marginality. It is against this backdrop that medieval prisons can be examined vis-à-vis a number of institutions that, by the fourteenth century, composed the landscape of urban otherness: the leper-house, the brothel, the almshouse, the hospital, and the Jewish quarter. The comparison itself was already drawn by contemporaries; in his chapter on jails and jailers, the author of *The Mirror of Justices* (perhaps Andrew Horn, d. 1328) asserted that

> as leprosy is a malady which disgraces the body of a man so that he may not be suffered to dwell among healthy folk, so mortal sin is a kind of leprosy which makes the soul abominable to God and severs it from the community of all holy folk.[16]

Leprosy may seem like an obvious analogue to crime, and on some level the instinct to rid society of its criminals strives to be just as effective as amputating an already degenerate limb. Practically, however, prisoners were seldom cut off from free society. Nor, for that matter, were lepers, despite regulations governing their movement and dress, and leprosaria's usual (but not exclusively) suburban or extramural location. As Nicole Bériou, François-Olivier Touati, Anne Lester, and Carole Rawcliffe have amply shown, not only was there a frequent and socially constructive interaction between urban residents and lepers, but the latter also came to be seen as part of the urban fabric: by the fourteenth century, urban magistrates stressed the location of leprosaria "iuxta civitatem" (near the city) in contrast to their earlier designation as "extra civitatem" (outside the city), thereby solidifying these facilities' status as urban extensions.[17] Likewise, contemporary English municipalities, despite having little or no involvement in the foundation of leper-houses, were increasingly mounting claims regarding their jurisdiction over these compounds.[18] In brief, across Europe, cities' political autonomy augmented rather than reduced the social inclusion of marginals, for whom indeed "[s]eclusion ... spelt disaster."[19]

A similar proclivity for regulating rather than banishing urban marginals was beginning to characterize coeval attitudes, for instance, toward the sick and the poor, prostitutes, Jews, and criminals.[20] True, the motivations behind such shifts were diverse, running the gamut from charity to greed, and follow somewhat different chronologies in different regions. Yet to look beyond persecution and social segregation within the medieval city is to discover their less celebrated counterpart, namely, containment or, to borrow a term from another context, "rough tolerance."[21] Thus, comparing criminals to lepers speaks to the role of medieval prisons as part of a drive to accentuate order over social sanitation, and underscores a preference of regulated interaction over social destruction.

Before proceeding to explore the significance of medieval prisons for urban social order, it is important to acknowledge that comparing prisons to other "marginalizing" institutions is problematic on two counts. First, what appears to set apart hospitals, leprosaria, Jewish quarters, and brothels from prisons was the latter's physical location. For while red-light districts were occasionally central (as in Toulouse and Venice), and although hospitals were gradually becoming less peripheral (as in England), prisons were established habitually at the city's physical and political heart. In this respect, London's Newgate Prison, embedded within the city walls, is the exception that proves the rule, though it, too, was hardly marginal, being located on a busy thoroughfare. However, and notwithstanding medieval cities' modest size, the prison's accessibility was more pragmatic than ideological, considering its usual development from an appropriated holding cell in or near the main government compound. Accordingly, separate, purpose-built prisons remained rare throughout and well after the fourteenth century. The prison's centrality, moreover, meant that, at least initially, few or no new guards had to be hired to supervise the inmates, and that prisoners could rely more easily on free society for some of their basic needs. Above all, the prison's location purported to increase the local court's efficiency and improve the facility's monitoring. For, as opposed to all other marginalizing institutions (including municipally run brothels), this institution was particularly integral to the machinery of justice.

But a second and even greater obstacle to comparing prison inmates with other marginal groups is the social constitution of the prison community, with its strong element of propertied debtors, the woof of the urban social fabric. And in fact, the social segregation that prison wardens were supposed to enforce bears witness to a heterogeneous inmate community, whose well-being depended on a carefully scripted interaction. Still, and despite the continuous impoverishment of prison communities, it would be inaccurate to infer that since inmates did not necessarily constitute an underclass, they were not socially marginal, that is, "partly belonging to two differing societies or cultures, but not fully integrated into either."[22] For in their daily routine it was the privileged inmates in particular who were partly extracted from their former lives, but not fully integrated into their new environment: they were constricted and incapacitated; their safety depended on the goodwill, compliance, or corruptibility of their social unequals; and, however affluent debtors may have been, their experience was far worse than when at large. However much prisons were created in the merchant's image, incarceration itself was widely known to entail inconveniences that were at odds with bourgeois life.

There is a further and equally important justification for situating prisons within the landscape of urban marginality. Inmates as a group and the edifice in which they dwelled were unique symbols of political or, in the case of episcopal and inquisitorial prisons, religious authority. Despite their internal hierarchy, prison communities comprised a social group that, from a legal perspective, either dissented from prescribed norms or was labeled as having done so. Furthermore, the inmates' state was a perceived consequence of their individual willingness to perpetrate an offense such as contracting excessive debts or refusing to pay them. In this sense prisoners approximated prostitutes in that they misused their available agency to conduct a virtuous life, unlike lepers, women, and Jews, or life-cycle marginals such as children and the elderly, who could scarcely control their diverse predicaments.[23] Accordingly, it is understandable that prisoners were imaged as straddling a gap between conformity and dissent, and that their place of arrest served civic propagandists in promoting the virtues of local regimes.

To return to the above analogy between lepers and criminals, it seems that urban incarceration (and immuring in general) meant much more than neutral, sterile sequestering. Prison walls, rather than severing the inmate community from the outside world, actually helped structure prisoners' interaction with various members of free society. One argument developed in chapter 3 was that the continuity of social commerce between inmates and society at large underscores the former's existence as one of being perched between two social systems, a condition that, in modern terms, rendered them marginal but not liminal. A similar economy underpins the interaction between free or "mainstream" society and other groups such as lepers, religious minorities, prostitutes, the poor, and the infirm, all of which had to accept, among other restrictions, intermittent immuring as part of their routines, and occasionally as a means to safeguard their well-being.[24] But, as in the case of incarcerating criminals, segregating minorities expanded rather than curbed interaction, and immuring the "other" can be seen as a compromise solution between acceptance and rejection. As Robert Bonfil asserts, "[B]efore it became a symbol of the desire to segregate the Jews, the institution [in 1516] of the ghetto in Venice *marked the abandonment of the traditional policy of excluding* Jews from the city."[25] What we are dealing with in the case of the first ghetto, then, is the culmination of a tendency, already evident by the fourteenth century, toward sequestering as part of an overall effort to contain, maintain, and even protect urban marginals and minorities, not conceal, banish, or destroy them.

This observation is demonstrably true and best articulated in the case of religious heretics incarcerated in episcopal and inquisitorial prisons, which were mostly urban facilities. As James Given argues, imprisonment developed as an effective tool in the inquisitors' "kit" for producing confessions.[26] Yet men and women who admitted their adherence to and practice of heterodox doctrines, but whose offenses did not merit the customary range of penitential measures (let alone execution), gradually began languishing in prisons for interminable durations. Thus, post-trial incarceration of heretics was a means originally devised to procure further confessions or effect contrition, either of which would have supplied the local tribunal with firmer grounds for imposing a determined penalty. Over time, however, this category of heretics grew exponentially, and the length of their incarceration extended ever further. Under these circumstances imprisonment became, for the first time in western European history, a common punitive measure for laymen: over half the penalties meted out by Bernard Gui, inquisitor in Toulouse in the early fourteenth century, were sentences of incarceration under various regimens.[27]

From a religious-doctrinal perspective, unrepenting heretics were excommunicate, not just marginal. Yet in practice, even among inquisitors, the physical and social maintenance of many heretics became routinized within the city's center. Like their counterparts in municipal prisons, incarcerated heretics could live under various conditions, were subject to gender segregation, and had access to free society, upon which they often relied for their sustenance.[28] Inquisitorial prisons, in sum, were another instance in which heterogeneity, or in this case, heterodoxy, was kept at bay: regimented and tolerated, but not rejected.

All this is not to argue that late-medieval prisons were born of benign intent or even neglect. Their foundation and management owed much to local regimes' expanding prosecutorial capacities, including the use of torture, a process underwritten in and beyond Italy by the encroachment of inquisitorial on accusatorial procedures.[29] In this context the duration of accusatorial procedures created a pressing need for more custodial spaces. Moreover, as suggested in chapter 2, de facto punitive incarceration could often be a coercive measure gone sour or a sub-rosa penalty. But regardless of the formal grounds for their arrest, many prison inmates experienced a temporary, nondestructive marginalization. It would be far-fetched to claim that this had been the explicit intention of urban magistrates (or religious inquisitors) everywhere when founding local prisons. Yet the growing recourse to incarceration, when compared with socially severing measures such as banishment, execution, and even dismemberment, and which remained common throughout the high and late Middle Ages, indicates a significant shift in contemporary practices of social control.

It has long been argued that the homogeneity of Latin Europe came at the expense of social solidarity and religious tolerance, and that this internal closing of the ranks sowed the ideological and logistical seeds of later (indeed, much later) calamities.[30] Yet the type of regulation to which urban criminals (and social and religious deviants in general) were gradually being subjected reflects greater tolerance and a more nuanced attitude toward indexing "in" and "out."[31] As long as urban magistrates could uphold their prerogative of maintaining social order, they preferred calculated inclusion to righteous exclusion, for instance, by accepting fees from prostitutes rather than insisting on their expulsion.[32] In contrast, when a policy of social cleansing was intermittently adopted by the rulers of England and France, vagabonds and Jews, mostly found in urban centers, were harshly uprooted.[33] But despite periodic and indeed brutal persecutions, which may or may not reflect urban governments' desire for social sanitation, late-medieval urban life, with its regulated brothels, proliferating hospitals and leprosaria, unofficial Jewish quarters, and, of course, central prisons, exhibits a kind of "rough tolerance" toward social marginals, including criminals.

According to Bronisław Geremek, the great historian of medieval marginality, civic death took the place of physical death by the late Middle Ages.[34] Limiting the underclasses' access to courts and organized labor, and the physical reclusion of the poor, sick, and deviant, defined and essentially created a group of dishonored and dispossessed. In Geremek's view (shared, incidentally, by some of the modern prison's critics), incarceration constituted only a pseudopenal measure, a means to the end of social oblivion. In other words, the prison's historical role was to warehouse, indeed to starve, the poor.[35]

But was it civic death that actually or completely replaced physical death, or can we detect a broader shift in attitudes toward deviancy? For the creation of prisons, among other marginalizing institutions, afforded the extension, rather than the contraction, of civic life. To recognize this process is to avoid confusing the form and content of medieval incarceration, or to understand medieval prisons through the prism of their modern, "total" heirs. Like brothels, leprosaria, and Jewish quarters, prisons reified marginality and otherness. Yet the *manner* in which these institutions were designed, governed, and perceived meant that urban marginals could constructively engage surrounding society, rather than be suffocated or outcast, however temporarily. In this sense, marginalizing institutions institutionalized, and thus, in an important sense, normalized and accepted marginality.

A PRISON INVENTORY FROM BOLOGNA, 1305

PRISON SCRIBES routinely drafted a list of existing inmates at the end of an administrative term (see chapter 2). It was on such an occasion that a certain Bolognese notary adjoined the following inventory of artifacts that the outgoing custodians passed on to their replacements.[1] The document offers a unique view of the facility's layout and a glimpse of prison furniture and utensils.

Item, [the retiring warden] dedit et consignavit eis [i.e., to the incoming wardens] infrascriptas res et massaratica. In primis, in fundo dicte carceris in muro anteriori, unam fenestram de ferro cum fenestra de ligna, clavatura,[2] cistello[3] et clavi; item, unum çeppum[4] cum catena et clavi a bocca bocolaris;[5] item, unam lampadem; item, unam scalam a petiis et unam a pirolis[6] causa eundi in fundo dicte carceris; item, unum portellum de asis duplum cum clavatura, catenaçia[7] et clavi pro seratura dicti fundi; item, unum altrum portellum de spranghis[8] ad dictum fundum cum clavatura, cistello et clavi; item, unum poticum[9] cum muraliis, seclario[10] fenestris et aliis ... cum ipso potichu; item, duas assides super seclarium cum ma[no]polliis[11] de ferro ab apendendis situlis;[12] item, duas situlas ab agna feratas cum una caça[13] de ramo et baçolo[14] ipsarum sitularum; item, unum lavetum[15] magnum de lapide; item, unum lavetum meçanum de lapide; item, unum parolum[16] de ramo; item, duas catenas ab igne; item, unum canedonçellum[17] ab igne; item, unam ramiolam[18] de ferro ad menestrandum; item, unum spetum[19] de ferro magnum cum vulgituro[20] et pede; item, unum altrum spetum de ferro ... et unum de ligno; item, unam concham[21] ad pestandum herbas cum pestatura; item, unam bacolam a[...]; item, unam padellam[22] de ramo cum caçola[23] de ferro; item, unum scutilenum[24] cum prelibi scudellis et masoriis;[25] item, unum discum magnum pro cochena;[26] item, unum catinum[27] magnum ab abluendo parasides[28] et masorios; item, unum camarotum[29] super fundo dicte carceris cum portello duplo, clavatura, cistello et clavi; item, unum scrineum[30] magnum a pane[31] cum clavatura et clavi; item, unum capsotum[32] pro scripturis[33] retinendis; item, unum scanellum[34] a scribendo cum quodam dischito super qua retinetur; item, duas tabulas cum quatuor trispidis et tres banchas; item, unum portellum in introytu dicti carceris cum clavibus ipsius et hostij anterioris; item, unam

sprangatam cum portello, clavatura et cistello scale inferioris; item, unam
aliam sprangatam cum po[r]tello de spranghis, clavatura, cistello et clavi
scale de medio; item, unam sprangatam magnam de spranghis de abeto[35]
ad porticum anteriorem dicte carceris; item, duas lampadas, unam in
caminata inferiori et alliam in caminatam de medio; item, hostium
novum ad caminatam de medio cum chistello et clavi; item, duo hostia
qui sunt ad cameras superiores factas de novo cum clavatorum chistello
et clavibus; item, unum mastellum[36] magnum ab aqua pro cochena cum
coperelo in duobus petiis; item, unam manariam[37] a scelando lignas;
item, unam fenestram ad fundum dicte carceris versus scalam cum
clavatura, cistello et clavi; item, unum botatium[38] a sale; item, unam
vacuxiam[39] a formatico; item, unam palettam de ferro ab igne; item,
tria paria de ferris traversagne;[40] item, octo paria de ferris a passo; item,
unam anguçinellam[41] de ferro ab [sic] inferiandum; item, unum par de
tenaglis[42] magnis ab inferiando et desferiando; item, unum cassaturum
ab inferiando; item, unum martellum ab inferiando; item, septem paria
de passis a ferris.

POEMS FROM THE PRISON

THE FOLLOWING IS a selection of Italian prison-related poetry from the fourteenth to the sixteenth centuries, with facing English translations. A work's unavailability or relative inaccessibility in modern print served as the main criterion for inclusion. The few interpretative essays on medieval prison poetry are noted at the end of chapter 3 and throughout chapter 4.

DINO DI TURA (D. 1373)

Famous mostly for his prison satire, Dino di Tura (also known as Dino di Tucca or dall' Allacci) spent some months during 1343–44 incarcerated at Le Stinche, allegedly for debt. His entry in the prison's register was uncovered and transcribed by Domenico Manni, but was forever lost in 1966, when the Florentine archives were flooded.[1]

UNTITLED (FRAGMENTS)

Avendo io girato a tondo a tondo	Having turned it round and round
Col cervello, ho conchiuso in conclusione,	In my mind, I have conclusively concluded,
Che in le prigioni è il meglio star del Mondo.	That the prison is the best place in the world.
Ove può farsi vita più contenta?	Where can one lead a better life?
Ove passar i giorni più felici?	Where are happier days spent?
Pazzo è certo chi d' essa si lamenta.	Mad is he who complains about it.
Questa ci tien sicuri da' nemici:	It keeps us safe from enemies:
Che non era così quando non ci era;	Which was not so when I wasn't here;
Quì si conosce i falsi, e i veri amici.	Here true and false friends are recognized.
Il dir, che quì ci è stato Imperatore,	To say that emperor, duke, and marquis
Duca, e Marchese, e di tutte le sorte,	And all types have been here
Sarebbe un voler dir, che l' uomo ha 'l cuore;	Is just like saying that man has a heart;

È noto a tutti; e se qualcun per sorte

Non lo sapesse, legga l' Ariosto,

Vedrà, che per ognun s' apron sue
  porte.
Ci è uno star da Principi l' Agosto,

Perchè non ci è mai freddo di quel
  tempo,
Giacchè la tramontana sta discosto:

Non ci piove giammai tardi, o per
  tempo,
Se voi ci steste mille settimane;

Se 'l volete veder, voi siete a tempo:

Se avete fame, a vita si dà il pane;

Se avete sete, quì si dà da bere;
Se un c'entra oggi, e ci muor, n' esce
  domane.
Fanno conto di voi, più d' un podere
Quei, che tengon le chiavi del
  palazzo;
Non è questo davvero un ben olere?
Come va? dissi a un, ch' era in
  catene.
Esso rispose: così steste voi!
Cioè, che gli pareva di star bene.
Voleva far provare ancor a noi,
O dirò meglio, a me, quel gran
  contento,
E fin messo m' avria ne' piedi suoi.

Il Guidaiuol delle Stinche Bobione

Le pecore, che stanno in quell'ovile,
Ciascuna nel suo grado tien sottile,
Massime quelle, a cui dà
  il boccone.

Everyone knows; and if by chance
  someone
Were to disagree, let him read
  Aristotle:
He will see that its doors are open to
  anyone.
In August one lives here like a
  prince,
For it is never cold in that season,

Since the wind from the north keeps
  away:
It never rains late or on time,

[Even] if you remain for a thousand
  weeks;
If you wish to see it, you still have
  time:
If you hunger, there is bread for a
  lifetime;
Thirsty? Here there is drink;
If one enters today and dies, he's out
  tomorrow.
On you, not on their own estates, rely
Those masters, who hold the
  building's keys.
Truly, is this not brotherly love?
How is it going? I ask a chained man.

He responds: You should be here!
That is, life seemed good to him.
He wished us—or better yet, me—to
  have that great joy;

He would rather have placed me in
  his shoes.
The guardian of Le Stinche, Bobione,

Holds caringly each of these sheep
That lies in his fold,
Especially those to whom he gives
  food

Quest' è perchè fa del voler ragione;	For he turns his will into law;
Ignudo va, o con vestimento vile;	He goes around bare, or with filthy garb;
Ipocrita barbuto, e signorile.	With bearded hypocrisy and lordship,
Dio porta in collo, e 'l Diavol succollone;	Bearing God on his neck, and the Devil in his heart;
Egli ha fatto un poder già d' otto moggia;	He has already bought an eight-moggia farm;
Grande in Mugello, u' si chiama a Figliano,	A large estate in Mugello, precisely in Figliano,
E tuttodì di nuovo ve n' appoggia.	Which he expands daily.
De' poveri prigion viene in sua mano	The poor prisoners' charity reaches
La carità, e ne tien nuova foggia:	His hand, whence it is transformed:
Noi, che siamo in prigion, ce ne avveggiamo.	We, who are in prison, notice it.
Con quei, che regna sì si sa portare,	With rulers he knows how to comport himself,
Che ogni volta si fa raffermare.	So that he is reappointed every time.

ADOARDUS DE ASISSI (MIDDLE TO LATE FOURTEENTH CENTURY)

The following *scongiuro*, or "invocation of death," is attributed to Adoardus, vicar to the papal legate at Bologna, who was "deservedly sent to the prisons" there in 1362.[2]

Po' che fortuna tanto	Since Fortune so
crudelmente de sotto m'à rivolto,	Cruelly cast me down,
pregote, morte, molto,	I pray to you, Death, earnestly,
che puni fine al doloroso pianto.	To end these sorry tears.

BURCHIELLO (1404–49)

A famous Florentine burlesque poet, Burchiello was imprisoned in the Sienese prisons roughly from May to December 1439, for unpaid fines and contumacy.[3] The poems below are reproduced from Mazzi's 1879 edition, since they were not included in the recent critical edition of Burchiello's sonnets. The latter collection, however, does include other prison-related poems.[4]

Io vuo che sappi ov' io sono arrivato[5]

Io vuo che sappi ov' io sono
arrivato,
bontà della mia mente trista
e chioccia;
acqua non posso aver se non per
doccia,
nè aver lo sole se non è scaccato:
Non posso aver pan se non
desperato.
se io ebbi mai piacer, il mal mi
noccia:
la casa mia ha sì doppia la boccia,
non ho pensier dal lupo esser
mangiato.
Io imbotto il vino giù senza bicchiere

ad uno arpion ch'i 'l vo' per
un coiaio,
che 'l trementin si è meglio al mio
parere,
Secondo che mi dice un galigaio
com'io sto ad agio, omai il puoi
sapere!
e Dio amoroso mi dia pace e gaio,

E con festa e con maio.
Mosche e zanzar di gennaio ci ho
trovate;
tu dei pensar quel che sarà
di state!

I want you to know where I've
come to,
Thanks to my sad and rasping mind;

I have no water except for the roof
drops,
Nor the sun if it is not checkered.
I can't have bread unless of
affliction;
If I was ever happy, let evil kill me:

My skin has so doubled in
thickness,
[That] I don't worry of being eaten
by a wolf.
I guzzle wine, dispensing with the
glass,
To a hook befitting a tanner;
[Wine,] methinks, worse than
turpentine,
From what a shoemaker tells me.
Now you know how comfortable
I am![6]
And God beloved gave me peace
and joy,
With the feast of spring.
I've found here flies and mosquitoes
in January;
Imagine what will be here in the
summer!

O voi ch' entrate dentro a questo chiostro[7]

O voi ch' entrate dentro a questo
chiostro,
se i miseri abitanti guarderete
con gli occhi della mente, voi direte

che non è alcun dolor simile al nostro.
Siamo in calamità, ch' ora v' è
mostro;

Oh you who enter this enclosure,

If you look at the wretched inmates
With your mind's eye, you
would say
That there is no sorrow like ours.
We are in misery, as I'll show,

a patir caldo, fame, freddo,
    e sete:

Suffering heat, hunger, chill, and
    thirst:

e liberi già fummo come siete

We were once free like you are

e non ci pesa dello stato vostro.

And we don't mind your state.

Ma ben preghiàn che 'n voi pietà s'
    accenda

But we pray to kindle your pity

a porger prieghi al sommo
    Creatore

So that you may offer prayers to the
    almighty Creator

che nostra libertà tosto ci renda.

To restore our freedom soon.

E per carità vostra, atto d'amore,

And by your charity, an act of love,

ciascun di voi la man pietosa stenda

May each of you extend a pious hand

a farci della borsa alcun favore.

And help us with some favors from
    your purse.

Deh fatel per onore!

Please do so, for honor's sake!

Chè Dio, in cento più, merto ne rende

For God a hundredfold rewards

a chi per i suoi poveri gli spende.

A man who spent money on His
    poor.

"LETTER" TO BURCHIELLO FROM ROSELLO ROSELLI[8]

Caro Burchiello mio; se il vero ho
    inteso,

My dear Burchiello, if it's true what
    I hear,

parmi che facci compagnia coi topi;

It seems you're in the company of
    mice;

chè tutte le prigion convien che scopi,

For you have to sweep all the prisons:

tanto mal da piccin fusti ripreso.

So badly were you scolded since
    childhood.

Con ben mille ragion io t' ho difeso,

With over a thousand petitions
    I defended you,

le quai ti mando tutte che le copi,

All of which I send you to copy,

dicendo, sol pietà ch' ha' de gli inopi

Saying, only the pity you have for
    the poor

t' ha fatto si al furar il braccio teso.

Made you stretch your hand so
    much to steal.

Veggo che scusa omai non ci val
    nulla,

I see that excuses are by now
    pointless,

e fa' come dee far ogn' uom virile,

So do what any worthy man must,

che render voglia infino a una frulla

Who wants to return down to the
    penny

quel che togliesti in mala consienza.

What he took in bad conscience.

E non aver temenza;

And do not fear;

chè se t' acconci ben d'ogni peccato

For if you pay for all your sins

senza fallo nïun sarai salvato

Certainly you will be saved.

Francesco Berni (1497/8–1535)

Berni was another Tuscan burlesque poet of the early sixteenth century, who spent his early and late career in Florence. Despite the autobiographical voice of the following poem—a satire in praise of debt, and thus of Le Stinche—it is unknown whether Berni was ever incarcerated.

In Lode del Debito (excerpt)[9]

O gloriose Stinche di Firenze;
Luogo celestial, luogo divino,
Degno di centomila riverenze.

A voi ne vien la gente à capo chino,
E prima che la vostra scala saglia
S'abbassa in su l'entrar dell'usciolino.
A voi nessuna fabrica s'agguaglia,
Sete piu belle assai che 'l Culiseo

O s' altra à Roma piu degna anticaglia.
Voi sete quel famoso Pritaneo
Dove teneva in grasso i suoi baroni

Il popol che discese da Teseo.
Voi gli tenete in stia come i capponi;

Mandate il piatto lor publicamente,
Non altrimenti che si fà à lioni.
Com'uno è quivi, è giunto finalmente
A quello stato ch' Aristotil pose,

Che'l senso cessa, e sol opra la mente.
Voi fate anche le genti industriose:
Chi cuce pelle, chi lavora fusa,

Chi stecchi, e chi mille altre belle cose.

O glorious Stinche of Florence;
Celestial place, divine place,
Worthy of a hundred thousand reverences.

To you men come with bowed heads,
And before they climb your stairs
They stoop at your doorstep.

No building equals you,
You are more beautiful than the Coliseum
Or any other worthy ruin of Rome.

You are that famous Prytaneum
Where the people descended from Theseus
Used to fatten their lords.
You hold men there like hens in a coop;
You give them their dishes in public,
Just as is done with lions.
Being there, one finally reaches
That state which Aristotle described:
Sensation ceases, and only the mind works.
You also render men industrious:
Some stitch pelts, other spindle, dry [meat], or
Perform a thousand other odd jobs.

Non vi ha né l'ozio, né 'l negozio
    scusa;
L'uno e l'altro ricapito vi truova.
Di tutti suoi v'è la scienzia infusa.
S'alla città vien qualche buona
    nuova,
 Voi sete quasi de' primi à sapella:
Par che corrieri addosso il ciel vi
    piova.
Et vi si sente un romor di martella,

Di picconi, e di travi per mandare

Libero ogniuno in questa parte e'n
    quella.
Ma s'io vi son, lasciatemivi stare;
Di questa pietà vostra, io non
    mi curo,
Appena morto me ne voglio andare.

Non sò piu bel che star drento à un
    muro
Quieto agiato, dormendo à chiusi
    occhi,
Et del corpo et dell' anima sicuro.
Fate parente mio pur de gli scrocchi,

Pigliate spesso à credenza,
    a'nteresse,
Et lasciate ch'à gl'altri pensier tocchi,
Che la tela ordisce un, l'altro
    la tesse.

There is release from neither
    idleness nor work;
Both have their home address there.
All present have innate wisdom.
If some good news reaches the city,

You are almost the first to know it:
It seems like the heavens rain
    envoys upon you.
There you can hear the noise of
    hammers,
Of picks, and of beams [working] to
    send
Free anyone hither and thither.

But if I am there, let me stay;
I need not this charity of yours—

Only when I die, I want to leave this
    place.
There is nothing better than staying
    behind a wall,
Comfortably at rest, sleeping with
    eyes shut,
Safe in body and soul.
Borrow, my friend, even from the
    swindlers,
Take out loans on credit, at interest,

And let others worry about it,
For one lays out the cloth, another
    weaves it.

ZUANE MANENTI (EARLY TO MIDDLE SIXTEENTH CENTURY)

An obscure Venetian poet, Manenti completed his literary voyage through the Venetian justice system at the encouragement of the Venetian Council in 1541, that is, just before the construction of the Pozzi. In form, it follows the Dantesque division into (worldly) Hell, Purgatory, and Paradise. The scene of worldly Hell is set within the palace's ground-floor prisons.

SPECCHIO DE LA GIUSTITIA, PART 1: "INFERNO DEL MONDO" (EXCERPTS)[10]

Io me ne vo, ne le Pregion oscure
Per veder gli'nfelici Malfattori
Che per lor vitii portan pene dure.

I am going to the dark prisons
To see the unhappy malefactors
Who suffer harsh pains for their vices

Io me ne vo in loco de fetori
Tra molti tormentati, et crudo Inferno
Nel cui patiscon pen'è [sic] gran martori.
Tanto amar, che poco piu è l'eterno;

I am going to the place of fetors,
Among the tormented, and the foul Inferno,
Where men suffer pains and great tortures.
It is so bitter that eternal [Hell] is hardly more so;

E'tal, che ne l'intrar con la mia scorta

And such, that entering with my escort,

Gli dissi, omei, che luce non discerno.
Et egli a me, passiam quest'altra porta
Che livi troverem la gran Liona

I said to him, Alas! for I see no light.

And he to me: Let us pass this other door
For there we will find the great Liona [ward]

Piena di gente, nel mal far accorta.
Hor quivi intrati, il stormo assai risuona
Da le voci d'afflitti, et dolorati

Full of people, cunningly evil.
Once we entered, the flock resounded
With the voices of the afflicted and suffering

Che biastemando adhor mia testa intuona.
Et piu de gli altri, alcuni disperati

Whose swearing makes my head ring.
And more than others, some desperate men

Ci venner contra con turbata voce
Gridando qui tra noi per che ne intrati.
Mia guid'a quegli, tal venire non nuoce
A tanti vitii, quanti in voi si atrova
Che per ben far, gia mai vi festi Croce.
Alhor tutti ver noi pur si rinova
Le diverse sue voci conturbate
Dicendo cui vi mand'a far tal prova.
Et io a quegli, tanto hor non gridate

Accosted us with angry voices,
Yelling, "Why have you come here among us?"
My guide to them: "Coming here does not worsen
The many vices there are among you,
Who to do good, have crossed yourselves not once.
Then they all launched against us
Their many angry voices,
Saying: "Who sends you to be tried so?"
And I to them: "But do not shout now!

Qui non venim'a farvi mal alcuno,

Ne meno vi torem quant'aspettate.

A ditto numerai ben quarant'uno
Che sconsolati stan'in tal pregione

Con lagrime il suo mal
    godend'ognuno.
Et io a mia guida, dimmi qual
    cagione
Et qual Fortun'è stata, che costoro
Qui dentro stian, in tal desperatione.
Et esso a me, quasi con modo ploro

Rispos'io [sic], io ti dirò quel
    c'hanno fatto
Isciagurati che mal fu per loro.
Dieci ne son, ch'in tal modo han
    robato
Con sotil arte, capi di centura

Tagliando molt'argento han rapinato.
Costor dal Boglia, haran gran
    battitura
Per che Giustitia vol che cotal genti
Tal fraude purghi, con simel penura.

Anchor per causa di armi, ne son
    vinti,
Che piu mortali in molti varii modi

Egli han feriti, e di gran dolor cinti.
Questi molti dinar, per simel frodi

Converranni pagar, et si non paga

Staranno sempre qui, con mal suoi
    lodi.
Undeci il resto, che con mortal piaga

De l'altrui robba, a tempo loro tolse

We have not come here to hurt
    anyone,
Nor will we steal from you what
    you await."
I counted some forty-one men
Who stayed in that prison
    disconsolate,
Each wallowing in his pain with
    tears.
And I to my guide: "Tell me, what
    reason
And what fate have led these men
In here, in such despair?"
And he to me, almost weeping,
    responded:
"I will tell you what those wretches
    have done,
Which was their undoing.
Ten of them are here for having
    cunningly
Robbed so much; who, by snipping
    purses off
Belts, have stolen much silver.
Such men will be thrashed by the
    executioner,
For Justice desires that such people
    be purged from such a crime,
    with similar scarcity.
Then, on account of arms, there are
    twenty men
Who have wounded more mortals
    in various ways
And afflicted them with great pain.
[All] these men, for similar crimes,
    will be made
To pay a great sum, and those who
    do not pay
Will always remain here, with evil as
    their praise.
The remaining eleven, who with
    mortal blows
Robbed from others, they removed a
    while ago,

Et hor stando qui dentro quegli paga.

And now they pay, languishing here inside."

Di questi assai mi doglio, ch'i rivolse

I am quite pained for them, how their path

Il camin lor, contra la rea Fortuna …
Dimmi scorta gentil, dimmi Signore

Turned against evil Fortune …
"Tell me, kind escort, tell me, my lord,"

Gli dimandai accio piu fusse certo
Di quel ch'ambiguo stava il mesto core.
Denno sempre costor star al coperto

I asked him in order to be more sure
About what remained vague in my sad heart:
"Are such men always condemned to the cover of such darkness, if they are unable

Di tanta scurita, n'havendo possa

To pay what had been assessed against them?"

Di satisfar a quel che gli han proferto?
Et egli a me, conven sue carni et ossa
Qui dentro tanto stiam, fin che vorranno
Color a cui gli aspettan tal riscossa.

And he to me: "It behooves that their flesh and bones
Remain here so long as it pleases
Those who await the recovery of their goods.
For Justice wants them to suffer a similar pain,

Per che Giustitia vol simel affanno
Patiscan lor, accio suoi creditori
Non se disperi, per patir tal danno.
E anchor di ciò, ben molti han gran terrori
Che guardan il principio, meggio, et fine
Per non cascar in tal dannosi errori.
Et io a lui, di tal prave confine
Ti prego uscian, e andian for in disparte
Laudand'ogn'hor l'alte gratie divine

So that their creditors would not despair
To suffer such harm.
And for this, many who well observe the Beginning, middle, and end,
Fear lest they fall into such harmful errors."
And I to him: "From such wretched quarters,
I beg you, let us depart, and keep away,
Always praising the divine graces of high,

Lascian sto loco, et gimo in altri parte.

Let us leave this place and head elsewhere."

LE STINCHE, A RECONSTRUCTION[1]

LE STINCHE WAS destroyed in 1833, after serving as Florence's main prison for over five hundred years. The trapezoid plot occupied by the compound was initially taken up by a residential building, but this was later converted into the present-day Teatro Verdi.

The reconstruction in figures A.1, A.2, and A.3 is based on the prison's ground plan appended to Fruttuoso Becchi's 1839 study, and on information that attests the compound's state prior to its demolition.[2] Five centuries of activity since Le Stinche's foundation, circa 1300, must have entailed many alterations, renovations, and adaptations. Yet fourteenth-century sources confirm that in its final years the prison still

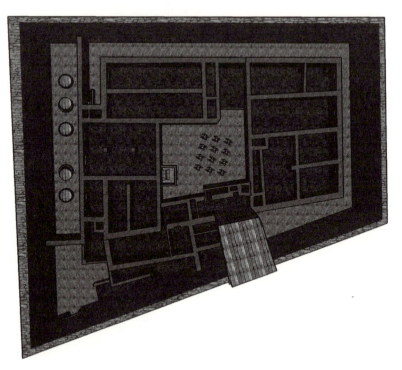

Fig. A.1. A reconstruction of Le Stinche, bird's-eye view, southern orientation.

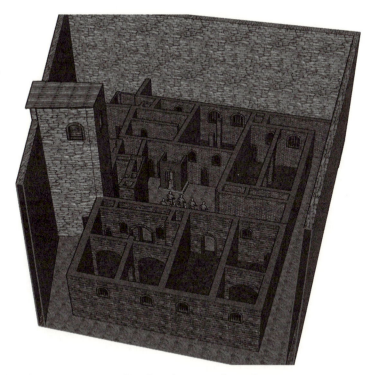

Fig. A.2. A reconstruction of Le Stinche, view from the west.

maintained many of its original features. In any case, the images in the figures are intended to be merely suggestive of the early layout.

Le Stinche had a single administrative entrance and one service gate, both from the north. The former led directly into the wardens' quarter, which consisted of the wardens' lodgings and offices, the watchtower, and a storage room. The wider service gate could let a handcart pass, and a low ramp afforded an easy climb from that entry into the storage room. This part of the compound was interconnected, with one passage leading into the inner court. There was another lodge (perhaps for the chaplain or the guards) across the courtyard.

The inmates' wards surrounded and opened into an inner courtyard, which contained the small prison chapel. The wards were separated from the outer wall by a peripheral sleeve or walk, accessible only from the administrative area, and which ended in an enclosure that contained several wells. Many bones were discovered in this area when the prison was destroyed, suggesting that at some point it began serving as a graveyard as well. The wards themselves differed somewhat in

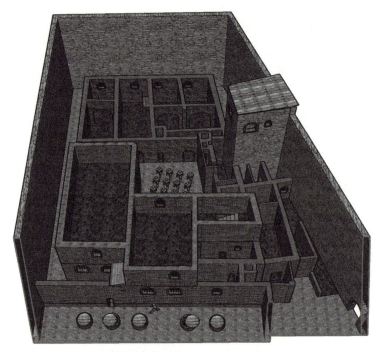

Fig. A.3. A reconstruction of Le Stinche, view from the east.

size. Each room seems to have contained sleeping benches, a latrine, some storage space, and one or more windows. At least one ward (the malevato) had two stories, the upper hosting the Esecutore's weekly tribunal. John Howard's 1778 description notes that both the infirmary and the women's ward were also on the second floor as well, but this may well have been a later development.

ABBREVIATIONS AND ARCHIVES

PRINTED ARCHIVAL SOURCES

B.St. 1245–67   *Statuti di Bologna dell'anno 1245 all'anno 1267*. Ed. Luigi Frati. 3 vols. Bologna: Regia Tipografia, 1869–77.

B.St. 1288   *Statuti di Bologna dell'anno 1288*. Ed. Gina Fasoli and Pietro Sella. 2 vols. Studi e Testi nos. 73, 85. Vatican City: Biblioteca Apostolica Vaticana, 1937–39.

B.St. 1352–57   *Gli Statuti del Comune di Bologna degli anni 1352, 1357; 1376, 1389 (Libri I–III)*. Vol. 1. Ed. Valeria Braidi. Bologna: Deputazione di Storia Patria per le Provincie di Romagna, 2002.

B.St. 1376–89   *Gli Statuti del Comune di Bologna degli anni 1352, 1357; 1376, 1389 (Libri I–III)*. Vol. 2. Ed. Valeria Braidi. Bologna: Deputazione di Storia Patria per le Provincie di Romagna, 2002.

F.St. 1322–25   *Statuti della Repubblica Fiorentina 1322–25*. Ed. Romolo Caggese. Rev. ed. by Giuliano Pinto et al. 2 vols. Florence: Leo S. Olschki, 1999.

F.St. 1415   *Statuta populi et communis florentiae … anno salutis MCCCCXV*. 3 vols. Freiburg: M. Kluch, 1778.

MC Cessi   *Deliberazioni del Maggior Consiglio di Venezia*. Ed. Roberto Cessi. 3 vols. Bologna: N. Zanichelli, 1931–50.

X Zago   *Consiglio dei Dieci: Deliberazioni miste*. Ed. Ferruccio Zago. 3 vols. Venice: Il Comitato, 1962–93.

XL Lombardo   *Le deliberazioni del Consiglio dei XL della Repubblica di Venezia*. Ed. Antonino Lombardo. 3 vols. Monumenti storici pubblicati dalla Deputazione di Storia Patria per le Venezie, n.s., vols. ix, xii, xx. Venice: Deputazione di Storia Patria per le Venezie, 1957–67.

UNPRINTED ARCHIVAL SOURCES

ASB   Archivio di Stato di Bologna
                  AO   Archivio degli Ospedali

	SMM	Ospedale di S. Maria della Morte, Opera de Carcerati: XI/5, XI/16
CC		Camera del Comune
	DA	Difensori dell'Avere: bb. 82–83, 90
	PC	Procuratori del Comune: bb. 1, 4, 8
	SDC	Soprastanti, Depositari e Conduttori dei Dazi: XXIII/1, XXIII/3
	TC	Tesoreria e Controllatore di Tesoreria: 1–17, 19–27
CP		Capitano del Popolo
	Giud.	Giudici: 49, 94, 639
CS		Uffici a Competenza Specifica
	SP	Soprastante alle Prigioni: b. 1
Dem.		Corporazioni Religiose Soppresse (Demaniale)
	SD	S. Domenico (Frati Predicatori): bb.178/7512–194/7528
	SMM	S. Martino Maggiore (Carmelitani): bb.1/3483–3/3485, 5/3487–7/3489, 9/3491–10/3492, 12/3494–13/3495, 15/3497–16/3498, 18/3500, 20/3502–23/3505, 25/3507
EC		Estimi del Comune: Serie II, b. 3
Gov.		Governo
	RP	Riformagioni e Provvigioni
	CPM	Riformagioni del Consiglio del Popolo e della Massa: 126, 129, 132, 138–39, 150, 153, 159–60, 170, 178, 184, 187, 190, 192–93, 196, 198–200, 208
	RPsc	Riformagioni e Provvigioni (serie cartacea): bb. 221–26

Statuti   Statuti: VIII, X
SP   Signoria Pepoli: bb. 245–46
SVEB   Signoria Viscontea,
            Ecclesiastica e
            Bentivolesca

    RPc   Riformagioni e Prov-
                vigioni   (cartacee):
                bb. 276–80, 283,
                285–86, 289, 293,
                297

    RPsm Riformagioni e Prov-
                vigioni (serie mis-
                cellanea): b. 314

Pod.   Curia del Podestà
          CA   Corone ed Armi:
                  bb. 2, 3, 5, 11, 18, 28–29, 32,
                  35–37, 39–42
          GM   Giudici ad Maleficia
              CC   Carte di Corredo: b. 70
              LI   Libri   Inquisitionum:
                        bb. 20, 30, 179–200,
                        203–4, 246, 254, 433
          Sind.   Sindacato: bb. 2–3, 13, 16, 22
UM   Ufficio dei Memoriali: 57, 101, 110,
          238–40

ASF   Archivio di Stato di Firenze
   AE   Atti dell'Esecutore degli Ordinamenti
                  di Giustizia: 129, 148, 156, 269, 280,
                  298, 314, 324, 333, 350, 365, 373, 389,
                  407, 416, 429, 442, 454, 477, 489, 501,
                  515, 535, 538, 540, 573, 575, 675, 678,
                  690, 698, 712, 770, 785, 788, 790
   CC   Camera del Comune
                  CU   Camarlinghi, Uscita: 65, 67,
                          145–46, 197–98, 244, 294
   MR   Miscellanea Repubblicana: 8, no. 240
   OSM   Capitani di Or San Michele: 1–16, 145–
                  46, 148–50, 244–46, 248–56
   PR   Provvisioni, Registri: 1–32, 387–88
   PP   Provvisioni, Protocolli: 1–2, 8
   SS   Soprastanti alle Stinche

	Car.	Carcerati: 82–85, 88–91
	EU	Entrata e Uscita: 376, 380–83, 385–88, 390–95
	Statuti	Statuti del Comune di Firenze
	1355	Statuti del Podestà e del Capitano del 1355: 16

ASS		Archivio di Stato di Siena
	Bicc.	Biccherna
	EU	Entrata e Uscita: 152, 154–55, 157, 159, 162–63, 167
	CG	Consiglio Generale
	Del.	Deliberazioni: 99, 101–9, 120–21, 143, 158, 168
	OC	Offerte di Carcerati: 470–73
	Conc.	Concistoro
	SCC	Scritture Concistoriali: 2119, 2162
	SC	Soprastanti alle Carceri: 1–2

ASV		Archivio di Stato di Venezia
	AC	Avogadoria di Comun: 1, 21/4, 22/5, 3617/1, 3641–45
	CD	Consiglio di Dieci, Deliberazioni (miste): 8
	CI	Cancelleria Inferiore
	Misc.	Miscellanea, Notai Diversi: bb. 19–22
	Notai	Notai: bb. 17, 20
	CP	Cinque Anziani alla Pace, Capitolari: b. 1
	GP	Giudici di Petizion
	EN	Estraordinario Nodari: 2–4
	SI	Sentenze a Interdetti: 2
	MC	Maggior Consiglio, Deliberazioni: 9 (Magnus et Capricornus, copia), 11 (Presbiter, copia), 13 (Clericus et Civicus, copia), 16 (Fronesis, copia), 18 (Spiritus, copia), 20 (Novella, copia), 21 (Leona)
	SNC	Signori di Notte al Criminal: 5–7; bb. 1, 16–17

GENERAL

Batiffol
: Louis Batiffol. "Le Châtelet de Paris vers 1400." *Revue historique* 61–63 (1896–97): 225–64; 225–35; 42–55, 266–83.

Beltrani
: Martino Beltrani-Scalia. *Sul governo e sulla riforma delle carceri in Italia. Saggio storico e teorico.* Turin: C. Favale, 1868.

Dunbabin
: Jean Dunbabin. *Captivity and Imprisonment in Medieval Europe, 1000–1300.* New York: Palgrave Macmillan, 2002.

Given
: James Given. *Inquisition and Medieval Society: Power, Discipline, and Resistance in Languedoc.* Ithaca, NY: Cornell University Press, 1997.

Gonthier
: Nicole Gonthier. "Prisons et prisonniers à Lyon aux XIVe et XVe siècles." *Mémoires de la Société pour l'Histoire du Droit et des Institutions des anciens pays bourguignons, comtois et romands* 39 (1982): 15–30.

Pugh
: Ralph B. Pugh. *Imprisonment in Medieval England.* Cambridge: Cambridge University Press, 1968.

RIS2
: Rerum Italicarum Scriptores. Gen. ed. L. A. Muratori. Rev. ed. by Giosue Carducci et al. 34 vols. Città di Castello [later Bologna]: N. Zanichelli, 1900-75.

Small
: Carola M. Small, "Prisoners at the Castellany of Artois in the Early Fourteenth Century." *Histoire Social–Social History* 26 (1993): 345–72

NOTES

A Note on Dates and Money

1. The Calends of January marked the beginning of an administrative term in Bologna, not the calendar year.

2. Conversion rates follow Goldwaithe and Mandich, *Studi sulla moneta fiorentina*, table 3 (pp. 87–100); Lane and Mueller, *Money and Banking in Medieval and Renaissance Venice*, appendix D, table D.3 (pp. 573–617). Exchange rates between local currencies follow Spufford, *Handbook of Medieval Exchange*, pp. 1–116.

Prologue

1. Fineschi, *Istoria comendiata*, pp. 71–72.

2. di Coppo Stefani, *Cronaca fiorentina*, col. 497.

3. Between 1177 and 1761 the Arno overflowed fifty-four times. See Aiazzi, *Narrazioni istoriche*, p. v.

4. Villani, *Nuova cronica*, XII, i (3:3–12). Villani purportedly expressed a common opinion in construing the event as divine retribution for the Florentines' vices. See *Nuova cronica*, XII, ii (3:12–26); Pucci, *L'alluvione dell'Arno nel 1333*, pp. 44–63.

5. By 1333 the compound comprised five wards, in accordance with the original plans. Only one of these, the *malevato* prison, was divided into lower and upper wards. See chapter 1 and appendix 3.

6. Inmate turnover at Le Stinche could rise above four hundred per semester. See ASF, SS Car. 82–85, 88–91 and fig. 3.4 below. Distribution charts for individuals semesters are in Geltner, "Medieval Prisons," appendix 1.

7. di Coppo Stefani, *Cronaca fiorentina*, col. 497.

8. ASF, *PR* 26, 118, fol. 70r–v (12 November 1333): "ut evaderent mortem quam indubitenter incurrissent ex dicta inundatione et impetu aque, nisi tunc subito extracuti fuissent."

9. The events are related in the wardens' request for compensations over the fines they had lost with the prisoners' flight. The plea was accepted, but a city official went on to prosecute the wardens, guards, and several of their associates for allegedly collaborating to aid the escape. See ASF, *PR* 26, 173, fol. 108r–v (26 April 1334). Due to fear of prison breaks, the penalty for complicit personnel was set in 1299 at ten thousand lire. See ASF, *PR* 10, 114, fols. 166v–167r (7 November 1299). It was a steep fine, considering that a warden earned one hundred lire for a six-month term (see chapter 1). Although such fines were

occasionally enforced (e.g., ASF, *PR* 19, 59, fols. 82r–83r [18 March 1323]), in this case the charges against the wardens were dropped.

10. Although he never mentions it, Villani was later imprisoned at Le Stinche. See Arias, "Nuovi documenti su Giovanni Villani," p. 386.

11. Associated Press, 5 January 2005. The doors to all of the cells, however, were found unlocked.

12. *The Age*, 31 August 2005. By that time the inmates were rioting, escaping, and holding a deputy warden and his family hostage.

13. For the distribution of grounds for incarceration at Le Stinche, see table 2.1.

14. Based on ASF, *SS* EU 376 (1 April–30 September 1355), Le Stinche's earliest surviving fiscal record. Villani, *Nuova cronica*, XII, xcii (3:193), probably overestimated the prison's annual revenues around that time at one thousand gold florins, or thirty-one hundred lire. See chapter 2.

15. Boccaccio, *Decameron*, Introduction to Day One (p. 13); equivocated by di Pagolo Morelli, *Ricordi*, pp. 287–92. Wray, *Communities and Crisis*, exposes the incongruence of Boccaccio's description with social realities, at least in the Bolognese case, and justly underscores Boccaccio's use of literary tropes in order to convey a sense of disaster.

16. On responses to political and environmental crises, which abounded in the fourteenth century, see Aberth, *From the Brink of the Apocalypse*; Canning et al., *Power, Violence, and Mass Death*, pp. 9–89; and Cohn, *Lust for Liberty*, pp. 205–42.

17. The compound came to be known as the Isola delle Stinche, commemorated today by the alley running along its former western wall.

Introduction

1. ASS, *CG* Del. 104, fol. 43r (17 February 1327): "In quibus carceribus essent loca distincta in quibus teneantur per se maiorum criminum criminosi et in quibus minorum et in quibus illi quos contigent pro debito carcerari." The appellants stressed (fol. 43v) the "evidens utilitas immo neccesitas quod huiusmodi enorme peccatum et severa crudelitas amplius non procedat nec substineatur ab hominibus civitatum."

2. At a total cost of 425 lire for three private residences and 500 lire for another property, according to ASS, *CG* Del. 104, fols. 114r–116r (4 June 1327); and *Bicc.* EU 157, fol. 17v (19 February 1328). These payments exclude sums that the commune paid to have the church of San Luca in Palchetto demolished. According to Balestracci and Piccinni, *Siena nel Trecento*, p. 103 n. 5, the entire endeavor amounted to 2,500 florins, or roughly 8,375 Sienese lire.

3. ASS, *Bicc.* EU 155, fol. 57v (31 December 1327): 469 lire, 8s., 4d.; EU 157, fol. 68v (January–July 1328): 4,387 lire, 10s.; and EU 159, fol. 76r (July 1328–January 1329): 1105 lire. Ambroggio Monzanini, the master mason of the project in 1330, earned 6 lire monthly (EU 167, fols. 43r, 68 [11 October–14 December 1330]). In the second semester of that year expenses amounted to over 825 lire (EU 167, fols. 4v, 36v, 67, 72v [13 July–12 December 1330]).

4. di Tura del Grasso, *Cronaca maggiore*, pp. 454–55, 491; Mannucci, "Un antico diario," p. 91.

5. Anonymous, *Cronanca senese*, p. 142; di Tura del Grasso, *Cronaca maggiore*, p. 498. The magistrates continued to improve the compound: in 1340 they built a hospital, in 1360 they added a fountain, and in 1376 they refurbished the wardens' quarters. See di Neri, *Cronaca senese*, pp. 593, 663; di Tura del Grasso, *Cronaca maggiore*, p. 526; Anonymous, *Cronaca senese*, p. 159.

6. Donati, "Il Palazzo del Comune di Siena," p. 317. On the early history of the Sienese prisons see Pazzaglini, "Comparable Practices of Medieval Imprisonment."

7. Balestracci, "From Development to Crisis," pp. 200–201; Heers, *La ville au Moyen Âge*, pp. 423–41; Piccinni, "Modelli di organizzazione dello spazio urbano"; Redi, "Dalla torre al palazzo"; Redi, *Pisa com'era*, pp. 177–313. For diverging views of Siena's political and economic history see Waley, *Siena and the Sienese*; and Bowsky, *A Medieval Italian Commune*.

8. See Nirenberg, *Communities of Violence*, which challenges the view of late-medieval European society as imbued with a so-called persecutorial mentality, in contrast with Cohn, *Pursuit of the Millennium*; Cohn, *Europe's Inner Demons*; and especially Moore, *Formation of a Persecuting Society*.

9. See Bériou and Touati, *Voluntate Dei Leprosus*; Rawcliffe, *Leprosy in Medieval England*; Otis, *Prostitution in Medieval Society*; Henderson, *The Renaissance Hospital*; Haverkamp, "Jewish Quarters in German Towns." The parallels between these forms of enclosure and municipal prisons are discussed in the conclusion.

10. Wolfgang, "A Florentine Prison"; and especially Manikowska, "The Florentine Communal Prison," are important exceptions.

11. Cervi, "Evoluzione topografica della Piazza Grande di Parma," pp. 45–47; Banzola, *Parma, la città storica*, p. 114; Franzoi, *Le prigioni della Repubblica di Venezia*; Scarabello, *Carcerati e carceri*; Magherini and Biotti, *L'isola delle Stinche*; Fadalti et al., *Gli artigli del leone*.

12. Pollock and Maitland, *History of English Law*, 2:516.

13. Following the examples, for instance, of Cohen, *The Crossroads of Justice*; Muir and Ruggiero, *History from Crime*; Smail, *The Consumption of Justice*; Wickham, "*Fama* and the Law in Twelfth-Century Tuscany."

14. See Kotkin, *Magnetic Mountain*, pp. 198–237.

15. Soman, "Deviance and Criminal Justice."

16. Howard, *State of the Prisons in England and Wales*; Beltrani. And see Mayhew and Binny, *Criminal Prisons of London*; and Desmaze, *Le Châtelet de Paris*. Less thorough, but equally demonstrative of contemporary interest in prisons are Alboize and Maquet, *Les prisons de l'Europe*; Tarra, *Prigioni di stato*.

17. Aubert, "Le parlement et les prisonniers"; Moranvillé, "Note sur les prisons"; Batiffol; Biffi, *Sulle antiche carceri di Milano*; Bertoletti, "Prigioni e prigionieri in Mantova"; Laschi, "Pene e carceri nella storia di Verona."

18. Given Bohne's cut-off date of roughly 1925, I tended to cite collections of statutes published after that year when expanding beyond the four main case studies.

19. Bohne, *Freiheitsstrafe in den italienischen Stadtrechten*, 2:1.

20. von Hippel, *Strafrechtsreform und Strafzwecke*, pp. 14–15.

21. See Schmidt, "Gotthold Bohne"; Schmidt, *Einführung in die Geschichte*, nos. 51, 184 (pp. 64–65, 193–94); Dahm, *Das Strafrecht Italiens*, pp. 308–11. Bohne's interim response to Schmidt forms the preface to his second volume.

22. Finzsch and Jütte, *Institutions of Confinement*; Van der Slice, "Elizabethan Houses of Correction."

23. Grand, "La prison et la notion d'emprisonnement"; Grand, "Justice criminelle"; Porteau-Bitker, "L'emprisonnement dans le droit laïque"; Bassett, "Newgate Prison in the Middle Ages"; Bassett, "Fleet Prison in the Middle Ages"; Pugh, "The King's Prisons before 1250."

24. Later studies that were either stimulated by Pugh or share, modify, or elaborate on his conclusions include Nicholas, "Crime and Punishment in Fourteenth-Century Ghent"; Coopland, "Crime and Punishment in Paris"; Pazzaglini, "Comparable Practices of Medieval Imprisonment"; Schnapper, *Les peines arbitraires du XIIIe au XIVe*; Hanawalt, *Crime and Conflict in English Communities*, pp. 53, 284; Vincent-Cassy, "Prison et châtiments à la fin du Moyen Âge"; Ireland, "Theory and Practice within the Medieval English Prison"; Peters, "Prison before the Prison"; Gonthier, *La châtiment du crime au Moyen Âge*, pp. 84–94, 114–20; Dunbabin.

25. Rusche and Kirchenheimer, *Punishment and Social Structure*; Taylor et al., *The New Criminology*; Fine, "Birth of Bourgeois Punishment"; Melossi and Pavarini, *The Prison and the Factory*.

26. Jones, *The Italian City-State*, pp. 152–332.

27. Goffman, *Asylums*, p. xiii.

28. Dossat, *Les crises de l'Inquisition toulousaine*, pp. 247–68; Given, pp. 69–70. And see Lea, *History of the Inquisition*, 1:373, 484–86; Peters, *Inquisition*, pp. 66–67.

29. Peters, *Torture*, pp. 40–62.

30. Chiffoleau, *Les justices du Pape*.

31. A review of critiques launched against Foucault, primarily by modern historians, is Roth, "La prison e ses histoires."

CHAPTER 1
ITALIAN PRISONS: THREE PROFILES

1. ASF, *SS* Car. 82–85, 88–91; *SS EU* 376, 380–83, 385–88, 390–95.

2. ASB, *CS SP* 1, fasc. 5–6; ASS, *SC* 1–2.

3. Beltrani, pp. 211–348.

4. An example of the former is ASS, *CG OC* 470–73.

5. ASF, *AE* 129, 148, 156, 269, 280, 298, 314, 324, 333, 350, 365, 373, 389, 407, 416, 429, 442, 454, 477, 489, 501, 515, 535, 538, 540, 573, 575, 675, 678, 690, 698, 712, 770, 785, 788, 790.

6. For all of the above, see abbreviations and archives and the manuscripts section in the bibliography.

7. Roberti, *Le magistrature giudiziarie veneziane*, 1:272. An early mention of the women's ward dates to 19 December 1366. See XL Lombardo, Reg. 29, pt. 1, no. 197 (3:114).

8. This was probably the only operative division among the inmates, despite the official stipulation to separate criminals from debtors, honest men from thieves, and grave from minor offenders. See ASV, *AC* 3617/1, no. 678 (1377 copy of an earlier register). Thus, an informed testator such as Niccolò Faron of Santa Maria Formosa included the inmates of both the upper and the lower wards in his bequest. ASV, *CI* Misc. b. 19, 16.

9. For Casanova's entertaining if self-aggrandizing account, see his *Histoire de ma fuite des prisons*. As is shown in chapter 3, this was hardly the earliest escape from the Venetian prisons, notwithstanding tour guides' claims to the contrary.

10. On Venetian prisons in general see Franzoi, *Le prigioni della Repubblica di Venezia*; Scarabello, *Carcerati e carceri*; Mutinelli, *Delle antiche prigioni della repubblica di Venezia*; Mutinelli, *Annali urbani di Venezia*, pp. 262–67, 492–94; Zanotto, *Il Palazzo Ducale di Venezia*, 4:1–53; Molmenti, *La storia di Venezia nella vita privata*, 2:25–29; Tassini, *Curiosità veneziane*, pp. 526–27; Lorenzi, *Monumenti*, nos. 18, 38, 40–41, 60, 88–89, 99; Fadalti et al., *Gli artigli del leone*.

11. According to Pullan, "Relief of Prisoners," p. 221, the original *casoni* functioned as debtors prisons well into the sixteenth century. Prisoners' graffiti from the Piombi and Pozzi continue uninterrupted from at least the sixteenth to the twentieth century.

12. Liber consiliorum specialium personarum 107 (7 July 1275), MC Cessi, 2:162: "solvendo insuper custodes, qui eum custodierunt, et illos, qui deputati fuerint ad custodiendum ipsum per dominum Ducem et eius Consilium, antequam exeat de forcia domini Ducis."

13. Liber Çaneta 132 (4 November 1287), MC Cessi, 3:188; ASV, *AC* 1, fol. 70r (Cap. 138 [1272]).

14. Ruggiero, *Violence in Early Renaissance Venice*, pp. 43–53.

15. ASV, *MC* 16 (Liber Fronesis), fols. 68v–69r (22 June 1320), 106r (5 July 1321); *MC* 18 (Liber Spiritus), fols. 6r (2 March 1326), 329v–330r (22 January 1344), 331r–v (25 February 1344); *MC* 21 (Liber Leona), fols. 98r (17 May 1397), 103v (28 September 1398).

16. ASV, *MC* 9 (Liber Magnus), fol. 148v (8 November 1303).

17. On supervised family visitations see X Zago, Reg. II, no. 453 (11 January 1324) (1:168); Reg. III, no. 5 (May 1325) (2:8); Reg. V, no. 328 (12 November 1355) (3:125). The doge and councilmen's weekly visitations shifted from emphasizing procedure to questioning prisoners regarding their conditions. See X Zago, Reg. V, no. 531 (24 January 1358) (3:206). Within four months, however, these "onerous" visits were reduced from weekly to monthly. See Reg. V, no. 558 (16 May 1358) (3:215–16). On the doge's prerogative in allocating different cells for different offenses see ASV, *MC* 16 (Liber Fronesis), fol. 29r–v (30? June 1319). On granting a prisoner permission to write letters under supervision see X Zago, Reg. III, no. 309 (11 December 1328) (2:106–7). For deliberations on prison overcrowding see ASV, *MC* 18 (Liber Spiritus), fols. 98v–99r (5 February 1331).

18. According to Guzzetti, "Le donne a Venezia nel XIV secolo," pp. 70–71, between 1301 and 1325 forty-six women (2.3 percent of all donations) and four men (1.6 percent) left bequests to prisoners, as against eighty-six women (5.7 percent) and eight men (4.8 percent) who did so between 1376 and 1400. For several such bequests see Bernardi, *Antichi testamenti*, 1:28, 2:32, 4:10, 5:12, 7:24, 10:16.

19. Mocenigo, *Capitolare dei Signori di Notte*, nos. 120, 141, 202, 293 (pp. 88, 105, 158, 228); Crouzet-Pavan, "Recherches sur la nuit vénetienne." For the use of the prisons by the Five of Peace, see ASV, *CP* 1, Reg. 2, II, xxxviii (28 December 1300), xxxix–xxxx (2 March 1301), xliii (1 June 1307) (fols. 16–19).

20. Liber Çaneta 6 (8 March 1297), MC Cessi, 3:419.

21. For the guards' salaries see ASV, *MC* 16 (Liber Fronesis), fol. 115r (23 August 1321); *AC* 21/4, fol. 148r (23 August 1321); *AC* 22/5, fol. 45v (8 January 1327); *MC* 18 (Liber Spiritus), fol. 211r (23 May 1339); and Mocenigo, *Capitolare dei Signori di Notte*, no. 293 (p. 228). As elsewhere, however, the guards' salaries were relatively low. On 7 September 1318, Marco Fabri, a custodian in the lower prisons, received a *grazia* or special license to transport grain from Puglia to augment his salary, which, he claimed, was insufficient to support his large family. See *AC* 21/4, fol. 45r. Attempts to avoid potential corruption among the guards were never entirely successful. See *AC* 22/5, fol. 28v (10 July 1325); XL Lombardo, Reg. 22, no.1; Reg. 29, pt. 1, no. 52 (1:1; 3:72–73).

22. The prisons' *capitano* is also mentioned in XL Lombardo, Reg. 22, nos. 129–33 (1:36–37); and in X Zago, Reg. VI, nos. 367–68, 371 (4:82).

23. XL Lombardo, Reg. 22, nos. 129–133 (1:36–37). According to Muir, *Civic Ritual in Renaissance Venice*, p. 190, the prison notaries and *capitani* routinely marched in the first segment of formal processions, a place reserved for minor *cittadini* officials, at least since the *Serrata* of 1297. These functionaries, however, are absent from the detailed description of Venetian processions in Martin da Canal's *Les estoires de Venise*, 246–62, 282–304, written in the late thirteenth century.

24. ASV, *MC* 21 (Liber Leona), fol. 103v (28 September 1398).

25. On 23 September 1321, the Council of Ten decided to raise a poor prisoner's bread ration from one to two loaves daily. See X Zago, Reg. I, no. 252 (1:97).

26. Lazzarini, "L'avvocato dei carcerati poveri a Venezia."

27. Occasional amnesties were declared before an important battle, to celebrate its positive aftermath, or periodically to reduce crowding. See ASV, *AC* 3644, Reg. 2, fol. 46r (27 July 1389); *MC* 11 (Liber Presbiter), fol. 286r (13 June 1314); 20 (Liber Novella), fols. 190v–191r (9 July 1361), fols. 231v–232r (9 June 1364), fols. 277v–278r (15 May 1367), fol. 313r–v (22 November 1369), fol. 395r (1 April 1382); 21 (Liber Leona), fol. 27v (20 December 1388), fols. 49v–50r (21 March 1391). And see de Monacis, *Chronicon de rebus venetis*, p. 247.

28. Conditional pardons are ubiquitous among the Avogaria di Comun's records.

29. The Compagnia della Carità del Crocefisso, the first Venetian confraternity dedicated to the relief of prisoners, was founded in 1591. See Sagredo, *Il patronato dei carcerati in Venezia*; Pullan, "Relief of Prisoners," pp. 221–29. For confraternity donations to prisoners in sixteenth-century Venice see Pullan, *La politica sociale della Repubblica di Venezia*, 1:185–87, 202.

30. Franzoi, *Le Prigioni della Repubblica di Venezia*, pp. 69–74.

31. Petro Gato of Chioggia was released after falling ill. See *MC* 9 (Liber Magnus), fol. 125r (30 April 1303). His subsequent escape, compounded by the rise in requests for amelioration on account of illness may have convinced Venetian magistrates to abandon this practice and revert to separating sick from healthy

inmates. See *AC* 1, fols. 114r–115r (1309); and *MC* 13 (Liber Clericus et Civicus), fol. 272r–v (31 July 1318).

32. *MC* 20 (Liber Novella), fols. 46v–47r (3 January 1343), 60v (21 September 1353), 149v (3 July 1358), 195v–196r (13 July 1361).

33. Master Ricobaldo, a poor surgeon, apparently attended poor Venetian prisoners free of charge. See *AC* 22/5, fol. 101r (6 April 1329).

34. X Zago, Reg. VI, no. 629 (4:127).

35. Seven cases are reported for the period 1324–87 in the Avogaria di Comun records. See chapter 3.

36. See ASV, *SNC* 6, fol. 5r–v (29 December–20 February 1348).

37. As implied by Dunbabin, pp. 171–72.

38. Updated general histories of medieval Venice include Lane, *Venice*; Branca, *Storia della civiltà veneziana*; Delogu et al., *Longobardi e Bizantini*; Cessi, *Storia della Repubblica di Venezia*; Cracco, *Un "altro mondo"*; and vols. 1–3 of the recently completed *Storia di Venezia*.

39. Roberti, *Le magistrature giudiziarie veneziane*, 1:163 and passim.

40. Chojnacki, "In Search of the Venetian Patriciate"; Cracco, "La cultura giuridico-politica"; Romano, "Quod sibi fiat gratia"; Romano, *Patricians and Popolani*; Lane, "L'ampliamento del Maggior Consiglio di Venezia"; Rösch, "Serrata of the Great Council," pp. 67–88.

41. The Statutes of the Podestà for 1325 (I, 18; F.St. 1322–25, II [p. 53]) and for 1355 (I, 52; ASF, *Statuti* 1355, 16, fol. 43v) mention twelve guards. This is an exceptional number and is probably unrealistic. The highest recorded number of guards (six) appears in 1360. ASF, *CC CU* 145, fol. 22r (14 March 1360). Conversely, F.St. 1415, I, 71 (1:91–92) calls for the election of three guards—perhaps an optimistic assertion. These statutes also mention a fifth warden.

42. The chamberlain's position rotated among the city's sixths (and later quarters) and was nominated by the Seven Major Guilds. See F.St. 1322–25, I, 18 (p. 50); ASF, *Statuti* 1355, 16, I, 52, fol. 41v.

43. ASF, *PR* 15, 90, fol. 144r–v (9 March 1318); *PR* 19, 56, fol. 75r (28 February 1323). For the *pinzocheri* see also *PR* 25, 42, fols. 44v–45r (20 June 1329); Thompson, *Cities of God*, pp. 70–102.

44. ASF, *PR* 19, 56, fol. 75r (28 February 1323). The rector of San Simone, the parish church next to the prison's southern wall, received sixty lire annually for the chaplain's needs, but not the latter's salary (one hundred lire annually), which was paid by the commune. This practice continued into the fifteenth century. See F.St. 1415, I, 74 (1:98).

45. ASF, *SS EU* 380 (1 October 1359–10 February 1360); *SS EU* 381 (1 October 1362–31 March 1363).

46. ASF, *CC CU* 146, fol. 60r (8 August 1360). A further physician was occasionally employed. See *CC CU* 197, fol. 10v (31 October 1370).

47. ASF, *SS EU* 380 (1 October 1359–10 February 1360).

48. ASF, *PR* 12, 86, fol. 105r–v (29 February 1305); *PR* 12, 115, fol. 149r–v (4 May 1305).

49. The Esecutore's office was established in 1307, and the supervision of Le Stinche and the Volognana (see below) fell under his "extraordinary" responsibilities. See Zorzi, "I rettori di Firenze," p. 463.

50. *Statuti* 1355, 16, I, 52, fol. 44v. These men served for two months, apparently without pay. See also F.St. 1415, I, 72 (1:92–93), where the term is extended to four months, with the added responsibility of hiring the prison physician. The prison's almoners appointed (from among the prisoners, apparently) a podesta who could collect two soldi from each inmate to aid the *pinzocheri*'s work. Neither these funds, nor this functionary, however, appear in the prison's extant records.

51. ASF, *SS* EU 391 (5 October 1391–31 March 1392); *SS* EU 392 (5 April–7 October 1392). The office of the communal almoner, or *litoris*, is defined in F.St 1415, I, 82 (1:102–3).

52. At least 160 inmates were dispersed throughout the city's jails in 1298. See ASF, *PR* 9, 78–79 (16 July 1298). And see ASF, *MR* 8, no. 240, fols. 211r–214v (27 November 1292) on the regulation of these prisons.

53. Around 1300 these included the Pagliazza (the women's prison) and the Burelle, appropriated from a Byzantine tower and from the foundations of the Roman amphitheater, respectively. In 1290 the Bellanda Prison was demolished, and the Volognana, a room in the tower of the Palazzo del Podestà, was retained solely for brief custody. Even the recently established Magnati Prison (ca. 1294) would move ca. 1307–8 into Le Stinche's grounds. Beyond these recognized facilities, the commune used existing houses, inns, and courts at times of need, especially to detain large numbers of war prisoners. See Fraticelli, *Delle antiche carceri di Firenze*; Becchi, *Sulle Stinche di Firenze*; Uccelli, *Il Palazzo del Potestà*, pp. 142–59; Davidsohn, *Storia di Firenze*, 1:983–84, 3:247 n. 1, 247, 648–49, 4:98–100, 108, 403, 615–34, 7:547, 603; Fanelli, *Firenze architettura e città*, pp. 129–30; Manikowska, "The Florentine Communal Prison."

54. Although much smaller, a rural English stronghold dating to the middle of the thirteenth century claims the European title. See Saunders, "Lydford Castle, Devon," p. 164.

55. See Davidsohn, *Forschungen zur Geschichte von Florenz*, 4:525, for an exception to this rule.

56. ASF, *AE* 269, passim (1 August 1357–15 January 1358).

57. ASF, *AE* 298, fol. 52r (19 February 1359).

58. Uccelli, *Il Palazzo del Potestà*, pp. 154–55. And see Zorzi, "Politica e giustizia a Firenze."

59. Direct payments to prison guards by the commune are already evident in 1286. See ASF, *PP* 1, fols. 20v–21r (20 September 1286). However, according to *PR* 6, 33, fols. 35v–36r (5 June 1296), and *PR* 8, 62, fol. 71r (7 July 1297), it was probably an innovation.

60. In 1289 Bandino de Tebalducci was still leasing the Burelle and Pagliazza. See *PR* 2, 10, fol. 12r (2 July 1289).

61. ASF, *PP* 1, fols. 24r (6 December 1286), 76r (12 May 1287); *PP* 2, fol. 34v (26 March 1303).

62. ASF, *PR* 29, 130, fol. 113r–v (2 April 1339); *PR* 30, fol. 59r–v (9 March 1341). Lorenzo, Le Stinche's water-carrier in late 1369, was not paid for over seven months: ASF, *SS* EU 383 (5 October 1369–31 March 1370).

63. ASF, *CC* CU 197, fol. 9v (30 October 1370).

64. For the physician's salary see ASF, *CC* CU 146, fol. 60r (8 August 1360); *CC* CU 197, fol. 9v (30 October 1370); *CC* CU 244, fol. 2r (24 September 1380). Inmates

convicted of violent assault within the prison could also suffer amputations. See ASF, *Statuti* 1355, 16, I, 54, fol. 45v.

65. By 1387 the physician's salary (ten lire monthly) was paid directly from Le Stinche's treasury. See ASF, *SS* EU 390 (1 April–7 October 1387).

66. The first mention of a prison hospital is ASF, *AE* 269, fol. 78r (20 October 1357).

67. Niccolò Valori replaced Master Ambrogio in 1387, and remained in this post at least until 1392. See ASF, *SS* EU 390 (1 April–7 October 1387); *SS* EU 392 (5 April–7 October 1392).

68. For a dicussion of death rates at Le Stinche, see chapter 3.

69. Official administrators were also prohibited from assuming any position related to the prison for the following three years. See F.St. 1322–25, I, 18 (pp. 49–50); ASF, *Statuti* 1355, 16, I, 52, fol. 41r; F.St. 1415, I, 71 (1:91–92). The duration of guards' employment is never specified.

70. Except wardens and guards, the only permanent functionaries known before Le Stinche's foundation were the Burelle's scribe and the Pagliazza's custodian.

71. ASF, *SS* EU 390 (1 April–7 October 1387); *SS* EU 391 (5 October 1391–31 March 1392).

72. According to the podesta's 1325 statutes (F.St. 1322–25, I, 18 [2:51–52]), the rates were as follows: for fines or debts up to 100 lire, 3 soldi; between 100 and 500 lire, 4 soldi; between 500 and 1,000 lire, 6 soldi; 1,000 lire and above, 10 soldi. Prisoners incarcerated by the commune without an express sum were to pay according to the wardens' or chamberlain's decision, but never above 10 soldi per day. Major debtors could not obtain agevolatura without their creditor's permission. These rates were reduced and modified by 1355: 1 soldo for fines or debts under 100 lire; 2 soldi between 100 and 500 lire; 3 soldi between 500 and 1,000 lire; and 5 soldi for 1,000 lire and above. Men held without a specific fine were subject to a daily rate of 2 soldi. Citizens were allowed eight days from their initial agevolatura to pay their fees, while noncitizens were given fifteen days. See ASF, *Statuti* 1355, 16, I, 52, fol. 42r–v and F.St. 1415, I, 73 (1:95).

73. ASF, *AE* 515, fol. 2r (12 November 1368). The phrase is ubiquitous.

74. The deputy chamberlain Jacopo was fined five lire for allowing an "unauthorized woman" to enter the compound. See ASF, *AE* 573, fol. 18r (26 March 1369).

75. ASB, *CS SP*, fasc. 1 (1239) relates that in 1250 war prisoners from Modena and Parma were dispersed among several facilities that could hold no more than twenty prisoners each. According to B.St. 1245–57, X, 101 (3:203–4), the custodians and notary at each prison were ordinary commune officials, elected for one semester, and who were to earn ten lire each. On the variety of Bolognese *torri* see Finelli, *Bologna ai tempi che vi soggiornò Dante*, pp. 23–48; significantly revised by Fabbri, *Le fortificazione del Medio Evo a Bologna*, pp. 35–49; and Fanti, "Intorno alle mura e alle torri di Bologna."

76. A 1256 inventory of the commune's properties lists some dozen workshops and businesses "sub voltis dicti pallacii [= veteris] iuxta spondam prixionis communis" (ASB, *CC PC* 1, fasc. 7, fols. 1v–6r [1256]). The document is reproduced in Foschi, "I palazzi del Comune di Bologna," pp. 94–100. This

modifies earlier estimates that dated the palace prisons to 1270 at the earliest: Giudicini, *Cose notabili*, 2:411. And see Foschi, "I Palazzi del Podestà, di Re Enzo e del Capitano del Popolo," pp. 13–17. ASB, *Gov.* SVEB, RPsm 314, Reg. 2 (single folio from 2 June 1268), contains a decision to replace the *existing* prison (*carcer seu camera comunis bon.*) with a more suitable facilty.

77. On 8 February 1254, the treasury paid thirty soldi to a certain Albertino, son of Bernardo, for several maintenance works, including a repair "ad hostium carceris domini Roberti, et lapidibus poscitis ad dictam carcerem" (ASB, *CC* TC 1, fol. 4r). An entry from 1 June 1254 records two separate payments to two guards of the prison of Guido of Piacenza, both serving for fourteen days (ASB, CC TC 1, fols. 11v, 12r).

78. In 1470 seventy Milanese prisoners were divided among the city's eleven prisons, according to Biffi, *Sulle antiche carceri di Milano*, pp. 4–8.

79. Tega, *Storia illustrata di Bologna*, 1:366, 2:399.

80. B.St 1245–67, II, 40 (1:298–99). However, a variant 1252 reading discloses that convicted false witnesses were to be incarcerated in the "thieves' prison" (*carcer latronum*) in lieu of a two-hundred-lire fine. See B.St 1245–67, II, 5 (1:258).

81. B.St. 1245–67, X, 74 (3:168–70 [Cod. 60]).

82. B.St. 1245–67, X, 74 (3:168–70 [Codd. 62–67]).

83. ASB, *Pod.* Sind., Reg. 1286 I/1, fol. 31r (28 March 1286). Records of the *camera superioris* certainly predate those of the (lower) tower prison, but the former space is not necessarily identical to the prison mentioned in the 1256 inventory cited above. This modifies Ghirardacci, *Historia di Bologna*, 2:316, where the year 1294 marks the terminus ad quem for the establishment of both prisons.

84. Compare ASB, CC PC 4, Reg. 34, fol. 13r–v (11 August 1288), which lists twenty-nine prisoners, to the forty-four inmates mentioned in *Pod.* CA 11, Reg. 3 (1301).

85. The Palazzo del Podestà was completely remodeled in the middle of the fifteenth century. The first available ground plan dates to 1658.

86. ASB, *UM* 110, fol. 375r (7 January 1305). The document is transcribed in appendix 1.

87. Pini, "Problemi di demografia bolognese," dates medieval Bologna's demographic peak to the 1290s. The decline was only exacerbated, albeit dramatically, by the onset of the plague cycle from 1348.

88. The Predacolaria, probably named after the commune's homonymous countryside stronghold, is identified during the deliberations regarding a certain Fantinus de Fabianis, held by the podesta's entourage "in carcere comunis qui vocatur predacolaria, qui est in palatio veteri comunis bononie iuxta cameram ubi deponuntur et stant baliste comunis et iuxta porticum ambulationum per quam iter di palatio veteri ad palatium novum faciendo." ASB, *CP* Giud. 639, fol. 33r (4 January 1318). The ward is later mentioned in rubric IV, 35, of the 1335 statutes: ASB, *Gov.* Statuti X, fols. 69r–70r.

89. Neither Hubert, *Der Palazzo Comunale von Bologna*, pp. 13–29, nor Foschi, "Da magazzini di governo a centro amministrativo," mentions these prisons.

90. ASB, *Gov.* RP, *CPM* 200, Reg. XIV/3, fol. 386r–v (17 October 1326). The cells were completed within six months, according to an entry in the *Cronaca Villola* from 23 April 1327. See Sorbelli, *Corpus Chronicorum Bononiensum*, 2:381–82.

91. Giudicini, *Cose notabili*, 2:350; Fanti, *Gli schizzi topografici originali di Giuseppe Giudicini*, no. 295.

92. First attested on 3 April 1327 (ASB, *Gov.* RP, *RPsc* 221, Reg. 37, fol. 78r). Possibly the last reference to the lower prisons is ASB, *Gov.* RP, *CPM* 200, Reg. XIV/3, fol. 320v (14 March 1326). The new distinction holds throughout all subsequent deliberations, statutes, and fiscal records.

93. The number of custodians initially dropped to two per prison. See ASB, *Gov.* RP, *RPsc* 224, Reg. 44, fol. 41v (19 March 1330). The reduction may have intended to maintain a representation of all quarters. However, it soon rose back to three (ASB, *CC* TC 9, fol. 5v [8 May 1339]), and then back to four, as prescribed by the statutes. But see Dondarini, *Le "Descriptio civitatis Bononie,"* p. 62, which notes only three custodians, an executioner, and a notary.

94. According to Ghirardacci, *Historia di Bologna*, 3:75, in early 1443 Giacomo dal Lino and Azzo da Quarto leased the old prisons for two years for the sum of thirteen hundred lire and on condition that they construct the prisons anew, which they apparently did. And see Giudicini, *Cose notabili*, 2:412.

95. On 16 October 1283, Donna Tomasina, wife of a declared Lambertazzi "rebel," was discovered in the city, contrary to her ban. She was placed interminably in the custody of Sister Marina, prioress of the convent at Santa Maria della Misericordia (ASB, *CP* Giud. 49, fol. 20r). Three years later, under similar circumstances, Donna Sima, daughter of Jacomo, was imprisoned in the monastery of San Lorenzo (ASB, *CP* Giud. 94, fol. 5v [15 October 1286]).

96. ASB, *Gov.* RP, *CPM* 138, fol. 9v (26 April 1294): "Item, cum ex forma statutum comunis bon. mulieres non possint in carceribus cum hominibus detineri, sed nuncti debeant custodi[re] apud aliquem locum dominarum religiosarum, qui eas custodire penitu recusant. Et ita male muliercule et meretrices non timent facere maleficia neque venire contra statuta comunis bon., sed penitus spernunt mandatum officialum comunis bon. et recusant securitatem prestate, scientes quod non possunt personaliter detineri."

97. ASB, *Gov.* RP, *RPsc* 222, Reg. 41, fol. 39v (5 February 1328). Ciacco, *Il cardinal legato Bartrando del Poggetto*, pp. 52, 55–56, underscores the legate's attention to prison administration, including the establishment of a women's ward and the monitoring of the custodians' expenditure of the prisoners' alms. On the tower itself, see Foschi, "I palazzi del Comune di Bologna," pp. 87–88 and n. 52.

98. Giudicini, *Cose notabili*, 2:411. Zucchini, *Il Palazzo del Podestà*, pp. 51–52, claims that the women's prison was located on the ground floor of Re Enzo's palace, facing east.

99. B.St. 1245–67, X, 74 (3:168–71).

100. Exceptionally there could be less. See ASB, *CC* PC 4, Reg. 34, fol. 13r–v (11 August 1288).

101. ASB, *Gov.* RP, *RPsc* 226, Reg. 54, fols. 16r–17r (24 October 1334).

102. B.St. 1245–67, X, 74 (3:168).

103. B.St. 1288, II, 3 (1:46–47).

104. ASB, *CC* SDC XXIII/3, fasc. III, no. 38 bis (8 January 1289). Ciacco, *Il cardinal legato Bartrando del Poggetto*, 52, misattributes the institution of the tax to the cardinal's efforts. The *conduttore* or tax collector paid an annual fee of

425 lire for the office, and was always guaranteed payment; if a prisoner was condemned to death, his or her fees would be paid by the commune. See ASB, *Gov.* SVEB, *RPc*, Reg. 23, fol. 38v (15 November 1352).

105. For the tax collectors' activities see ASB, *CC* DA 82, fols. 119r–124r (May 1335), 134v (July 1340); 83, fols. 81r–v (August 1347), 144r (March 1370), 181v–182r (March 1375); 90, fols. 27r (July 1398), 28r (1399).

106. The earliest surviving reports by the prison supervisors are in ASB, *Pod.* Sind. 22 (1388–90).

107. To judge by its value against the Florentine florin, the Bolognese lira was in a slight but steady decline throughout this period. This may explain the rise in the wardens' required guarantees from 2,000 to 5,000 lire, but not its leap from 200 to 2,000 lire. Inflation, if such it was, would also underscore the continuous decline in the value of the wardens' salary. See Salvioni, *Il valore della lira bolognese.*

108. ASB, *Pod.* Sind., Reg. 1286 I/1, fol. 31r (28 March 1286). The 1288 statutes reconfirm this reduction, which remained in place during the following decades. See ASB, *Gov.* SP 245, Reg. 35, fols. 48v–49r (1347); 246, Reg. 38, fols. 42v, 44r–v, 46r, 47v, 48v (1348).

109. B.St. 1288, II, 17 (1:92–94). Such payments were common: on 5 September 1286, Galerano Del Ferro and his associate custodians at the upper prisons earned twenty soldi for performing a decapitation; five days later a further thirty soldi for flogging five men; and yet another forty soldi for two decapitations and five soldi for a flogging, all performed two weeks later. See ASB, *Pod.* Sind. 3, Reg. 1286 II/2, fols. 72r, 73v, 78v–79r. On 21 November of that year the same custodians received payments for one decapitation (20s.), one amputation of a leg (10s.) and two floggings (10s.), all performed recently (fol. 108v). And see Kantorowicz, *Albertus Gandinus*, nos. 36, 44, 134.

110. Statute IV, 64 (1335), in ASB, *Gov.* Statuti X, fols. 85r–86r; B.St. 1352–57, III, 28 (1:200); B.St. 1376–89, III, 23 (2:962–62). The older fee system remained in effect at least until 1295, when the expense accounts of six inmates only list payments of two soldi "per inferiatura et deferiatura" and two denari per diem. See ASB, *Pod.* GM, *LI* 433, Reg. 2, fols. 1r–2v.

111. Many cooking utensils feature on the prison's inventory from 1305, suggesting that meals were already offered previously, although at what price (if any) is unknown. See appendix 1.

112. The 1376 statutes reduced the waiting period to two years, perhaps in response to the revisitation of the plague, or to the difficulty of recruiting wardens. See B.St. 1376–89, III, 23 (2:962).

113. Gaudenzi, *Statuti del popolo di Bologna*, p. 30.

114. B.St. 1352–57, III, 28 <III, 34> (1:199).

115. For Florence, see above; for Perugia, see Degli Azzi, *Statuti di Perugia*, pp. 211–17.

116. Funds for the prisoners' daily bread-rations were temporarily channeled into the custodians' hands, according to ASB, *CC* TC 1, fols. 1v (3 July 1288), 2r (5 July 1288), 4v (8 July 1288). For the friars' reincorporation see ASB, *Gov.* RP *CPM* 192, Reg. XII/8, fols. 380v–381r (25 April 1320).

117. Grion, "La 'Legenda' del B. Venturino da Bergamo," p. 46.

118. ASB, *AO* SMM, XI/16, fols. 43–46. And see Zucchini, *Il Palazzo del Podestà*, pp. 1–3.

119. Fanti, "La Confraternita di Santa Maria della Morte," pp. 104–5.

120. Among the 1,108 wills deposited at the Dominican convent between 1270 and 1400, merely 11 contain donations to prisoners. There are a handful of similar bequests in the parallel depository of 400 wills surviving from the Carmelite convent (1288–1400). The confraternity of Santa Maria della Morte may have assumed responsibility for executing such bequests in the 1380s, but it certainly did not generate them ex nihilo, as Fanti's aforementioned study implies. And see Fortunato, "La raccolta dei testamenti," p. 200.

121. Gaudenzi, *Statuti del popolo di Bologna*, 1292 (pp. 202–3).

122. B.St. 1376–89, III, 25 (2:972–77).

123. There exists no modern comprehensive history of Bologna to follow Alfred Hessel's *Geschichte der Stadt Bologna von 1116 bis 1280*, although discrete periods have been examined, e.g., Rodolico, *Dal comune alla signoria*; Vitale, *Il dominio della parte guelfa in Bologna*; Ciacco, *Il cardinal legato Bartrando del Poggetto*; Larner, *The Lords of Romagna*; Bosdari, "Il Comune di Bologna alla fine del secolo XIV"; as well as several syntheses such as Fasoli, "Bologna nell'età medievale"; and Dondarini, *Bologna medievale*. Sarah Blanshei is currently completing a political and legal history of late-thirteenth-century Bologna.

CHAPTER 2

ASPECTS OF IMPRISONMENT

1. Italian urban history is an immense and highly regionalized field. A clear sketch of late-twelfth-century and thirteenth-century developments, including a substantial bibliography, is Pini, *Città, comuni e corporazioni*, pp. 22–40. Several recent additions that cover the fourteenth century as well, include Spilner, "'Ut civitas amplietur'"; Sznura, "Le città toscane nel XIV secolo"; Trachtenberg, *Dominion of the Eye*. General urban histories of medieval Europe include Hohenberg and Lees, *Making of Urban Europe*; Heers, *La ville au Moyen Âge*; Braunfels, *Urban Design in Western Europe*; Benevolo, *La città nella storia d'Europa*; Nicholas, *Growth of the Medieval City*; Nicholas, *The Later Medieval City*. None of these studies or surveys, however, offers even the briefest discussion of urban prisons. A unique, if brief, exception is Cunningham, "For the Honour and Beauty of the City," who argues (p. 29) that "[t]he siting of a prison within the headquarters of the [Sienese] chief officer of the judiciary is entirely logical." And see pp. 50–51.

2. Fabris, "La Cronaca di Giovanni da Nono," pp. 11–12; excerpted translation in Dean, *Towns of Italy*, pp. 19–21.

3. Hassler, *Fratris Felicis Fabri Evagatorium*, 2:409–10; de Monacis, *Chronicon de rebus venetis*, p. 279.

4. Alberti, *L'architettura*, V, 13 (1:397–99); Filarete, *Trattato di architettura*, VI, X (1:166, 2:276–77). Note, however, that while Alberti tried to balance between realism and idealism, Filarete's dialogical tractate is mostly imaginary. Later in the work (2:610–17), Filarete "describes" a penal colony outside the city, purportedly based on an ancient model.

5. Nagel, *The New Red Barn*, pp. 47–48. A further technique used in North American cities is simply to camouflage local prisons as ordinary government buildings (as in downtown Philadelphia, Chicago, and New York) or hotels (as in Los Angeles). See Home Office, *New Directions in Prison Design*, pp. 8–19; and Davis, *City of Quartz*, pp. 253–57.

6. An exotic (and later) example of this type is the so-called Prison Tree in Kimberly County, Australia. It is a hollow trunk of a baobab tree, which used to house up to thirty prisoners in transit.

7. Batiffol, p. 46; Small, pp. 345–72.

8. Bassett, "Newgate Prison in the Middle Ages"; Bassett, "Fleet Prison in the Middle Ages"; Saunders, "Lydford Castle, Devon."

9. Manca, "Istituti di pena," p. 2.

10. Newcomb, "Evolution of the Prison Plan"; Johnston, *Forms of Constraint*.

11. To replace the existing upper and lower prisons of Modena, the council asked "quod unus carcer fiat et fieri debeat de novo in domibus palatii ... vel inter ambo palacia comunis Mutine ubi melius videbitur consilio populi." Vicini, *Respublica Mutinensis*, 1:75. On Siena and Venice see above, introduction and chapter 1, respectively.

12. Laschi, "Pene e carceri nella storia di Verona," pp. 32–53.

13. ASV, MC 18 (Liber Spiritus), fols. 329v–330r (22 January 1344).

14. Balestracci, "From Development to Crisis," pp. 200–201.

15. Muir, "Idee, riti, simboli di potere," pp. 740–42.

16. Bernard Chevalier's passing mention of prisons in "La paysage urbain à la fin du Moyen Age," p. 12, is the exception that proves the rule of obliviousness.

17. This observation furthers, rather than relies on, Marvin Trachtenberg's seminal work on Florentine piazzas that, ironically, were never flanked by municipal prisons. As noted above, however, Le Stinche was exceptional; most urban prisons were located along and circumscribed by the city's main political square, affirming Trachtenberg's claim (*Dominion of the Eye*, p. 14) that "the trecento devised a highly evolved set of specific procedures, preferences, and principles that governed the shaping of its squares and provided them with a powerful form of spatial order and visuality." An equivocation of Trachtenberg's thesis is Henderson, *The Renaissance Hospital*. Note that despite both authors' use of the terms "early-modern" and "Renaissance," respectively, they are mostly concerned with construing the "medieval" fourteenth century as a watershed period in the history of urban planning.

18. Cassidy-Welch, "Testimonies from a Fourteenth-Century Prison." And see chapter 3.

19. Alberti, *L'architettura*, V, 13 (1:399): "[A]damantinum esse carcerem custodis ad vigilantis oculum."

20. Pini, "La 'burocrazia' comunale nella Toscana del Trecento."

21. ASS, SC 1, fols. 37r–38v (4 January–1 July 1395).

22. See chapter 1. A maximum of four guards and at least one part-time notary ran the Parma prisons, according to the *Statuta Communis Parmae anno MCCLXVI ad circiter MCCCIV*, pp. 172–74. Eight and ten Modenese guards overseeing, respectively, an upper and a lower ward in 1306 are named in Vicini, *Respublica Mutinensis*, 1:130, 188. The Arras prison staff comprised a jailer, a

porter, and a hangman, according to Small, p. 351. An even smaller outfit ran the Lyon prison (Gonthier, pp. 20–21). Staff at the Paris Châtelet consisted of one warden, three guards, and a notary (Batiffol, p. 50). English prison staffs were similarly basic (Pugh, pp. 140–64).

23. There were two short-lived attempts to lease the Sienese prison into private hands (ASS, CG Del. 143, fol. 24v [8 October 1348]; Del. 158, fol. 36r–v [26 November 1356]; Del. 168, fols. 11r–12v [23 August 1361]), but otherwise prisons were publicly run by wardens who changed frequently. In contrast, prison custody in England was usually purchased, although the office could be deputed by local sheriffs or awarded by the Crown. The English jailers' tenure was typically long and at times even hereditary. Still, it was particularly in towns, as Pugh notes, that "prisons were felt to be a part of the civic bureaucracy, controlled, and even subject to dismissal, by the common council" (p. 154). On English jailers' remuneration see Pugh, pp. 165–91.

24. See chapter 1. The Parisian prévôt was charged with visiting the Châtelet's inmates every Monday and reviewing the prison registers daily, according to Batiffol, p. 237. On the external supervision of English prisons see Pugh, pp. 186–91.

25. In contrast, the personnel of the few documented French prisons were more stable. See Gonthier, pp. 20–21.

26. According to Small, the Arras prison notary recorded the prisoners' movements and fees, although these registers do not seem to have survived. The earliest extant registers from Paris date to 1412. See Gauvard et al., "Le Châtelet de Paris."

27. Copies of oblate lists survive mostly in the minutes of the local council's deliberations. A collection of original Sienese lists, incompletely covering the years 1337–83, is ASS, CG OC 470–73.

28. Examples of fourteenth-century petitions are in ASS, Conc. SCC 2162 (Carcerati), fols. 1r–14v.

29. ASB, UM 101, fol. 502r (January 1301); UM 110, fol. 374v (7 January 1305).

30. ASB, UM 110, fol. 375r (7 January 1305). The document is transcribed in appendix 1.

31. Biblioteca Nazionale Centrale, Firenze, MS Magl. Cl. VII, no. 624 is probably a sole fourteenth-century survivor of such a series.

32. Lopez, "Crossroads within the Wall," p. 34.

33. At Arras, an annual fifty-lire profit was considered exceptionally high, according to Small, p. 350.

34. ASS, CG Del. 143, fol. 24v (8 October 1348); Del. 158, fol. 36r–v (26 November 1356).

35. ASS, CG Del. 168, fols. 11r–12v (23 August 1361). Nor did it prove to be a "lucrative" private business, as suggested by Falletti-Fossati, Costumi senesi, pp. 154–55. As we shall see, however, these systems overlapped.

36. Beltrani, pp. 303–7, describes three different fee systems: (1) according to social status (Savoy); (2) fixed rates (Rome); and (3) according to the nature of the offense (Lucca). According to the late-fourteenth-century Grand Coutumier de France, ed. Laboulaye and Dareste, pp. 183–84, Châtelet inmates paid radically different entry and exit fees according to their social status (from eight

denari *parisis* for most nonnobles, to ten lire for high nobility), but fairly similar daily fees (1–2d.) according to their level of accommodation. Meal prices were set by the prévôt, and renting a bed cost four denari, but neither was obligatory, and inmates could have these supplied from outside. See Batiffol, pp. 47–49. Daily fees at Arras were 12 denari *tournois* for standard accommodations and five soldi for a more comfortable room, according to Small, p. 353. On prison fees in England see Pugh, pp. 167–77.

37. According to Laschi, "Pene e carceri nella storia di Verona," p. 45, local inmates only paid entry and exit fees of six denari.

38. In case of execution, the tax collector would be compensated the full amount by the commune.

39. ASS, *CG* Del. 168, fols. 11r–12v (23 August 1361). The Sienese agevolatura cost twelve denari per day and six denari per night. Although agevolatura was optional, the charter obligated the prison's leasers to maintain eight poor prisoners at the agevolatura, implying that only the most unfortunate inmates in this medium-sized facility were chained.

40. For Bologna see chapter 1; for Siena see ASS, *SC* 1, fols. 37r–38v (4 January–1 July 1395). The jailer, porter, and hangman at the Arras prison cost the commune just over twenty-one livres *tournois* a year, excluding payments to the hangman for individual executions (Small, p. 351).

41. ASS, *SC* 1, fols. 37r–38v (4 January–1 July 1395).

42. See chapter 1 and Beltrani, pp. 309–11.

43. The claim by Villani, *Nuova cronica*, XII, xcii (3:193), that Le Stinche brought in one thousand gold florins (roughly thirty-one hundred lire) annually to the commune is highly exaggerated.

44. See Geltner, "Medieval Prisons," appendix 1.

45. Accordingly the average volume of unpaid private debts was between 37,200 and 74,400 lire per semester.

46. F.St. 1322–25, I, 18 (2:51–52).

47. ASF, *Statuti* 1355, 16, I, 52, fol. 42r–v and F.St. 1415, I, 73 (1:95).

48. Pound, "Law in Books and Law in Action." Two celebrated efforts to apply this juxtaposition in the case of medieval legal history are Bossy, *Disputes and Settlements*; and Davis and Fouracre, *Settlement of Disputes*.

49. See introduction. On punitive imprisonment in Late Antiquity see Garnsey, *Social Status and Legal Privilege*, pp. 147–52; Millar, "Condemnation to Hard Labour"; Krause, *Gefängnisse im Römischen Reich*, pp. 8–91.

50. See Peters, "Prison before the Prison"; Bartrand-Dagenbach et al., *Carcer*.

51. Ireland, "Theory and Practice within the Medieval English Prison," modifying, e.g., Cohen, "History of Imprisonment for Debt," p. 155.

52. Bellomo, *Common Legal Past of Europe*, pp. 195–202.

53. A typical statement is Bartolus de Sassoferrato, *Commentaria in digestum vetus*, Prima pars, liber II, De iurisdictione omnium iudicorum, par. Imperium iurisdictio, no. 8 (fol. 49v), where a discussion of perpetual incarceration concludes: "ut sit per iudices ecclesiasticos seu spirituales de iure canonico, sed de iure civili non debeat fieri."

54. *Digesta Justiniani* 48.19.8.9: "carcer enim ad continendos homines, non ad puniendos haberi debet." Even Ulpian, however, seems to have reacted to an

existing situation whereby Roman provincial governors were employing imprisonment as a form of punishment, as the immediately preceding sentence
reveals: "Solent praesides in carcere continendos damanare aut ut in vinculis
continentur: sed id eos facere non oportet. Nam huiusmodi poenae interdictae
sunt." Another staple prescript employed by medieval jurists is *Codex Theodosianus* 11.7.3: "Carcer poenalium, carcer hominum noxiorum est."

55. For instance, Lucas de Penna, *Commentaria in tres libros*, X, De exatoribus
tributorum, l. 2, nos. 1, 3, 10, 15 (fols. 30v–31v), XII, De curiosis, & stationariis
l. 1, 5–8 (fol. 281r–v), and XII, De erogatione militaris annonae, l. 17, nos. 6–8
(fols. 317v–323v). A fine review of medieval jurisprudence on this topic is Sarti,
"Appunti su carcere-custodia e carcere-pena."

56. Baldus de Ubaldis, *Commentaria in primam digesti veteris partem*, Liber I,
De iurisdictione omnium iudicorum, l. 2, additio 9 (fol. 73r): "Carcer dicitur
quadruplex ... carcerare est meri imperii, quia poenae illa aequiparatur morti....
Secundus est carcer modicae coertionis....Tertius est carcer custodiae.... Quar-
tus carcer est domesticus, qui non est licitus nisi in casibus expressis in iure."

57. ASB, *Pod.* Sind. 22, Reg. 1, fols. 11r (23 March 1388), 23v (29 May 1388), 67r
(10 July 1388); Reg. 2, fols. 16r (20 October 1388), 30v (19 November 1388), 33v
(29 November and 6 December 1388), 36r–v (15 and 20 December 1388), 41v–42r
(10 and 18 January 1389), 64v (31 January 1389), 66r (8 February 1389), 76r–v (24
January and 22 February 1389), 82v (28 February 1389).

58. The authorship of the treatise is disputed, and is variously attributed,
among other major fourteenth-century jurists, to Mathaeus de Matesilanis,
Bartolus de Sassoferrato, his student Baldus de Ubaldis, and the latter's brother,
Angelus. See Colli, "Le opere di Baldo," pp. 38–40. Of the twenty-eight manuscripts of *De carceribus* that I have traced so far, many are of Italian origin and
date to the early fifteenth century. The version of the treatise cited here is from a
compilation attributed to Baldus de Ubaldis, *Tractatus exquisitissimi*, fols. 8v–13r.

59. Baldus de Ubaldis, *De carceribus*, fol. 8v: "Usa legum precepta principali-
ter sunt inventa ne pauperes persone molestiis affligantur. ideo visum est quod
inter pauperes personas nulla adeo tristior et pauperior inventur quam persona
incarcerata."

60. Ibid., fol. 9r: "[C]arcer est locus securus horribilis repertus non ad penam
sed ad delinquentium vel debitorum custodiam."

61. Ibid., fol. 11v: "[A]n pro debito fisci possit incarcerari, respondeo quod
si non vult solvere... quod probatur ratione nam debitor fisci potest cedere
bonis.... Sed cessio bonorum sit ut cedens liberetur a carceribus."

62. Ibid.: "Dico tamen quod iudex propter paupertatem potest collectaneam
remittere."

63. Petrus di Bellapertica, *Repetitiones*, leg. Si non convitii, etc.: de injuriis,
no. 24 (pp. 151–52). The teachings of the Orleans professor were introduced into
Italy by Cino da Pistoia (1270–1336).

64. A decision from 1308 by the Parisian Parlement implies that six months'
incarceration were the equivalent of one hundred livres *tournois*. See Porteau-
Bitker, "L'imprisonnment dans le droit laïque," pp. 402–4.

65. Biblioteca Apostolica Vaticana, MS Capp. 290, fol. 217v: "ad perpetuum
carcerum nemo ingenuus condemnare de iure civilis ut c. de pen., l. incredibile

ff. et l. mandatis, sed ad temporalem sic … quia carcer non est inventus ut terminus pena, sed ubi alia pena non cadit ibi in subsidium potest intelligeri pena carceris."

66. Sarti, "Appunti su carcere-custodia e carcere-pena," pp. 82–99.

67. Vicini, *Respublica Mutinensis*, 2:202.

68. Falletti-Fossati, *Costumi senesi*, p. 159.

69. F.St. 1322–25, II, 18, III, 6 (1:94, 132–33).

70. F.St. 1322–25, III, 45 (2:192).

71. F.St. 1322–25, V, 128 (1:286–87) allows for a commutation of a prison so-journ into corporal punishment.

72. F.St. 1322–25, II, 23 (2:96).

73. F.St. 1322–25, I, 12 (2:43).

74. Besta and Predelli, "Gli statuti civili di Venezia anteriori al 1242," II, A, 36 (p. 225). The gloss to the parallel entry in Jacopo Tiepolo's 1242 statutes explains that the penalty does not substitute the fine or debt, but is a response to an individual's disobedience. See Cessi, *Gli statuti veneziani di Jacopo Tiepolo*, I, li (pp. 79–81).

75. ASV, *AC* 1, fols. 114r–115r (1339). Rubric 248 prescribes a two-month penalty.

76. Liber officiorum, I, XI, xx (27 February 1273), MC Cessi, 2:215.

77. ASV, *MC* 9 (Capricornus), fol. 389v (13 August 1308).

78. ASV, *MC* 16 (Liber Fronesis), fols. 108r–109v (14 July 1321), 112v–113r (30 July 1321).

79. Liber officiorum, II, II, viii (15 May 1269), MC Cessi, 2:225–26.

80. Liber Luna, 64 (3 June 1283), MC Cessi, 3:30.

81. ASV, *MC* 9 (Liber Magnus), fol. 148v. In practice, however, the conversion was somewhat more flexible: on 26 September 1304, for instance, the Great Council pardoned a certain Frizerino, a scribe from San Lio who was convicted of forgery. Originally fined 150 lire, by the time of his release Frizerino had spent twenty-eight months in prison. ASV, *MC* 9, fol. 180r.

82. "[A] libris centum supra non sit aliquis ordo … servato ordine predicati consilii, si ipsi solvent superfluum librarum centum, relaxeretur, et si qui sunt in carcere completo termino, solvant superfluum et relaxentur." ASV, *MC* 9 (Liber Capricornus), fol. 325r (1 June 1307).

83. ASV, *MC* 11 (Liber Presbiter), fol. 222r–v (3 April 1313). One hundred lire usually remained the upper limit, however long an inmate remained in prison prior to effecting the commutation. One Leonardo was absolved of 100 lire out of a fine of 148 lire even after spending six years and four months in prison. He was released on condition that he pay the remainder of his fine (minus 6 lire) in three annual installments. ASV, *AC* 22/5, fol. 89r (27 September 1328). But there were exceptions: Menico, a bricklayer from San Jacopo de Luprio, could choose between a 200-lire fine or a two-year incarceration for the attempted rape of his employer's wife. ASV, *AC* 3617/1, fol. 65r (15 March 1329).

84. Priori, *Prattica criminale*, pp. 125–26, 134, 195, 203; Leicht, "Lo stato veneziano e il diritto comune"; Pansolli, *La gerarchia delle fonti*; Cracco, "La cultura giuridico-politica"; Zordan, *L'ordinamento giuridico veneziano*; Ventura, "Politica

del diritto e amministrazione della giustizia"; Padovani, "La politica del diritto"; Rubini, *Giustizia veneta*, pp. 116–28.

85. ASV, *MC* 20 (Liber Novella), fols. 4r–v (11 April 1350), 126v (22 June 1357), 168r–v (21 September 1359).

86. Ibid., fols. 410v–411v (25 August 1382).

87. For numerous other examples, see Bohne, *Freiheitsstrafe in den italienischen Stadtrechten*, 2:9–104.

88. As mentioned earlier, further charges, sometimes in the dozens, were often added throughout one's imprisonment.

89. Note, however, the sharp decline in "bene custodia" incarcerations in the last three semesters.

90. Quoted in Origo, *The Merchant of Prato*, p. 127.

91. Erikson, *Wayward Puritans*, p. 116.

92. F.St. 1415, I, 83 (1:103–6).

93. ASV, *MC* 11 (Liber Presbiter), fol. 194v (21 September 1312). His original fine was twenty-five lire.

94. ASV, *MC* 11 (Liber Presbiter), fols. 214v–215r (1 March 1313). The original fine was one hundred lire. After four months in prison Francesco was still ineligible for release, but the councilmen allowed him to pay his fine in annual installments of twenty lire should he "volunteer" to join the fleet.

95. ASV, *MC* 11 (Liber Presbiter), fols. 228v–229r (11 June 1313). The original fine was set at two hundred lire. After one year had elapsed, Viviano was released on pledges that he would pay the remainder of his fine in annual installments of fifteen lire grossi.

96. ASV, *MC* 16 (Liber Fronesis), fol. 178r–v (9 August 1323). Piero was sentenced to three months in prison followed by perpetual exile from Venice. His master, who was apparently present at the incident, was given a two-hundred-lire fine.

97. ASV, *QC* 16, fol. 9v (7 November 1348). Sentenced to one month in prison.

98. ASV, *MC* 21 (Liber Leona), fol. 32r–v (23 June 1389). The original sentence was three years in prison and six hundred lire. Unable to pay the fine, by the time of his charitable release Michele had spent four years and two months "in maxima miseria."

99. According to Scarabello, *Carcerati e carceri*, pp. 9–10, of the 238 cases adjudicated by the Quarantia between 1342-54 and 1366-68, 25 percent resulted in imprisonment, and 29 percent in imprisonment along with other penalties (usually pecuniary). A further 23 percent ended with fines, which were commutable into imprisonment or resulting with it if not resolved. Of the remaining cases, 10 percent received outlawry sentences (occasionally in conjunction with other penalties such as loss of property), 5 percent received capital punishments, and 2 percent corporal punishments. A variety of other penalties constitute the remaining 5 percent. The annual average, then, stood at just over six prison sentences, ranging anywhere from several days to four years. The data is partial and somewhat misleading since it does not disclose distribution patterns within subperiods. Moreover, the Quarantia was not the only body capable

of sentencing offenders to punitive imprisonment. For instance, according to ASV, *AC* 3645, between March and September 1393, the magistrates of the Avogaria di Comun imprisoned twenty-one men and women for periods of between seven days and two years. And see Chojnacki, "Crime, Punishment and the Trecento Venetian State," pp. 195, 199–200, 210; Ruggiero, *Violence in Early Renaissance Venice*, pp. 43–53.

100. ASV, *MC* 11 (Liber Presbiter), fol. 48v (17 February 1310). For a similar negotiation in Bologna see ASB, *Gov.* RP, *CPM* 132, fol. 213v (28 February 1291).

101. On rare occasions the Great Council released inmates who appear to have been genuinely poor. See ASV, *MC* 9 (Liber Magnus et Capricornus), fol. 267r (28 May 1306); 11 (Liber Presbiter), fol. 56v (7 April 1310); Romano, "Quod sibi fiat gratia," pp. 260–61.

102. Schiera, "Legitimacy, Discipline, and Institutions."

103. Scholarship on the political history of the Italian city-states, whether individually or in common, is prolific. A magisterial synthesis, including a comprehensive bibliography, is Jones, *The Italian City-State*, pp. 333–650. Two essential compendiums that focus on the administrative aspects of communal regimes are *I ceti dirigenti dell'eta comunale nei secoli XII e XIII*; and *I ceti dirigenti nella Toscana tardo comunale*. A more recent contribution is Maire Vigueur, *I Podestà dell'Italia comunale*.

104. Peters, *Inquisition*, pp. 11–39, 317; Peters, *Torture*, pp. 40–62.

CHAPTER 3
PRISON LIFE

1. Nagel, *The New Red Barn*, pp. 47–49; Johnson and Toch, *The Pains of Imprisonment*, pp. 255–84.

2. Nagel, *The New Red Barn*, p. 139.

3. Wheeler, "Socialzation in Correctional Communities." "Prisonization" is defined by Clemmer, *The Prison Community*, p. 300, as the "[a]cceptance of an inferior rôle, accumulation of facts concerning the organization of the prison, the development of somewhat new habits of eating, dressing, working, sleeping, the adoption of local language, *the recognition that nothing is owed to the environment for the supplying of needs*, and the eventual desire for a good job [in prison]" (emphasis added).

4. Lévi-Strauss, *Tristes Tropiques*, p. 388. Lindner, *Stone Walls and Men*, p. 392, anticipated Lévi-Strauss in remarking that under "primitive" modes of punishment, "the offender, in spite of his offense, is part of the in-group, and hostility is reserved for the out-group."

5. van Gennep, *The Rites of Passage*, pp. 1–25; Turner, *The Ritual Process*, p. 95; Turner, "Variations on a Theme of Liminality."

6. ASV, *MC* 18 (Liber Spiritus), fols. 98v–99r (5 February 1331), 155v (26 February 1334).

7. ASB, *Gov.* RP, *CPM* 200, fols. 424v–425v (26 January 1327).

8. ASS, *CG* OC 470, fols. 2v–6v (23 December 1337). Comparatively briefer periods of incarceration are attested in fragments of 1412 Parisian prison register. See Gauvard et al., "Le Châtelet de Paris," pp. 576–77.

9. According to Petersilia, *When Prisoners Come Home*, p. 3, the recent (and rising) average term for U.S. inmates was two and half years. And see Flanagan, *Long-Term Imprisonment*, pp. 3–9; Liebling and Maruna, *The Effects of Imprisonment*, pp. 1–32.

10. ASB, *EC*, Serie II, b. 3, 135/133 (1296): "et adhuc non est relaxatus quia non potest satisfacere merita nec custodes." According to Small, pp. 353–59, the average length of incarceration at Arras during the first half of the fourteenth century was nine days. Yet even there poor inmates languished for at least sixty-five days.

11. In 1328 the convicted traitor Jacobino Quirino continued to conduct his wine business through supervised correspondence from his cell. See X Zago, Reg. III, no. 309 (2:106–7). ASV, *GP* EN 2, fols. 60r and 62v (14 September and 14 October 1315, respectively), offer a rare peek into the dynamics of a business venture once one of the partners was incarcerated. In another case (X Zago, Reg. V, nos. 439, 446 [3:166–67, 169]), despite a previous escape, Nicoletto Grasso de Mauriano was released eight days before the end of his sentence in order to receive payment from a ship that had just arrived. And see X Zago, Reg. V, no. 684 (3:263); ASB, *Pod.* GM *CC* 70, unnumbered folio (18 January 1322). Notarial records often reveal the activities of incarcerated merchants. See Zaninoni, *Il 1. registro di imbreviature di Rufino de Rizzardo*.

12. Origo, *The Merchant of Prato*, p. 146. The threat of Datini's incarceration was raised during his tax assessments.

13. In one description, artisans were plying their trades while incarcerated at Venice. See Hassler, *Fratris Felicis Fabri Evagatorium*, 2:410. In fifteenth-century Lucca the prison wardens were encouraged to allow artisans to continue working, while similar attempts in Florence failed. See Beltrani, pp. 286–87. In general, however, organized labor in medieval prisons is never mentioned in contemporary sources.

14. Mazzei, *Lettere di un notaro a un mercante*, 2:346: "E posto ch'io non sia mercatante, ma de' mercatanti amico." And see Geremek, *Margins of Society*, pp. 17–18. Status, wealth, and connections were similarly instrumental in securing beds in contemporary leper-houses, according to Rawcliffe, *Leprosy in Medieval England*, pp. 291–301.

15. See Aubert, "Le parlement et les prisonniers," p. 111; Pugh, pp. 318–26; Gonthier, pp. 21–22; Small, pp. 351–52, 355 and passim. On the place of the *opus caritatis* of aiding prisoners in the context of lay piety see Rosenthal, *The Purchase of Paradise*, pp. 109–10; Pullan, "Support and Redeem"; Henderson, *Piety and Charity in Late Medieval Florence*, pp. 245, 257; Swanson, *Religion and Devotion in Europe*, pp. 29, 210–13.

16. ASF, *OSM* 248, fol. 12v (18 October 1324); 146, fol. 31r (7 July 1351). And see *OSM* 8, fol. 6 (17 December 1372); 248, fols. 44v (1324), 51v (1324).

17. Origo, *The Merchant of Prato*, p. 309. On another occasion (pp. 311–14) the couple gave some material aid and later contributed to the release of a long-term inmate.

18. ASV, *MC* 11 (Liber Presbiter), fol. 48v (17 February 1310). See ASV, *AC* 22/5, fols. 2r (12 May 1324), 81v (29 May 1328), 85r (1 August 1328).

19. ASV, *MC* 11 (Liber Presbiter), fols. 202v (10 November 1312), 214v–215r (1 March 1313), 222r–v (3 April 1313); *GP* SI 2, fol. 42r (1 April, 1315).

20. ASV, *MC* 21 (Liber Leona), fols. 22v–23r (1 March 1388), 49v–50r (21 March 1391).

21. ASB, *Gov.* RP, *CPM* 138, fol. 41v (23 July 1294). During their seventeen days of imprisonment, six Bolognese inmates incurred expenses of between 30 lire, 18 soldi, 10 denari and 40 lire, 5 soldi each for prison fees and legal expenses. See ASB, *Pod.* GM, *LI* 433, Reg. 2, fols. 1r–2v (1295). In one contemporary tale, the families of three imprisoned Florentine merchants are forced to leave the city, "no longer knowing what to expect but a life of perpetual misery." Boccaccio, *Decameron*, II, III (p. 91).

22. XL Lombardo, Reg. 25, no. 34 (11 April 1353) (3:12).

23. ASV, *AC* 3644, Reg. 1, fol. 8v (27 October 1378). Cervo, a sailor incarcerated for three months, managed to convert his sentence into two months of unpaid labor aboard a state galley. See X Zago, Reg. VI, nos. 28–31 (3:16). Such pleas, however, were not always accepted. See X Zago, Reg. V, no. 67 (3:34). Giovanni Paduani of the Giudecca confessed immediately to the night guards who caught him that he was on his way to collect a debt, "timens ne duceretur ad carcerem." ASV, *MC* 13 (Liber Clericus et Civicus), fol. 106v (8 August 1316). In southern France, a heretical priest's messenger advised one of the faithful, on the night before his impending arrest: "[S]ay you fell off the ladder in your house; pretend you have broken bones everywhere. Otherwise it's prison for you." Quoted in Le Roy Ladurie, *Monataillou*, p. 56.

24. Small, p. 364.

25. I, viii (1 December 1249), MC Cessi, 2:21; ASB, *Gov.* RP, *RPsc* 286, Reg. 44, fol. 10r (21 January 1381).

26. Contumacy in general, however, was frequent enough in Venice to raise concerns: on 13 March 1341, the Great Council promised to reward citizens who seized contumacious criminals. See ASV, *MC* 18 (Liber Spiritus), fols. 265v–266v. And see Dean, *Crime in Medieval Europe*, pp. 10, 42.

27. For a rare instance see ASB *Pod.* GM, *LI* 191, Reg. 4, fol. 106r (30 August 1360). A further case documented for 1461 Lyon is in Gonthier, pp. 17–18, 23.

28. Sacchetti, *Il trecentonovelle*, CXXXIX (pp. 423–24).

29. On "fag-making" see Kaminski, *Games Prisoners Play*, pp. 41–46, 134–38. Similar rituals are mentioned in Nelson, *Prison Days and Nights*, pp. 158–60, 164–65; Thomas, *Down These Mean Streets*, p. 267; Buckner, *The Animal Factory*, p. 12. And see Fishman, *Sex in Prison*, pp. 83–85; Hefferman, *Making It in Prison*, pp. 92–97; Wooden and Parker, *Men behind Bars*, pp. 1–3, 74–76, 91–92, 101–6.

30. Toch, *Living in Prison*, pp. 50–57; Richmond, "Fear of Homosexuality"; Abbott, *In the Belly of the Beast*, p. 79; Wooden and Parker, *Men behind Bars*, pp. 106–20; Applebaum, *Gulag*, pp. 288–89, 482; Lerner, *You Got Nothing Coming*, pp. 152–56.

31. Barbi, *Novella del grasso legnaiuolo*, p. 140.

32. Lindner, *Stone Walls and Men*, pp. 420–21; Garfinkel, "Conditions of Successful Degradation Ceremonies"; Gibbs, "The First Cut Is the Deepest," pp. 97–114; Zamble and Porporino, *Coping, Behavior, and Adaptation*, pp. 76–91.

33. Respectively, Goffman, *Asylums*, pp. 69–70; and Clemmer, *The Prison Community*, p. 297.

34. Filipepi, *Cronaca*, p. 502: "Et, gionto quivi, lo fecero loro capitano novello, cantando tutti allegrissimamente per un poco di ricreatione. Et, essendo a quel modo cosí ben vagheggiato da la forza, lo misero in capo di tavola con un'altra mitra nova et maggiore della prima. Il povero Pacchierotto piangeva per la vergogna, et per il duolo delle scoreggiate; ma, vedendo poi, tra quei ribaldi, chi marchiato nella fronte, chi senza naso et senza orecchie, chi moncherino, et altri che stavano peggio di lui, so racconsolò alquanto. Et cosí, in tal luogo, stette qualche anni assai honoratamente." Rocke, *Forbidden Friendships*, p. 278 n. 188, identifies the protagonist as Lorenzo di Zanobi del Magno.

35. McCorckle and Corn, "Resocialization within Walls."

36. Hayner and Ash, "Prison as a Community"; Schrag, "Leadership among Prison Inmates"; Irwin, *The Jail*, pp. 59–66.

37. On the nature/nurture debate over the origins of modern inmate culture, see Sykes, "Men, Merchants and Toughs"; Garabedian, "Social Roles and Processes of Socialization"; Mathiesen, *Defences of the Weak*; Giallombardo, *Society of Women*; Jacobs, "Stratification and Conflict among Prison Inmates"; Johnson, *Hard Time*, pp. 97–118.

38. ASS, *Statuti*, no. 4, fols. 326r–327r. Quoted in Pazzaglini, "Comparable Practices of Medieval Imprisonment," pp. 165–66. In 1361 the Sienese prison was divided into the *agevolatura grossa*, *agevolatura comune*, *orsa*, *capaccia*, the women's ward, and the hospital. ASS, *CG* Del. 168, fol. 11r–v (23 August 1361). The Parmese likewise insisted that "mali debitores non ponantur cum latronibus et malefatoribus." *Statuta Communis Parmae anno MCCLV*, pp. 76–77. For a similar link between social hierarchies and a premodern prison layout, see Botsman, *Punishment and Power in the Making of Modern Japan*, pp. 61–69. By contrast, according to the Dominican friar Raymond of Peñafort (d. 1275), an early ideologue of the papal inquisition, such divisions (including that between heretics and Catholic inmates) are less crucial than the prisoners' general safety and welfare. See Baraut, "Els inicis de la inquisició a Catalunya," p. 426.

39. See chapter 1. According to Gauvard et al., "Le Châtelet de Paris," p. 573, separating debtors from criminals at the Châtelet was a modern development.

40. According to Bowker, *Prison Victimization*, p. 30, "[I]t is no accident that prisoners living in dormitory setting have higher blood pressure than prisoners living in single cells." Violence in modern dormitory environments is generally higher.

41. Zug Tucci, "Venezia e i prigionieri di guerra nel Medioevo," pp. 42–46, notes that status and wealth could improve a war captive's conditions.

42. di Tura del Grasso, *Cronaca maggiore*, p. 498; Villani, *Nuova cronica*, VIII, xix (1:442); de Monacis, *Chronicon de rebus venetis*, p. 279.

43. ASS, *CG* Del. 104, fols. 43r–44v (17 February 1327). Le Stinche's original provision from 27 April 1297 (ASF, *PR* 8, 41, fol. 51r) required a separation of women, debtors, and children sent to prison by their parents: "[F]iant… carceres in quibus condempnati dicti communis in quodam carcere per se; ac etiam debitores spatium personarium in quodam alio carcere per se; et mulieres in

quodam alio carcere per se; nec non iuvenes et male se gerentes qui aliquando eorum carcerationem ad petitionem eorum parentum carcerantur in quodam carcere per se."

44. For Venice, Florence, and Bologna see chapter 1; for Padua see Fabris, "La Cronaca di Giovanni da Nono," pp. 12–13; for San Gemigniano see Brogi, *Gli albori del Comune di San Gimigniano*, Dist. I, i (p. 70); for Reggio-Emilia see Cerlini, *Consuetudini e Statuti Reggiani del secolo XIII*, Statuti del 1265, III, xxxi (p. 227). On similar divisions in England, see Pugh, pp. 351–60; and the corroborating report in Saunders, "Lydford Castle, Devon," pp. 160–64. Prisoners at the Châtelet in Paris were classified into fourteen different wards of varying conditions according to status, allegation, or the judge's decision. Overflow custodial space was occasionally designated at the Petit Châtelet. See Batiffol, pp. 46–49.

45. Beltrani, pp. 272–79.

46. O'Brien, "Crime and Punishment as a Historical Problem," p. 516.

47. According to Gonthier, p. 21, "[T]he detainee depend[ed] on the generosity or avarice of his guard," a situation that could entail grave abuses, including the physical and sexual violation of incarcerated prostitutes and the abandonment of bare inmates to freeze in their cells (p. 24). Pugh, pp. 179–81, lists unnecessary chaining, malevolent placement, and physical brutality as common abuses among English prisons.

48. Lorenzi, *Monumenti*, no. 160 (p. 69). In 1359, the Quarantia authorized Franceschino dalle Boccole to serve the remainder of his two-year sentence in a *camerella* attached to the lower prisons. The decision was later overruled (no. 99 [p. 36]). For a similar decision in 1356 that was not revoked see X Zago, Reg. V, no. 420 (3:160–61).

49. ASV, *AC* 1, 278, fol. 142r–v.

50. Even at the modest prison of Arras the rich usually separated themselves from the poor by paying a fee (Small, p. 370).

51. Female prisoners were a small minority in Arras as well, though less so specifically among the indigent inmates (Small, pp. 368–70). Today, women still comprise a fraction of prison populations across Europe (from 2.4 percent in Ireland to 4.8 percent in Italy) and the United States (about 3 percent). Cells or wards are commonly appropriated ad hoc, sometimes without real gender segregation, and hold all types and ages of offenders. See Baldwin, "Women in Prison."

52. ASB, *Pod.* GM, *LI* 197, Reg. 4, fol. 83r–v (20 October 1363).

53. Under interrogation, Niccolò admitted to having had sex with Constantia in return for money, claiming that she was a known prostitute. But he failed to produce reliable witnesses to support his case. See ASB, *Pod.* GM, *LI* 203, Reg. 5, fols. 66r–68v (9 September 1366).

54. ASF, *AE* 382, fol. 4r (30 October 1367). And see ASF, *SS* EU 388, fol. 1r (4 October 1376).

55. ASF, *Statuti* 1355, 16, I, 52, fol. 43v, which states that women can only be admitted in the presence of the prison's penitential friars. Similar practices are attested in Degli Azzi, *Statuti di Perugia*, p. 213. On gender separation in premodern prisons see Bertoletti, "Prigioni e prigionieri in Mantova," pp. 59–60; Portenari, *Della Felicità di Padova*, pp. 102–3.

56. ASB, *Gov.* RP, *RPsc* 226, Reg. 54, fols. 16r–17r (24 October 1334).

57. Cohen, *Evolution of Women's Asylums*, pp. 142–52.

58. The first mention of a prison hospital appears in ASF, *AE* 269, fol. 78r (20 October 1357); and the first hired physician is mentioned in ASF, *CC* CU 146, fol. 60r (8 August 1360). The insane (*macci*) ward was founded by 1355 (ASF, *Statuti* 1355, 16, I, 52, fol. 43v). See Magherini and Biotti, *L'isola delle Stinche*. Infirmity and old age were likewise grounds for release before Le Stinche's foundation. See ASF, *PR* 6, 31, fol. 35r–v (5 June 1296).

59. ASV, *AC* 22/5, fol. 101r (6 April 1329).

60. ASV, *AC* 22/5, fol. 77r (21 February 1328); *MC* 9 (Liber Magnus), fol. 201v (30 March 1305); 13 (Liber Clericus et Civicus), fol. 93r (22 June 1316). The solution was eventually abandoned, partly since inmates occasionally never returned. See ASV, *MC* 9 (Liber Magnus), fol. 125r (30 April 1330). For similar practices in Paris see Aubert, "Le parlement et les prisonniers," pp. 107, 112; Moranvillé, "Note sur les prisons," p. 76.

61. ASV, *MC* 13 (Liber Clericus et Civicus), fol. 272r–v (31 July 1318); 20 (Liber Novella), fols. 46v–47r (3 January 1353), 60v (21 September 1353), 195v–196r (13 July 1361).

62. X Zago, Reg. V, no. 420 (3:160–61). An infirmary was first established at the New Prisons.

63. ASB, *Gov.* RP, *CPM* 200, fol. 320v (14 March 1326).

64. ASB, *Dem.* SD 193/7527, 18 (20 August 1348)

65. di Tura del Grasso, *Cronaca maggiore*, p. 526. It is unclear whether inmates such as Mona Agnola, described as "pazza et non in sana mente," were held there. See ASS, *Conc.* SCC 2162, fol. 9r–v (late fourteenth century).

66. Howell, "Spaces of Late Medieval Urbanity."

67. ASS, *CG* Del. 168, fols. 11r–12v (23 August 1361).

68. Foucault, *Discipline and Punish*, p. 160.

69. Zamble and Porporino, *Coping, Behavior, and Adaptation*, pp. 76–77.

70. As Given, p. 82, notes, this is true even for inquisitorial prisons, despite their explicitly penitential goals.

71. Additions to an inmate's initial entry in the extant logbooks usually date to the first few days or weeks of incarceration. While this chronology does not necessarily reflect the range of legal activities engaged in, it does indicate a decline in such activity insofar as it was consequential. For a rare rejection of an inmate's request to attend the trial of one of his debtors, see X Zago, Reg. VI, no. 272 (3:64).

72. ASB, *Gov.* RP, *CPM* 200, fols. 334v (25 April 1326), 424r (23 January 1327); X Zago, Reg. V, A. 16 (3:322).

73. X Zago, Reg. VI, no. 570 (3:117).

74. Mazzei, *Lettere di un notaro a un mercante*, 1:61.

75. Ibid., 2:343; Tommaseo, *Della bellezza educatrice*, p. 313.

76. Mazzi, *Il Burchiello*, p. 69: "acqua non posso aver se non per doccia, / nè aver lo sole se non è scaccato: / Non posso aver pan se non desperato. / Se io ebbi mai piacer, il mal mi noccia."

77. Manni, *Le veglie piacevoli*, 2:38: "le prigioni è il meglio star del Mondo ... per ognun s' apron sue porte."

78. Frati and Sorbelli, *Matthaei de Griffonibus*, pp. 65–66: "Po' che fortuna tanto / Crudelmente de sotto m'à rivolto, / Pregote, morte, molto, / Che puni fine al doloroso pianto." For later examples of prison poetry from France and England, see respectively Menage, "Deux poètes en prison"; and Mooney and Arn, *The Kingis Quair and Other Prison Poems*. And see chapter 4.

79. Five hundred years of Venetian prison graffiti are currently being catalogued by Giandomenico Romanelli, general director of the Musei Civici Veneziani.

80. ASF, *AE* 501, fol. 14v (11 May 1367); 540, fol. 21v (4 April 1368).

81. ASF, *SS* EU 382, fol. 4r (30 October 1367); 388, fol. 1r (4 October 1376).

82. X Zago, Reg. VI, nos. 406, 443–45, 599 (3:89, 95, 121); ASF, *AE* 501, fols. 18v–19r (2 July 1367).

83. ASV, *MC* 20 (Liber Novella), fol. 404v (6 June 1382). Some officials had abused this benefit for their own profit, leading to stricter supervision. In Parma, guards were warned against allowing inmates to visit local taverns. See *Statuta Communis Parmae ab anno MCCLXVI ad circiter MCCCIV* , p. 174.

84. ASF, *AE* 538, fols. 4v–5r (19 May 1368). Under investigation, the two men involved revealed the names of two further "sodomites." And see ASF, *AE* 538, fol. 8r–v (16 June 1368).

85. ASF, *SS* EU 382, fol. 7r (27 November 1367); *AE* 501, fol. 30v (17 September 1367); 515, fols. 18v (25 February 1368), 22v (17 March 1368); 540, fols. 6v (25 February 1368), 16r (17 March 1368); 573, fol. 18r (27 March 1369); 678, fols. 54r (27 August 1372), 55v (3 September 1372); 698, fols. 22v–23r (17 March 1373); 770, fol. 15r (20 March 1377); 790, fol. 18r (16 October 1377). Needless to say, all of these events involved multiple participants, blasphemy, and usually violence. There is no record for the participation of female inmates in gambling sessions at Le Stinche. On gambling in general see Zdekauer, "Il gioco in Italia nei secoli XIII e XIV," pp. 3–22.

86. ASF, *Statuti* 1355, 16, I, 54, fol. 45v.

87. ASF, *AE* 538, fols. 19v–20r (29 August 1368). It is often unclear how consensual such activities were.

88. X Zago, Reg. III, nos. 510–11 (3 January 1330) (2:172).

89. ASF, *AE* 489, fol. 12r–v (27 November 1366).

90. An inmate named Rosso hit Filippo di Piero on the chest (ASF, *AE* 515, fol. 20v [3 March 1368]); Angelo di Lorenzo and Stagio of Santa Maria de Vergano fought "with empty hands" (fol. 22v [17 March 1368]); a certain Andrea hit Leonardo di Ricci in the face (538, fols. 2v–3r [5 May 1368]); Antonio, a Neapolitan inmate, suffered a bleeding wound in the face at the hand of Niccolò di Giorgio, a Venetian inmate, who retaliated by grabbing his aggressor's testicles (538, fol. 5v [2 June 1368]). And see ASF, *AE* 538, fols. 8v (16 June 1368), 15v (11 August 1368); 19v–20r (28 August 1368); 540, fols. 15v (17 March 1368), 34r (5 May 1368); 573, fol. 12v (9 March 1369); 575, fol. 29v (15 June 1369); and ASF, *RP* 15, 185, fol. 267v (30 December 1318).

91. Chojnacki, "Crime, Punishment and the Trecento Venetian State," pp. 224–25 n. 110, relates a rare case of homicide among inmates.

92. Cohen et al., *Prison Violence*; Johnson and Toch, *The Pains of Imprisonment*, pp. 63–93; Sparks et al., *Prisons and the Problem of Order*; Edgar et al., *Prison Violence*.

93. Nacci and Kane, "Incidence of Sex and Sexual Aggression"; Braswell et al., *Prison Violence in America*.

94. Ellis et al., "Violence in Prisons."

95. ASB, *Pod.* CA 29, Reg. 1332II (20 August 1322); ASF, *PR* 33, fols. 6v–7r (9 June 1344), respectively. And see Villani, *Nuova cronica*, XIII, xvii (3:333–34). The enraged crowds that torched Le Stinche and the Châtelet in 1378 and 1381, respectively, likewise seem to have left the staffs unharmed. See Cohn, *Popular Protest*, pp. 209, 290. Buonaccorso Pitti reported that "[b]y God's grace the danger of riots was averted," when, in 1399, a number of religious enthusiasts aborted an attempt to storm Le Stinche's gates. Quoted in Brucker, *Two Memoirs of Renaissance Florence*, p. 62. Carniello, "Rise of an Administrative Elite," pp. 344–45 and n. 94, claims that prison notaries were difficult to recruit in Bologna because of their fear of violence, but I have found no supporting evidence for their claim.

96. Herlihy, "Psychological and Social Roots of Violence"; Heers, *Le clan familial au Moyen Age*; Smail, "Common Violence"; Dean, "Marriage and Mutilation"; Zorzi, "La cultura della vendetta"; Gauvard, *Violence et ordre public*, pp. 214–26.

97. Sofsky, *Saggio sulla violenza*, p. 5. And see Nirenberg, *Communities of Violence*.

98. Sparks et al., *Prisons and the Problem of Order*, p. 2; King and McDermott, "My Geranium Is Subversive."

99. Zola, "Observations on Gambling in a Lower-Class Setting."

100. Compare the openings of ASF, *AE* 129 (1349) and that of *AE* 489 (1366).

101. Dunbabin, pp. 42–43.

102. See chapter 1. In Arras a hangman was a permanent and rather busy member of the staff (Small, pp. 351, 365–66)

103. Hassler, *Fratris Felicis Fabri Evagatorium*, 2:409–10.

104. Beebe, "Felix Fabri and His Audiences." And see Rubiés, "Travel Writing as a Genre."

105. ASV, *MC* Del. 18 (Liber Spiritus), fols. 329v–330r (22 January 1344).

106. Niccolini di Camugliano, *Chronicles of a Florentine Family*, p. 48.

107. ASB, *CC PC* 1, Reg. 7, fols. 1v–6r (1256), reproduced in Foschi, "I palazzi del Comune di Bologna," pp. 94–100.

108. ASS, *CG* Del. 104, fols. 43r–44v (17 February 1327).

109. Moranvillé, "Note sur les prisons," p. 74.

110. Barbi, *Novella del grasso lagnaiuolo*, pp. 138–39. Similar practices prevail in present-day Indonesia. See Sujinah, *In a Jakarta Prison*, p. 52.

111. For institutional charity in Florence see ASF, *OSM* 9, fol. 52r (27 October 1373); 11, fol. 31r (27 January 1380); 244, fol. 39v (4 March 1347); 245, fols. 66r–67r (3–23 June 1343); 248, fol. 62v (1324). For individual aid to Venetian inmates see, for instance, ASV, *CI* Misc., bb. 19, 10 (4 July 1313), 16 (7 July 1320), 19 bis (13

September 1326), 26 (8 September 1334), 30 (8 November 1338), 33 (22 September 1339), 34 (5 March 1340), 36 (8 January 1341), 37 (10 September 1341), 39 (7 July 1342), 43 (1 July 1343), 64 (10 December 1346), 74 (30 December 1347), 80 (3 August 1360). And see Thompson, *Cities of God*, pp. 106, 195.

112. ASB, *Gov.* RP, *CPM* 160, fol. 150v (7 August 1304); *CC* TC 3, fols. 1v (3 July 1288), 2r (5 July 1288), and 4v (8 July 1288) record typical payments for inmates' daily bread rations. The provisions were later calculated on a monthly basis: *CC* TC 4a, fols. 4r (24 January 1296), 25r (17 March 1296). Testators infrequently left donations for feeding and aiding Bolognese inmates: ASB, *Dem.*, SMM 9/3491, 34 (26 January 1329); 13/3495, 21 (28 October 1341); 16/3498, will of Bertolazzo q. ser Paolo (25 March 1350); SD 178/7512, 34 (14 December 1274), 86 (1 March 1282); 180/7514, 2 (12 February 1294), 18 (13 September 1295); 181/7515, 62 (9 May 1300); 182/7516, 47 (8 March 1301) (donation to prisoners in the testator's native Florence); 188/7522, 58 (5 June 1323); 190/7524, 16 (11 June 1329), 26 (20 October 1330); 192/7526, 25 (6 April 1346), 29 (19 February 1347); 193/7527, 18 (20 August 1348), 37 (19 February 1356). By the end of the fourteenth century the confraternity of Santa Maria della Morte monitored the inmates' material and spiritual welfare. Throughout France, both the commune and friends and family provided the inmates with bread. See Moranvillé, "Note sur les prisons," p. 73; Gonthier, p. 22; Small, pp. 351–52.

113. Grion, "La 'Legenda' del B. Venturino da Bergamo," pp. 46 and 71; and Waley, *Siena and the Sienese*, p. 143.

114. On 12 November 1355, six months into his five-year sentence, Nicoletto Bono, a convicted traitor, was granted visitation rights: his relatives and children could speak to him "quotiens fuerit opportunum" without the presence of a notary, as long as he received only one visitor at a time, and in the presence of a warden or guard. X Zago, Reg. V, no. 328 (3:125). At Le Stinche, the supervisory committee's charter specified *illicit* contacts with the outside world rather than visits in general. ASF, *AE* 489 (1366). And see Aubert, "Le parlement et les prisonniers," p. 103.

115. Toch, *Living in Prison*, pp. 52–56; Cordilia, *Making of an Inmate*, pp. 31–46; Bondesson, *Prisoners in Prison Societies*, pp. 158–59. On the impact of incarceration on prisoners' families see Morris, *Prisoners and Their Families*; Matthews, *Forgotten Victims*; Shaw, *Children of Imprisoned Fathers*; Shaw, *Prisoners' Children*. "Pains of imprisonment" is a term introduced by Sykes, *The Society of Captives*, pp. 68–83, and continuously revisited ever since. See Johnson and Toch, *The Pains of Imprisonment*; Liebling and Maruna, *The Effects of Imprisonment*.

116. Human Rights Watch, *Prison Conditions in the United States*, pp. 58–60. According to Sykes, *The Society of Captives*, p. 65, some 41 percent of the inmates at Trenton, in the early 1940s, received not a single visitor over the course of one year. The picture emerging from Zamble and Porporino's study of Canadian prisons in the 1980s (*Coping, Behavior, and Adaptation*, pp. 81–82), is marginally better.

117. Devereux and Moos, "Social Structure of Prisons"; McCorkle and Korn, "Resocialization within Walls," pp. 95–96; Wheeler, "Socialization in Correctional Communities," pp. 697–98; Koscheski et al., "Consensual Sexual Behavior."

118. Blackler, "Primary Recidivism in Adult Men"; Fitzgerald, "The Telephone Rings"; Lochhead, *Outside In*, pp. 26–33.

119. Lembo, "Relationship of Institutional Disciplinary Infractions"; Jamieson and Grounds, "Release and Adjustment," pp. 41–42.

120. Saleebey, *The Non-Prison*, pp. 20–24.

121. ASF, *SS* Car. 82–85, 88–91. See Geltner, "Medieval Prisons," appendix 1.

122. Respectively, ASS, *CG* Del. 104, fols. 43r–44v (17 February 1327); di Tura del Grasso, *Cronaca maggiore*, p. 526. ASV, *AC* 3641, fols. 112r (22 January 1332), 173r (4 September 1337); 3642, fol. 49v (3 March 1343); 3644, Reg. 1, fols. 22v–23r (13 September 1380), 41r–v (21 April 1382), 78v (16 August 1385), Reg. 2, fol. 11r (30 January 1387).

123. ASV, *AC* 3641, fols. 112r (22 January 1332), 173r (4 September 1337); 3642, fol. 49v (3 March 1343); 3644, Reg. 1, fols. 22v–23r (13 September 1380), 41r–v (21 April 1382), 78v (16 August 1385), Reg. 2, fol. 11r (30 January 1387).

124. Villani, *Nuova cronica*, XIII, lxxii (3:483–84); ASF, *SS* Car. 82, 91. Only two deaths were recorded at the Arras prison in the first half of the fourteenth century (Small, p. 365). In contrast, death rates in English prisons seem to have been consistently higher: Pugh, p. 331; Bennett, *Pastons and Their England*, pp. 175–76.

125. Murray, *Suicide in the Middle Ages*, 1:154–60, 185–91, 295–304, lists several dozen cases of inmate suicides from English and French sources. A singular incident regarding an alienated Italian Jew is reported in 1484 Venice: Hassler, *Fratris Felicis Fabri Evagatorium*, 2:410. The only case of self-injury I came across concerns the serial thief Piero Ugoli, who struck himself on the head with a stone, causing serious bleeding. See ASB, *Pod.* GM, *LI* 204, Reg. 8, fol. 131v (8 October 1367). On modern rates see Liebling, *Suicides in Prison*, pp. 24–25; Matthews, *Doing Time*, pp. 69–72; Toch, *Men in Crisis*, pp. 127–43; and Danto, *Jail House Blues*.

126. ASS, *Conc.* SCC 2162, fol. 11 (late fourteenth century).

127. A chisel drop-off at Venice is recorded in ASV, *AC* 22/5, fol. 68v (20 September 1327); and XL Lombardo, Reg. 22, nos. 48, 209, 211 (1:16, 64).

128. Vendramino, a former servant and guard at the Venetian prisons was incarcerated under similar circumstances in 1366. See XL Lombardo, Reg. 29, pt. 1, no. 52 (3:72–73). In 1290, a group of Bolognese inmates smuggled a letter (written in the vernacular) out to their relatives in the city, with precise instructions for a breakout. See ASB, *Pod.* GM, *LI* 20, Reg. 10, fol. 24r (1 August 1290).

129. Chiaretto was from the Casentino, Goro and Domenico resided in Castelnuovo di Berardenga.

130. Berni, *Il primo libro del l'opere Burlesche*, fol. 53r: "Et vi si sente un romor di martella, / Di picconi, e di travi per mandare / Libero ogniuno in questa parte e'n quella."

131. Personnel's reported complicity in escapes or illicit releases are recorded for Venice in XL Lombardo, Reg. 22, nos. 129–33 (1:36–37); Reg. 25, no. 54 (3:18); X Zago, Reg. V, nos. 405–6, 448–49 (3:157, 169–71); for Bologna in ASB, *Gov.* RP, *CPM* 221, fol. 50v (5 September 1321); RP, *RPsc* 225, Reg. 49, fol. 103v (1 April 1333); *Pod.* CA 3, Reg. 3, fol. 32r (29 August 1291); 18, Reg. 4, fols. 79r–80r (27 August 1310); 28, Reg. 1332II, fol. 27r (20 August 1322); *UM* 101, fol. 502r (January 1301); for Florence in ASF, *RP* 19, 59, fols. 82r–83r (18 March 1323); 20, 33, fol. 47r–v (12 December 1323); 27, 173, fol. 108r–v (26 April 1334); 27, 142, fols. 65v–66r (26 July 1336); and for Siena in ASS, *CG* Del. 106, fols. 120v–122v

(27 December 1328). Corruptibility, in fact, was the chief motivation for establishing prison supervision committees. The first *sindaco* of Le Stinche's wardens was nominated immediately following the escape of several war captives. See ASF, *RP* 12, 86, fol. 105r–v (28 February 1305). For French parallels see Gonthier, p. 20; and Géraud, *Chronique latine de Guillaume de Nangis*, 1:339, which relates an accusation brought against several Dominican inquisitors who were bribed into releasing accused heretics in 1303 Toulouse.

132. Waley, *Siena and the Sienese*, p. 25.

133. For Venice, see ASV, *MC* 13 (Liber Clericus et Civicus), fol. 119v (4 September 1316); X Zago, Reg. III, nos. 148, 187, 197 (4 June, 19 August, 30 September 1327) (2:59, 71, 74); Reg. V, nos. 405, 439 (11 May–3 August 1356) (3:157, 166–67); XL Lombardo, Reg. 22, nos. 1, 30, 48 (20 September, 25 October, 11 December 1342) (1:1, 11, 16); Reg. 25, no. 54 (7 May 1353) (3:18); Reg. 29, nos. 173, 489 (9 December 1366, 10 May 1368) (3:106–7, 182–83); ASV, *CD* 8, fol. 13r (10 September 1393). There were three attempted escapes from the Bolognese prisons during a sample decade (1355–64): ASB, *Pod.* GM, *LI* 185, Reg. 5, fol. 37r (15 July 1357); 193, Reg. 3, fol. 87r (28 January 1362); and 194, Reg. 2, fols. 33r–34v (23–25 July 1362). Several escapes outside this period are recorded in ASB *Gov.*, RP *CPM* 138, fol. 6r (23 April 1294); *Pod.* CA 36, Reg. 1357I, fols. 11r–12r (26–28 June 1357) with related records in fols. 13r–v (26 June 1357), 15r–17r (15 May–16 June 1357). For Arras, see Small, p. 364. Several escape attempts are reported for Siena: ASS, *CG* Del. 106, fols. 120v–122v (27 December 1328); 108, fols. 22v–23r (12 August 1329); *Conc.* SCC 2162, fol. 11 (fourteenth century); and for Florence: ASF, *RP* 12, 86, fol. 105r–v (28 February 1305); 19, 59, fols. 82r–83r (18 March 1323); 20, 33, fol. 47r–v (12 December 1323); 22, 19, fols. 23v–24r (11 October 1325); 26, 118, fol. 70r–v (12 November 1333); 27, 173, fol. 108r–v (26 April 1334); 27, 142, fols. 65v–66r (26 July 1336); 33, fols. 6v–7r (9 June 1344), though this is by no means a comprehensive list. A curious case is reported in Lansing, *Power and Purity*, p. 98. According to Wakefield, "Friar Ferrier," escapes from the royal prison at Carcassone were also rare, despite allegedly harsh conditions. For two incidents at Rethel and Tours see Moranvillé, "Note sur les prisons," p. 75. Pugh, pp. 219–24, on the other hand, claims that escapes from English prisons were fairly common.

134. See Smail, "Common Violence," p. 48. According to Applebaum, *Gulag*, pp. 355–70, the mere reputation of the Siberian wilderness kept many prisoners at bay. The force of this myth, often perpetuated by inmates who returned to their camps after an initially successful attempt, appears to have been real: some of the more remote facilities had no fence.

135. The likelihood of non-Bolognese avoiding their trial or fleeing from prison may have been predicated on their high rates of prosecution. According to Blanshei, "Crime and Law Enforcement in Medieval Bologna," p. 123, foreigners were three times more likely than Bolognese citizens to be "captured, tortured, convicted, and actually punished." Conversely, the predominantly rural provenance of the inmates studied by Mathieu, "Prisons et prisonniers en Anjou," helps to explain their relatively frequent escapes.

136. ASS, *CG* OC 470, fols. 2v–6v (23 December 1337).

137. See Koenig, "Prisoner Offerings, Patron Saints and State Cults." On similar practices in France see Batiffol, p. 49; Gonthier, p. 19 n. 5; Small, p. 363; LeDieu, "Restitutions de prisonniers à Abbeville."

138. ASV, *AC* 3644, Reg. 2, fol. 46r (27 July 1389); *MC* 11 (Liber Presbiter), fol. 286r (13 June 1314); 20 (Liber Novella), fols. 190v–191r (9 July 1361), 231v–232r (9 June 1364), 277v–278r (15 May 1367), 313r–v (22 November 1369), 395r (1 April 1382); 21 (Liber Leona), fols. 27v (20 December 1388), 49v–50r (21 March 1391). And see de Monacis, *Chronicon de rebus venetis*, p. 247.

139. ASB, *Gov.* RP, *RPsc* 223, fols. 98v–99v (5 April 1328), 108v (25 May 1328), 120r–v (28 June 1328); 224, fols. 164v–166r (21 February 1332); 225, Reg. 46, fols. 60r–v (17 April 1332), 93r–v (6 June 1332), 103r–v (27 June 1332), Reg. 47, fols. 18r–19r (14 August 1332), 85v–87v (24 October 1332), Reg. 49, fols. 44v–45v (23 December 1332).

140. ASS, *CG* Del. 99, fols. 119v–121r (11 April 1324); 101, fols. 46r–49r (13 August 1324), 183v–186r (24 December 1324); 105, fols. 84r–85r (30 March 1328); 106, fols. 22v–24r (12 August 1328), 117v–119r (22 December 1328); 107, fols. 76v–77v (20 April 1329); 108, fols. 22v–25v (12 August 1329), 91v–95r (22 December 1329); 120, fols. 53r–58v (10 April 1337); 121, fols. 17r–20r (13 August 1337); *CG* OC 470, fols. 2v–6v (23 December 1337); 473, fols. 19r–25r (March–December 1361).

141. ASF, *PR* 2, 87, fol. 76v (22 March 1290), 120, fol. 94r (22 June 1290), 205, fol. 161r (31 December 1290). For typical discrepancies between the potential and actual number of oblates see *PR* 19, 51, fols. 67v–68v (3 February 1323); 28, 57, fols. 142r–143v (17 March 1337).

142. Two biblical prison scenes decorate the Baptistery. The central bronze door features an image of St. John in Herod's prison, and a mural tracing Joseph's life-cycle depicts him in Pharaoh's prison. These are, however, instances of unjust incarceration. Both date to the fourteenth century at the latest.

143. Filipepi, *Cronaca*, pp. 501–2; Muir, *Civic Ritual in Renaissance Venice*, pp. 245–49.

144. Thompson, *Cities of God*, pp. 304–8.

145. ASF, *PR* 12, 142, fol. 194r–v (2 March 1306). For a sample of such provisions see *PR* 12, 89, fols. 107v–108r (4 December 1304); 13, 3, fols. 9v–11r (26 July 1306); 14, 13, fols. 35r–36v (10 February 1309); 15, 3, fol. 4r–v (27 July 1316); 16, 12, fols. 13v–14r (22 January 1319).

146. Smith, "Bare Facts of Ritual," p. 125: "Ritual is a means of performing the way things ought to be in conscious tension to the way things are in such a way that this ritualized perfection is recollected in the ordinary, uncontrolled, course of things. Ritual gains its force where incongruity is perceived."

147. Trexler, *Public Life in Renaissance Florence*, pp. 240–70; Muir, *Civic Ritual in Renaissance Venice*, pp. 189–211.

148. Huxley, "Variations on *The Prisons*," p. 195.

149. Pini, *Città, comuni e corporazioni*, p. 34; Mollat, *Les pauvres au Moyen Âge*, pp. 93–106. The highly regulated *fondaco*, described by Constable, *Housing the Stranger*, pp. 306–54, was exceptional.

150. Skinner, "Material Life," pp. 148–49; Dyer, *Standards of Living*, pp. 200, 203; Schiaparelli, *La casa fiorentina e i suoi arredi*, 1:7–9. Some of the

Venetian prisons developed from and later reverted back to private residences. See ASV, *MC* 16 (Liber Fronesis), fols. 68v–69r (22 June 1320), also published in Lorenzi, *Monumenti*, no. 38 (p. 13). And see Franzoi, *Le prigioni della Repubblica di Venezia*, p. 63.

151. On medieval urban hygiene in general see Thorndike, "Sanitation, Baths, and Street-Cleaning"; Jarry, "Diététique et hygiène"; Keene, "Rubbish in Medieval Towns"; Sjoberg, *The Preindustrial City*, pp. 92–95; Bocchi, "Regulation of the Urban Environment"; and, more by implication, Vigarello, *Concepts of Cleanliness*.

152. van Gennep, *The Rites of Passage*, p. 18; Turner, *The Ritual Process*, p. 95. And see Turner, "Variations on a Theme of Liminality."

CHAPTER 4

THE PRISON AS PLACE AND METAPHOR

1. da Certaldo, *Libro di buoni costumi*, pp. 159–60, 186–87.

2. Ibid., pp. 101–2: "Pensa, se to fossi in pregione e fossi abbandonato da parenti e amici e mai a te non venisse persona, e uno che ti non sapessi chi e'si fosse ti venisse a vicitare e traesseti di pregione, quello che te ne parebbe: così è de l'anime abbandonate, chi priega o fa pregare per loro."

3. See Meneghetti, "Scrivere in carcere nel medioevo."

4. Jauss, *Toward an Aesthetic of Reception*, pp. 3–46; Iser, *The Implied Reader*, pp. 274–94.

5. Curtius, *European Literature*, p. 157; Hyde, "Medieval Descriptions of Cities"; Fasoli, "La coscienza civica nelle 'Laudes civitatum.'"

6. Respectively, Gen. 39:20ff.; 2 Chron. 16:10; 1 Kings 22:27; 2 Chron. 18:25; Jer. 20:2, 32:2, 37:15–21; Matt. 13:3–12 (and synoptic parallels); Acts 5:17–20, 12:1–19.

7. Libanius, *Oratio* 45, in *Selected Works*, 2:160–93; Chrysostom, *Homilies on St. John*, 60 (2:144–50).

8. *Codex Theodosianus* 9.3.1: "ne poenis carceris perimatur, quod innocentibus miserum, noxiis non satis severum esse cognoscitur"; *Digesta Justiniani* 48.19.8.9: "carcer enim ad continendos homines, non ad puniendos haberi debet."

9. See Paulinus of Nola, *I carmi*, 15:230ff. (1:252–60); Reymond and Barns, *Four Martyrdoms*; Musurillo, *Acts of the Christian Martyrs*, 15.4, 28; Heffernan and Shelton, "*Paradisus in carcere*."

10. Prudentius, *Peristephanon* 6, vv. 25–27 (2:204): "carcer Christicolis gradus coronae est, / carcer provehit ad superna caeli, / carcer conciliat Deum beatis."

11. See Clement of Rome, *First Epistle to the Corinthians* 59.4 and Ignatius of Antioch, *Epistle to the Smyraeans* 6.2, both in *The Epistles of St. Clement of Rome and St. Ignatius of Antioch*, pp. 46, 92; Justin Martyr, *1 Apologie* 67.7 (p. 170); Eusebius, *Ecclesiastical History* 6.3.4 (p. 16).

12. According to Dix, *Shape of the Liturgy*, p. 193, the Greek and Syriac *Liturgy of St. James*, which expands on a fourth-century Jerusalemite text, asks God to remember "those of our fathers and brethren that are in bondage and in prisons, in captivity or exile, in the mines, in torture or in bitter slavery." The Paschal

liturgical cycle of the *Missale Gothicum* includes an *oratio pro exulibus*, "pro fratribus, et sororibus nostris captivitatibus elongatis, carceribus detentis, metallis deputatis [for our sisters and brothers far away in captivity, held in prisons, confined to the mines]" (*Liturgia gallicana* III, Patrologia Latina, ed. Jacques-Paul Migne, 221 vols. [Paris, 1844–64], 72:271). A Christmas-cycle prayer contained in the *Vetus Missale Gallicanum* is offered "ut cunctis mundum purget erroribus … aperiat carceres, vinc[u]la dissoluat [so he may purge the world from all errors … open the prisons, loosen the chains]" (72:359). A Paschal-cycle prayer in the same collection is offered *pro captivis, vel qui in carcere detinentur* (72:367).

13. Musurillo, *Acts of the Christian Martyrs* 15.4, 28; Cyprian, *Letters*, 20.2, 27.1–2 (1:101–2, 112–13).

14. Chrysostom, *Homilies on St. John*, 60 (2:144–50); Cassian, *Institutiones*, 10.22 (p. 233); Cassian, *Conlationes*, 18.7.6 (p. 641); Palladius, *The Lausiac History*, 14.3, 32.9, 54.2, 68.2 (pp. 50, 94, 134); Gerontius, *Vie de Sainte Mélanie*, 9 (pp. 142–44); Paulinus of Nola, *Letters*, 13.14 (p. 130); John of Ephesus, *Lives of the Eastern Saints*, 12 (p. 172).

15. Tertullian, *Ad martyras*, 2.8–9 (*Opera*, 1:4–5): "Hoc praestat carcer Christiano, quod eremus prophetis … Auferamus carceris nomen, secessum vocemus. Etsi corpus includitur, etsi caro detinetur, omnia spiritui patent."

16. Cameron, *Christianity and the Rhetoric of Empire*, p. 70; Malone, *The Monk and the Martyr*; Frend, *Martyrdom and Persecution*, pp. 547–50.

17. Stancliffe, "Red, White and Blue Martyrdom."

18. Syncletica 20, in Ward, *Sayings of the Desert Fathers*, p. 234. See Paulinus of Nola, *I carmi*, 15, 16 (1:235–85).

19. *Select Letters*, 22.7 (p. 67). Despite his efforts, however, Jerome often found himself "surrounded by bands of dancing girls."

20. Ammonas 1 (Ward, *Sayings of the Desert Fathers*, p. 26).

21. Bessarion 12 (Ward, *Sayings of the Desert Fathers*, p. 42).

22. Tertullian, *Apologeticum*, 27.5–7 (*Opera*, 1:139); Musurillo, *Acts of the Christian Martyrs* 14.6; de Vogüé, *Histoire littéraire du mouvement monastique*, 1:94.

23. Penco "Monasterium-Carcer"; Leclercq, "Le cloître est-il une prison?"; Ferrante, "Images of the Cloister"; Herzman and Kennison, "Jacopone Da Todi."

24. de Jong, "Power and Humility in Carolingian Society"; de Jong, "Monastic Prisoners or Opting Out?"; Brown, "Vers la naissance du purgatoire"; Geltner, "*Detrusio*."

25. See McAvoy and Hughes-Edwards, *Anchorites, Wombs, and Tombs*.

26. Sensi, "Incarcerate e penitenti a Foligno."

27. *Codex Theodosianus* 9.3.7; 16.2; *Codex Justinianus* 1.4.22–23.

28. John of Ephesus, *Lives of the Eastern Saints*, 12 (p. 183); *Chronique de Michel le Syrien*, 2:336–37.

29. Gatier, "Nouvelles inscriptions de Gerasa," pp. 298–99.

30. Krause, *Gefängnisse im Römischen Reich*.

31. Graus, "Die Gewalt bei den Anfängen des Feudalismus"; Graus, *Volk, Herrscher und Heiliger*, 61–156. But see James, "Beati pacifici," pp. 34–36, 41–43; Wiesheu, "Bischof und Gefängnis."

32. Gregory of Tours, *Histoire des Francs*, 5.8, 6.8, 10.6 (pp. 161, 217, 418). Quoted here from *The History of The Franks*, trans. Lewis Thorpe (Harmondsworth, England: Penguin, 1974), pp. 264, 338, 553.

33. *Acta Sanctorum*, iii, November, 149–55; Arbellot, *Vie de saint Léonard*; Sargent, "Religious Responses."

34. See Acts 5:17–20, 12:7–11.

35. Clay, *Mediæval Hospitals of England*, pp. 261–62; Sargent, "Religion and Society in Late Medieval Bavaria."

36. Among the twenty-two saints currently associated with aiding criminals, prisoners, or captives are Dismas the Good Thief, Joan of Arc, Vincent de Paul, and Jacinta Marto, the child visionary of Fatima.

37. Rodriguez, *Captives and Their Saviors*.

38. Le Goff, *The Birth of Purgatory*, pp. 3–4, 130–234. Le Goff dates the "spatialization" of Purgatory to around 1150.

39. See Mall, "Zur Geschichte der Legende vom Purgatorium des heiligen Patricius," p. 157 (both versions). The text was written by an English Cistercian monk sometime during the reign of King Stephen (1135–54).

40. Bériou, "La prédication au béguinage de Paris," pp. 124, 129.

41. Le Goff, *The Birth of Purgatory*, p. 319.

42. For a rare string of exceptions see Drees, "Sainthood and Suicide."

43. Fabris, "La Cronaca di Giovanni da Nono," pp. 12–13: "Unum palaciorum, quod est occidentem versus, Novus Carcer dicetur, qui fortissimus erit. Hoc palacium in tres dividetur partes. In prima parte ponentur homines, qui penes alios erunt obligati pecunia, aut qui Communi Padue erunt obligati pro aliquibus bampnis pecuniariis, aut propter ipsius redditus. Et hec pars Lymbo poterit assimilari. In secunda parte ponentur hii qui aliqua facient maleficia et hec pars Purgatorio poterit equiparari. In tercia parte ponentur homicide, latrones, depredatores et ceteri malefactores, postquam potestati de illorum delictis erit manifestum. Et hanc terciam partem tenebrosam, in qua nulla lux unquam apparebit, Inferno vere poteris assimilare." On Padua's medieval prisons see also Portenari, *Della Falicità di Padova*, pp. 102–3.

44. "Statuta civitatis Brixiae MCCCXIII," Rub. CLII (col. 1628): "[C]ivitates factae sunt ad similitudinem paradisi." The passage forbids the destruction of buildings on account of city's alleged physical perfection. The early-fifteenth-century chronicler Goro di Stagio Dati described Florence on the Feast of St. John as paradise on earth. See Guasti, *Le feste di S. Giovanni Batista in Firenze*, pp. 4–8. For an abridged translation see Dean, *Towns of Italy*, pp. 72–75.

45. Dante, *Purgatorio*, p. xv.

46. Mazzi, *Il Burchiello*, pp. 70–71: "a porger prieghi al sommo *Creatore* / che nostra libertà tosto ci renda" (emphasis added).

47. Mazzei, *Lettere di un notaro a un mercante*, 1:345.

48. Laschi, "Pene e carceri nella storia di Verona," p. 46; Davey, *The Tower of London*, p. 40; Hastings, *Court of Common Pleas*, pp. 143–44.

49. Manenti, *Opera nuova in versi volgare*, unnumbered pages: "Io me ne vo, ne le Pregion oscure / Per veder gli'nfelici Malfattori / Che per lor vitii portan pene dure. / Io me ne vo in loco de fetori / Tra molti tormentati, et crudo Inferno / Nel cui patiscon pen'è [sic] gran martori. / Tanto amar, che poco piu è l'eterno; / E'tal, che ne l'intrar con la mia scorta / Gli dissi, omei, che luce non discerno." The prisons that Manenti describes are essentially those founded in the late thirteenth and fourteenth centuries.

50. Ibid.: "Hor quivi intrati, il stormo assai risuona / Da le voci d'afflitti, et dolorati / Che biastemando adhor mia testa intuona."

51. *The Poetical Works of Coleridge*, pp. 214–15.

52. Oscar Wilde, *De profundis, The Ballad of Reading Gaol, & Other Writings*, pp. 52, 58, 63.

53. See Bailey, *Hellholes*, p. 1; Ives, *History of Penal Methods*, pp. 171–72; Sjoberg, *The Preindustrial City*, p. 248; Toch, *Living in Prison*, p. 8; Zamble and Porporino, *Coping, Behavior, and Adaptation*, p. 21.

54. From the *Thirteenth Annual Report* of the prison inspectors for the Eastern Penitentiary in Philadelphia, p. 6, quoted from Barnes and Teeters, *New Horizons in Criminology*, p. 402.

55. Braswell et al., *Prison Violence in America*, p. 1.

56. Introduction to Abbott, *In the Belly of the Beast*, p. x. Mailer later adds that the prison was "an infernal machine of destruction, a design for the Dispose-All anus of a prodigiously diseased society" (p. xi).

57. Photograph reproduction in Nagel, *The New Red Barn*, p. 188. The grammatical and spelling errors are original.

58. Manni, *Le veglie piacevoli*, 2:38–54: "Avendo io girato a tondo a tondo / Col cervello, ho conchiuso in conclusione, / Che in le prigioni è il meglio star del Mondo"; "Ci è uno star da Principi l' Agosto, / Perchè non ci è mai freddo di quel tempo, / Giacchè la tramontana sta discosto: / Non ci piove giammai tardi, o per tempo, / Se voi ci steste mille settimane; / Se 'l volete veder, voi siete a tempo: / Se avete fame, a vita si dà il pane; / Se avete sete, quì si dà da bere; / Se un c'entra oggi, e ci muor, n' esce domane."

59. Berni, *Il primo libro del l'opere Burlesche*, fols. 52r–53r: "O gloriose Stinche di Firenze; / Luogo celestial, luogo divino, / Degno di centomila riverenze … Non sò piu bel che star drento à un muro / Quieto agiato, dormendo à chiusi occhi, / Et del corpo et dell' anima sicuro."

60. Ibid., fol. 53r: "Voi gli tenete in stia come i capponi; / Mandate il piatto lor publicamente, / Non altrimenti che si fà à lioni. / Com'uno è quivi, è giunto finalmente / A quello stato ch' Aristotil pose, / Che'l senso cessa, e sol opra la mente."

61. Ibid.: "Et vi si sente un romor di martella, / Di picconi, e di travi per mandare / Libero ogniuno in questa parte e'n quella."

62. Hassler, *Fratris Felicis Fabri Evagatorium*, 2:409–10: "Carceres enim reorum sub deambulatorio palatii sunt contra publicam plateam respectum habentes, patentibus fenestris lucidi, quae ferreis cancellis sunt clausae, per quas captivi respicere possunt et manus extendere et cum astantibus colloquium habere, et si sunt pauperes, eleemosynam a transeuntibus petere possunt. Vidi in uno carcere ultra XL pauperes transeuntes inclamantes pro misericordia. In alio vidi sedentes machanicos captivos, qui manibus nihilo minus laborabant in suis artibus et denarios lucrabantur. In alio carcere vidi divites negotiatores inclusos, qui simul ludebant in alea et scacho, et domicellae uxores eorum cum ancillis et servis ante cancellos stabant colloquentes eis. In alio singulari inclusorio vidi Judaeum quendam senem, captivum ratione debitorum, qui se ipsum in custodia strangulavit … [Custodes] multos etiam captivos cum industria minus caute custodiunt et aufugiendi opportunitatem tribuunt, praesertim cum partem

adversam crudeliorem justo sentiunt … Verum, qui pro enormibus excessibus, qui morte plectendi sunt, in carceribus detinentur arctioribus, tolerabilibus tamen."

63. Ibid., 2:410: "Inter multas crudelitates Teutonicorum est illa una, quod reorum carceres sunt inhumani, terribiles, obscuri, in profundis turrium, humidi, frigidi, et nonnumquam serpentibus et bufonibus pleni, longe a hominibus sequestrati, nec aliquis accedit consolator ad miseros illos, nisi tortores crudelissimi, qui terreant, minentur et torqueant."

64. Beebe, "Felix Fabri and His Audiences," chap. 3.

CONCLUSION
"MARINALIZING" INSTITUTIONS, INSTITUTING MARGINALITY

1. There are exceptions, such as Rome's Regina Coeli prison, still lodged at Trastevere's heart.

2. The graphic series *Oz* has recently terminated a remarkable six-year career on HBO, but successful series set in prisons still take up prime-time slots in England, Germany, and Australia, not to mention countless feature films, documentaries, plays, and works of literary fiction.

3. Davis, *City of Quartz*, pp. 253–57. The Federal Penitentiary in downtown Philadelphia is a further example of modern-day prisons' struggle for invisibility, as are detention centers in New York, San Diego, and Chicago. See Home Office, *New Directions in Prison Design*, pp. 8–19.

4. Ireland, "Theory and Practice within the Medieval English Prison."

5. Green, *Medieval Civilization in Western Europe*, p. 233, was too captivated in his own preconceptions on this matter to notice the important evidence that he produces to the contrary: "Conditions [in prisons] must often have been appalling. *When* a prisoner was placed in the *worst quarter* of the prison, according to Fleta and Britton, he could expect to lay upon the bare earth, sustained only by bread and water every other day. Living in an atmosphere suffused by the stench of decay and excrement (*though even by 1281 Newgate had a systematic drainage system and numerous privies*), often in the dark, damp and cold, the prisoner suffered horribly" (emphases added). Likewise, Dupré Theseider, "L'eresia a Bologna nei tempi di Dante," p. 266, considered burning at the stake a more humane punishment than perpetual incarceration given "the miserable conditions of prisons at that time."

6. Gallo and Ruggiero, *Il carcere in Europa*, p. 27. See Langbein, "Historical Origins of the Sanction of Imprisonment," pp. 35–39.

7. Garcia, "History of Prisons," pp. 415–16.

8. Dunbabin, pp. 171–72. And see Peters, "Prison before the Prison."

9. Galtung, "Social Functions of a Prison."

10. Strayer, *Medieval Origins of the Modern State*; Bartlett, *The Making of Europe*, pp. 281–91; Moore, *Formation of a Persecuting Society*. For the conceptual underpinnings of these theses, see Weber, *Theory of Social and Economic Organization*; Elias, *The Civilizing Process*.

11. According to Katz, "Origins of the Institutional State," p. 6, creating institutions, along with "the training of specialists, and the certification of their monopoly over a part of our lives," are typically modern capitalist responses. But the latter two processes can be gleaned well before the nineteenth century (for instance, in monasticism and medieval universities as well as among certain guilds), and institutionalization itself certainly predates the modern state and even mercantilism.

12. Blumer, "Social Problems as Collective Behavior."

13. Goffman, *Asylums*.

14. Foucault, *Naissance de la clinique*; Foucault, *Madness and Civilization*; Rothman, *Discovery of the Asylum*; Grob, *Mental Institutions in America*; Ignatieff, *Just Measure of Pain*. And see Ignatieff's bold self-critical essay, "State, Civil Society, and Total Institutions."

15. Recent works include Orme and Webster, *The English Hospital*; Sweetinburgh, *Role of the Hospital in Medieval England*; Mollat, *Histoire des hôpitaux en France*; Cohen, *Evolution of Women's Asylums*; Bailey, *Almshouses*; Otis, *Prostitution in Medieval Society*; Rossiaud, *Medieval Prostitution*; Scarabello, "Per una storia della prostituzione a Venezia"; Finzch and Jütte, *Institutions of Confinement*. The medieval origins of other institutions such as banks, universities, chanceries, leprosaria, and of course monasteries, are uncontested.

16. Horn, *The Mirror of Justices*, p. 52: "E si com lepre est une maladie revillaunt cors de homme taunt qe il nest mie suffrable a demoerer entre senz genz, aussi est pecche mortel une manere de lepre qe fet lalme abhominable a deu e la del part del commun de totes seinz gentz."

17. Bériou and Touati, *Voluntate Dei Leprosus*; Touati, *Maladie et société au Moyen Âge*, pp. 267–80; Lester, "Gender and Social Networks in Medieval France"; Rawcliffe, *Leprosy in Medieval England*, pp. 252–343.

18. Satchell, "Emergence of Leper-Houses," pp. 126–32.

19. Rawcliffe, *Leprosy in Medieval England*, pp. 308–9.

20. Crouzet-Pavan, "Police des mœrs"; Manikowska, "Polizia e servizi d'ordine a Firenze"; Trexler, "La prositution florentine au XVe siècle"; Otis, *Prostitution in Medieval Society*, pp. 15–39; Rossiaud, *Medieval Prostitution*, pp. 55–71; Karras, "The Regulation of Brothels"; Varanini and De Sandre Gasparini, "Gli ospedali dei 'malsani'"; Anversa, "L'Ospedale Rodolfo Tanzi di Parma"; Watson, "*Fundatio, Ordinatio* and *Statuta*"; Henderson, *The Renaissance Hospital*; Toaff, *Vino e la carne*; Mentgen, "'Die Juden waren stets eine Randgruppe.'"

21. See MacEvitt, *Crusades and the Christian World of the East*.

22. *Oxford English Dictionary*, 2nd ed., s.v. "marginal," 3c. See Stonequist, *The Marginal Man*.

23. See Shahar, *The Fourth Estate*; Shahar, *Childhood in the Middle Ages*; Shahar, *Growing Old in the Middle Ages*.

24. The obligatory concentration of Jews (and in Iberia, of Muslims) in designated neighborhoods was rare throughout the Middle Ages. However, Jews were routinely forbidden from appearing in public during certain liturgical periods such as Holy Week, the occasion for much interreligious violence. See

Stacey, "Conversion of Jews to Christianity," pp. 264–66; Nirenberg, *Communities of Violence*, pp. 200–230.

25. Bonfil, *Jewish Life in Renaissance Italy*, p. 70 (emphasis added). And see Haverkamp, "Jewish Quarters in German Towns"; Elukin, *Living Together, Living Apart*, pp. 75-134.

26. Given, pp. 52–65; Pegg, *The Corruption of Angels*, pp. 23, 33 and passim.

27. Given, p. 69. And see Dossat, *Les crises de l'Inquisition toulousaine*, pp. 247–68; Roach, "Penance and the Making of the Inquisition."

28. Le Roy Ladurie, *Monataillou*, pp. 6, 55, 64, 235–36, 251, 269–73.

29. Peters, *Inquisition*, pp. 11–39; Peters, *Torture*, pp. 40–62.

30. Most famously (and repeatedly) by Cohn, *Pursuit of the Millennium*; Cohn, *Europe's Inner Demons*; and by Moore, *Formation of a Persecuting Society*.

31. Goodich, *Other Middle Ages*, p. 3.

32. Otis, *Prostitution in Medieval Society*, pp. 19–24; Scarabello, "Per una storia della prostituzione a Venezia," pp. 22–26; Reverchon and Schneider, "Die Metzer Rotlichtbezirke," pp. 203–31.

33. Stow, *Alienated Minority*, pp. 281–308; Geremek, "La lutte contre vagabondage."

34. *The Margins of Society*, p. 20.

35. Geremek, *La pietà e la forca*, pp. 217–19. And see Wacquant, *Punishing the Poor*.

Appendix 1
A Prison Inventory from Bologna, 1305

1. Source: ASB *Mem.* 110, fol. 375r (7 January 1305).
2. Lock.
3. Chest.
4. Fetters.
5. Fetters.
6. One disassembled ladder, a rung-ladder.
7. Bolt.
8. Slide bars.
9. Tap room.
10. Basin.
11. Hooks.
12. Buckets.
13. Chest.
14. Small bucket.
15. Basin.
16. Pot.
17. Unknown.
18. Ladle.
19. Spit.
20. Turnhandle.

21. Bowl.
22. Small dish.
23. Small ladle.
24. Low bowl.
25. Utensils.
26. Cooked food.
27. Bowl.
28. Unknown.
29. Vaulted room.
30. Chest.
31. Bread.
32. Small chest.
33. "Pro scripturis" repeated.
34. Bench.
35. Fir.
36. Vat.
37. Axe.
38. Keg.
39. Vessel.
40. Interlocked? (from *traversino*).
41. Perhaps a hook or a buckle.
42. Pincers.

Appendix 2
Poems from the Prison

1. Manni, *Le veglie piacevoli*, 2:38–54. A fragment of the poem is included in Crescimbeni, *L'istoria della poesia volgare*, 2:181. Early witnesses are Biblioteca Nazionale Centrale, Firenze, MS Magl. Cl. II, I, 343, fol. 5v (late fourteenth century); and Biblioteca Apostolica Vaticana, MS Chigi L IV 131, fol. 340r (fifteenth or sixteenth century).

2. Fraticelli, *Delle antiche carceri di Firenze*, pp. 65–66.

3. Mazzi, *Il Burchiello*, pp. 66–82. For Burchiello's formal condemnations and his petition to the Sienese General Council, see pp. 123–36.

4. Zaccarello, *I sonetti del Burchiello*. See especially LXIII—Magnifici e potenti Signor miei; LXXVI—Lievitomi in sull'asse come 'l pane; LXXVII—Ficcami una pennuncia in un baccello; LXXVIII—Un gatto si dormiva in su un tetto; CXXVIII—Signori, in questa ferrëa graticola.

5. Mazzi, *Il Burchiello*, pp. 69–70.

6. An alternative (but so far unattested) order of the last five lines would translate: "I guzzle wine, dispensing with a glass— / A wine that, according to what a shoemaker tells me, / Is worse than turpentine. / Now you know how comfortable I am, / Hanging on a hook that I would recommend to a tanner."

7. Mazzi, *Il Burchiello*, pp. 70–71.

8. Ibid., pp. 71–72 n. 1.

9. Berni, *Il primo libro del l'opere Burlesche*, fols. 52r–53r.
10. Manenti, *Opera nuova in versi volgare*, pages unnumbered.

Appendix 3
Le Stinche, a Reconstruction

1. In collaboration with designer Yuval Samuelov (London and Tel Aviv) and architect Andrea Magnaghi (Rome).
2. Becchi, *Sulle Stinche di Firenze*. And see Howard, *State of the Prisons in England and Wales*, p. 107; and Fraticelli, *Delle antiche carceri di Firenze*.

BIBLIOGRAPHY

A bibliography of printed and unprinted archival sources is given in abbreviations and archives

MANUSCRIPTS

Biblioteca Apostolica Vaticana: Capp. 290; Chigi L IV 131; Vat. Lat. 5569.
Biblioteca Nazionale Centrale, Firenze: Magl. Cl. II, I, 343; Magl. Cl. VII, no. 624; Magl. Cl. XXV, no. 45; II, I, 269.
Biblioteca Nazionale Marciana, Venezia: It. VII 295 (10047); It. VII 2205 (9580).

PUBLISHED SOURCES

Aiazzi, Giuseppe. *Narrazioni istoriche delle più consideravoli inondazioni dell'Arno.* Florence: Tipografia Piatti, 1845. Reprint, Florence: Forni, 1996.
Alberti, Leon Battista. *L'architettura [De re aedificatoria].* Ed. Giovanni Orlandi. 2 vols. Milan: Polifilo, 1966.
Alighieri, Dante. *Purgatorio.* Trans. Jean Hollander and Robert Hollander. New York: Doubleday, 2003.
Anonymous. *Cronanca senese dei fatti riguardanti la città e il suo territorio di autore anonimo del secolo XIV.* In *Cronache senese.* Ed. Alessandro Lisini and Fabio Iacometti. RIS2 15, pt. VI, no. 1. Bologna: N. Zanichelli, 1931.
Barbi, Michele, ed. *Novella del grasso legnaiuolo nella relazione di codice Palatino 200.* Florence: Academia della Crusca, 1968.
Bernardi, Jacopo, ed. *Antichi testamenti tratti dagli archivi della Congregazione di Carità di Venezia.* 12 fasc. Venice: Società di Mutuo Soccorso, 1882–93.
Berni, Francesco. *Il primo libro del l'opere Burlesche di M. Francesco Berni.* Ed. Anonymous. Florence, 1552.
Besta, Enrico, and Riccardo Predelli, eds. "Gli statuti civili di Venezia anteriori al 1242." *Nuovo Archivio Veneto* 41 (1901): 5–117, 205–300.
Boccaccio, Giovanni. *Decameron.* Milan: Rizzoli, 2001.
Brogi, Mario, ed. *Gli albori del Comune di San Gimignano e lo statuto del 1314.* Siena: Cantagli, 1995.
Brucker, Gene A., ed. *Two Memoirs of Renaissance Florence: The Diaries of Buonaccorso Pitti and Gregorio Dati.* Trans. Julia Martines. New York: Harper and Row, 1967.
Casanova, Giacomo. *Histoire de ma fuite des prisons de la République de Venise, qu'on appelle les Plombs.* Leipzig: Chez le Noble de Schönfeld, 1788.
Cassian, John. *Conlationes.* Trans. Boniface Ramsey. New York: Paulist Press, 1997.
———. *Institutiones.* Trans. Boniface Ramsey. New York: Newman Press, 2000.

Cerlini, Aldo, ed. *Consuetudini e Statuti Reggiani del secolo XIII*. Milan: U. Hoepli, 1933.

Cessi, Roberto, ed. *Gli statuti veneziani di Jacopo Tiepolo del 1242 e le loro glosse*. Venice: C. Ferrari, 1938.

Chronique de Michel le Syrien: Patriarche jacobite d'Antioche (1166–1199). Ed. and trans. J.-B. Chabot. 4 vols. Paris: Ernest Leroux, 1899–1910.

Chrysostom, John. *Homilies on St. John*. Trans. Sister Thomas Aquinas Goggin. Fathers of the Church, vols. 33, 41. New York: Fathers of the Church, 1957–60.

Codex Justinianus. Ed. P. Kreuger. Berlin: Weidmann, 1954.

Codex Theodosianus. Ed. T. Mommsen and P. Meyer. Berlin: Weidmann, 1905.

Cohn, Jr., Samuel K., ed. and trans. *Popular Protest in Late Medieval Europe*. Manchester: Manchester University Press, 2004.

Cyprian of Carthage. *Letters*. Trans. G. W. Clarke. 4 vols. New York: Newman Press, 1984–89.

da Canal, Martin. *Les estoires de Venise. Cronaca veneziana in lingua francese dalle origini al 1275*. Ed. Alberto Limentani. Florence: Leo S. Olschki, 1972.

da Certaldo, Paolo. *Libro di buoni costumi*. Ed. Alfredo Schiaffini. Florence: Le Monnier, 1945.

de Monacis, Lorenzo. *Chronicon de rebus venetis ab U. C. ad annum MCCCCLIV*. Ed. Flaminio Corner. Venice: Remondini, 1758.

de Penna, Lucas. *Commentaria in tres libros*. Lyons, 1586.

de Ubaldis, Baldus. *Commentaria in primam digesti veteris partem*. Venice, 1616.

———. *De carceribus*. In *Tractatus exquisitissimi. De questionibus et tormentis secundum Baldum*, fols. 8v–13r. Paris: I. Barbier, 1508.

Dean, Trevor, ed. and trans. *The Towns of Italy in the Later Middle Ages*. Manchester: Manchester University Press, 2000.

Degli Azzi, Giustiniano, ed. *Statuti di Perugia dell'Anno MCCCXLII*. Vol. 1. Rome: Ermanno Loescher, 1913.

di Bellapertica, Petrus. *Repetitiones in aliquot divi Iustiniani imperatoris Codici leges*. Frankfurt, 1571.

di Coppo Stefani, Marchione. *Cronaca fiorentina*. Ed. Niccolò Rodolico, RIS2 30, pt. I. Città di Castello: S. Lapi; Bologna: N. Zanichelli, 1903–55.

Digesta Justiniani. Ed. T. Mommsen. Rev. ed. by P. Krueger. Berlin: Weidmann, 1963.

di Neri, Donato. *Cronaca senese*. In *Cronche senesi*. Ed. Alessandro Lisini and Fabio Iacometti. RIS2 15, pt. VI, nos. 7–8. Bologna: N. Zanichelli, 1936–37.

di Pagolo Morelli, Giovanni. *Ricordi*. Ed. Vittore Branca. Florence: Le Monnier, 1956.

di Sassoferrato, Bartolus. *Commentaria in digestum vetus*. Lyons, 1533.

[di Tura del Grasso, Agnolo]. *Cronaca maggiore*. In *Cronache senesi*. Ed. Alessandro Lisini and Fabio Iacometti. RIS2, pt. VI, nos. 3–6. Bologna: N. Zanichelli, 1936–37.

Dondarini, Rolando, ed. *Le "Descriptio civitatis Bononie eiusque comitatus" del cardinale Anglico (1371). Introduzione ed edizione critica*. Bologna: Deputazione di Storia Patria per le Provincie di Romagna, 1990.

The Epistles of St. Clement of Rome and St. Ignatius of Antioch. Trans. James A. Kleist. Westminster, MD: Newman Press, 1949.

Eusebius. *Ecclesiastical History*. Trans. J.E.L. Oulton. London: William Heinemann and G. P. Putnam's Sons, 1932.

Fabris, Giovanni. "La Cronaca di Giovanni da Nono." *Bollettino del Museo civico di Padova*, n.s. 10 (1932): 1–33; 11 (1933): 167–200; 12–17 (1934–39): 1–31.

Filarete, Antonio Averlino. *Trattato di architettura*. Ed. Anna Maria Finoli and Liliana Grassi. 2 vols. Milan: Polifilo, 1972.

Filipepi, Simone. *Cronaca*. In *Scelta di prediche e scritti di fra Girolamo Savonarola con nuovi documenti intorno all sua vita*, ed. Pasquale Villari and E. Casanova, pp. 453–518. Florence: Sansoni, 1898.

Fineschi, Vincenzo. *Istoria comendiata di alcune carestie antiche e dovizie di grano occorse in Firenze cavata da un diario ms. in cartapecora del secolo xiv*. Florence: P. G. Viviani, 1767.

Frati, Lodovico, and Albano Sorbelli, eds. *Matthaei de Griffonibus memoriale historicum de rebus bononiensium*, RIS2 18, pt. II. Città di Castello: S. Lapi, 1902.

Gaudenzi, Augusto, ed. *Statuti del popolo di Bologna del secolo XIII*. Monumenti storici pertinenti alle Provincie della Romagna, Statuti, vol. 6. Bologna: Merlani, 1888.

Géraud, H., ed. *Chronique latine de Guillaume de Nangis et de ses continuateurs*. 2 vols. Paris: Jules Renouard, 1843.

Gerontius. *Vie de Sainte Mélanie*. Ed. and trans. Denys Gorce. Paris: Éditions du Cerf, 1962.

Ghirardacci, Cherubino. *Historia di Bologna*. 2 vols. Bologna: Rossi, 1605–69.

———. *Historia di Bologna*. Vol. 3 and index. Ed. Albano Sorbelli. Bologna: N. Zanichelli, 1933.

Goodich, Michael, ed. and trans. *Other Middle Ages: Witnesses at the Margins of Medieval Society*. Philadelphia: University of Pennsylvania Press, 1998.

Gregory of Tours. *Histoire des Francs*. Ed. Henri Omont and Gaston Collon. Rev. ed. by René Poupardin. Paris: Picard, 1913.

Grion, A., ed. "La 'Legenda' del B. Venturino da Bergamo secondo il testo inedito del codice di Cividale." *Bergomum*, n.s. 30 (1956): 11–110.

Guasti, Cesare, ed. *Le feste di S. Giovanni Batista in Firenze descritte in prosa e in rima da contemporanei*. Florence: Galletti e Cocci, 1908.

Hassler, Cunradus Dietericus [Konrad Dieterich], ed. *Fratris Felicis Fabri Evagatorium in Terrae Sanctae, Arabiae et Egypti Peregrinationem*. 3 vols. Stuttgart: Sumtibus societatis literariæ stuttgardiensis, 1843–49.

Jerome. *Select Letters*. Trans. F. A. Wright. London: William Heinemann; Cambridge: Harvard University Press, 1954.

John of Ephesus. *Lives of the Eastern Saints*. Ed. and trans. E. W. Brooks. Patrologia Orientalis 17. Paris: Firmin-Didot, 1923.

Justin Martyr. *Apologie*. Ed. and trans. Giuseppe Girgenti. Milan: Rusconi, 1995.

Laboulaye, Edouard, and Rodolphe Dareste, eds. *Le Grand Coutumier de France*. Paris: A. Durand et Pedone-Lauriel, 1868.

Libanius. *Selected Works*. Trans. A. F. Norman. 2 vols. Cambridge: Harvard University Press, 1969.

Lorenzi, Giambattista, ed. *Monumenti per servire alla storia del Palazzo Ducale di Venezia*. Venice: M. Vistentin, 1868.

Mall, Ed. "Zur Geschichte der Legende vom Purgatorium des heiligen Patricius." *Romanische Forschungen* 6 (1891): 139–97.

[Manenti, Zuane]. *Opera nuova in versi volgare, intitulata specchio de la giustizia.* Venice, 1541.

Manni, Domenico M. *Le veglie piacevoli.* 2nd ed. 8 vols. Florence: G. Ricci, 1815–16.

Mannucci, G. B. "Un antico diario senese (1055–1613)." *Bullettino senese di storia patria* 29 (1922): 89–99.

Mazzei, Ser Lapo. *Lettere di un notaro a un mercante del secolo XIV con altre lettere e documenti.* Ed. Cesare Guasti. 2 vols. Florence: Le Monnier, 1880.

Mazzi, Curzio. *Il Burchiello. Saggio di studi sulla sua vita e sulla sua poesia.* Bologna: Tipografia Fava e Garagnani, 1879.

Mocenigo, Filippo Nani, ed. *Capitolare dei Signori di Notte esistente nel Civico Museo di Venezia.* Venice: Tipografia del Tempo, 1877.

Mooney, Linne F., and Mary-Jo Arn, eds. *The Kingis Quair and Other Prison Poems.* Kalamazoo, MI: Medieval Institute Publications, 2005.

Musurillo, Herbert, ed. and trans. *The Acts of the Christian Martyrs.* Oxford: Clarendon Press, 1972.

Palladius. *The Lausiac History.* Trans. Robert T. Meyer. London: Newman Press, 1965.

Paulinus of Nola. *I carmi.* Ed. and trans. Andrea Ruggiero. 2 vols. Naples: Libreria Editrice Redenzione, 1996.

———. *Letters.* Trans. P. G. Walsh. Westminster, MD: Newman Press, 1966.

Portenari, Angelo. *Della Felicità di Padova.* Padua: Tozzi, 1623.

Priori, Lorenzo. *Prattica criminale secondo il rito delle leggi della Serenissima Repubblica di Venetia.* Venice: F. Brogiollo, 1663.

Poetical Works of Coleridge, Shelley, and Keats. Philadelphia, 1831.

Prudentius. *Peristephanon.* Ed. and trans. H. J. Thomson. 2 vols. London: William Heinemann; Cambridge: Harvard University Press, 1953.

Pucci, Antonio. *L'alluvione dell'Arno nel 1333 e altre storie popolari di un poeta campanaio.* Ed. Alessandro Bencistà. Reggello: FirenzeLibri, 2006.

Reymond, E.A.E., and J.W.B. Barns, eds. and trans. *Four Martyrdoms from the Pierpont Morgan Coptic Codices.* Oxford: Clarendon Press, 1973.

Sacchetti, Franco. *Il trecentonovelle.* Ed. Valerio Marucci. Rome: Salerno, 1996.

Scanaroli, Giovanni Battista. *De visitatione carceratorum libri tres.* Rome, 1655.

"Statuta civitatis Brixiae MCCCXIII." In *Monumenta Historiae Patriae*, vol. 16. Turin: Fratres Bocca, 1876, cols. 1585–1914.

Tertullian. *Opera.* Ed. E. Dekkers. 2 vols. Turnholt: Brepols, 1954.

Vicini, Emilio Paolo, ed. *Respublica Mutinensis (1306–1307).* 2 vols. Milan: U. Hoepli, 1929–32.

Villani, Giovanni. *Nuova cronica.* Ed. Giuseppe Porta. 3 vols. Parma: Fondazione Pietro Bembo / U. Guanda, 1990–91.

Ward, Benedicta, ed. and trans. *The Sayings of the Desert Fathers.* Rev. ed. Kalamazoo, MI: Cistercian Publications, 1984.

Wilde, Oscar. *De profundis, The Ballad of Reading Gaol, & Other Writings.* Ware, Hertfordshire: Wordsworth Editions, 1999.

Zaccarello, Michelangelo, ed. *I sonetti del Burchiello*, Collazione di opere inedite o rare 155. Bologna: Commissione per i testi di lingua, 2000.

Zaninoni, Anna, ed. *Il 1. registro di imbreviature di Rufino de Rizzardo, 1237–1244*. Milan: A. Giuffrè, 1983.

Modern Studies

Abbott, Jack Henry. *In the Belly of the Beast: Letters from Prison*. London: Hutchinson, 1982.

Aberth, John. *From the Brink of the Apocalypse: Confronting Famine, War, Plague, and Death in the Later Middle Ages*. New York: Routledge, 2000.

Alboize, M. M., and A. Maquet. *Les prisons de l'Europe*. 8 vols. Paris: Administration de librairie, 1845.

Anversa, Elisabetta. "L'Ospedale Rodolfo Tanzi di Parma nei documenti membranacei di privilegi, indulgenze e concessioni (1214–1368)." Tesi di Laurea, Università degli Studi di Bologna, 1986.

Applebaum, Anne. *Gulag: A History of the Soviet Camps*. London: Penguin, 2003.

Arbellot, Abbé. *Vie de saint Léonard, solitaire en Limousin: Ses miracles et son culte*. Paris: Jacques LeCoffre, 1863.

Arias, Gino. "Nuovi documenti su Giovanni Villani." *Giornale storico della letteratura italiana* 34 (1899): 383–89.

Aubert, Félix. "Le parlement et les prisonniers." *Bulletin de la société d'histoire de Paris* 20 (1893): 101–14.

Bailey, Brian J. *Almshouses*. London: Hale, 1988.

———. *Hellholes: An Account of History's Most Notorious Prisons*. London: Orion, 1995.

Baldwin, Pamela. "Women in Prison." In *Imprisonment Today: Current Issues in the Prison Debate*, ed. Simon Backett et al., pp. 53–69. London: Macmillan, 1988.

Balestracci, Duccio. "From Development to Crisis: Changing Urban Structures in Siena between the Thirteenth and Fifteenth Centuries." In *The "Other Tuscany": Essays in the History of Lucca, Pisa, and Siena during the Thirteenth, Fourteenth, and Fifteenth Centuries*, ed. Thomas W. Blomquist and Maureen F. Mazzaoui, pp. 199–213. Kalamazoo, MI: Medieval Institute Publications, 1994.

Balestracci, Duccio, and Gabriella Piccinni. *Siena nel Trecento. Assetto urbano e strutture edilizie*. Florence: CLUSF, 1977.

Banzola, Vincenzo, ed. *Parma, la città storica*. Parma: Cassa di Risparmio di Parma, 1978.

Baraut, Cebrià. "Els inicis de la inquisició a Catalunya i les seves actuacions al bisbat d'Urgell (segles XII–XIII)." *Urgellia* 13 (1996): 407–38.

Barnes, Harry Elmer, and Negley K. Teeters. *New Horizons in Criminology*. 2nd ed. Englewood Cliffs: Prentice-Hall, 1955.

Bartlett, Robert. *The Making of Europe: Conquest, Colonization, and Cultural Change, 950–1350*. London: Allen Lane / Penguin Press, 1993.

Bartrand-Dagenbach, Cécile, et al., eds. *Carcer. Prisons et privation de liberté dans l'Antiquité classique. Actes de colloque de Strasbourg (5 et 6 décembre 1997)*. Paris: De Boccard, 1999.

Bassett, Margery. "Newgate Prison in the Middle Ages." *Speculum* 18 (1943): 233–46.

———. "The Fleet Prison in the Middle Ages." *University of Toronto Law Journal* 5 (1944): 383–402.

Becchi, Fruttuoso. *Sulle Stinche di Firenze e su'nuovi edifizi eretti in quel luogo.* Florence: Le Monnier, 1839.

Beebe, Kathryne. "Felix Fabri and His Audiences: The Pilgrimage Writings of a Dominican Preacher in Late-Medieval Germany." DPhil thesis, Oxford University, 2007.

Bellomo, Manlio. *The Common Legal Past of Europe, 1000–1800.* Trans. Lydia G. Cochrane. Washington, DC: Catholic University of America Press, 1995.

Benevolo, Leonardo. *La città nella storia d'Europa.* Rome: Laterza, 1993.

Bennett, H. S. *The Pastons and Their England: Studies in an Age of Transition.* Cambridge: Cambridge University Press, 1922.

Bériou, Nicole. "La prédication au béguinage de Paris pendant l'année liturgique 1272–1273." *Recherches Augustiniennes* 13 (1978): 105–229.

Bériou, Nicole, and François-Olivier Touati. *Voluntate Dei Leprosus. Les lépreux entre conversion et exclusion aux XIIème et XIIIème siècles.* Spoleto: Centro Italiano di Studi sull'Alto Medioevo, 1991.

Bertoletti, A. "Prigioni e prigionieri in Mantova dal secolo XIII al secolo XIX." *Bullettino ufficiale della Direzione Generale delle Carceri* 17 (1887): 51–70, 163–82.

Biffi, Serafino. *Sulle antiche carceri di Milano e del Ducato Milanese.* Milan: C. Rebeschini, 1884.

Blackler, Chairmian. "Primary Recidivism in Adult Men: Differences between Men on First and Second Prison Sentence." *British Journal of Criminology* 8 (1966): 130–69.

Blanshei, Sarah Rubin. "Crime and Law Enforcement in Medieval Bologna." *Journal of Social History* 16 (1982): 121–38.

Blumer, Herbert. "Social Problems as Collective Behavior." *Social Problems* 18 (1971): 298–306.

Bocchi, Francesca. "Regulation of the Urban Environment by the Italian Communes from the Twelfth to the Fourteenth Century." *Bulletin of the John Rylands Library* 72 (1990): 63–78.

Bohne, Gotthold. *Die Freiheitsstrafe in den italienischen Stadtrechten des 12.–16. Jahrhunderts.* Leipziger rechtswissenschaftliche Studien 4, 9. Leipzig: T. Weicher, 1922–25.

Bondesson, Ulla V. *Prisoners in Prison Societies.* New Brunswick, NJ: Transaction Publishers, 1989.

Bonfil, Robert. *Jewish Life in Renaissance Italy.* Trans. Anthony Oldcorn. Berkeley and Los Angeles: University of California Press, 1994.

Bosdari, Filippo. "Il Comune di Bologna alla fine del secolo XIV." *Atti e memeorie della Deputazione di Storia Patria per le Provincie di Romagna,* 4th ser., 4 (1914): 123–88.

Bossy, John, ed. *Disputes and Settlements: Law and Human Relations in the West.* Cambridge: Cambridge University Press, 1983.

Botsman, Daniel V. *Punishment and Power in the Making of Modern Japan.* Princeton: Princeton University Press, 2005.

Bowker, Lee H. *Prison Victimization*. New York: Elsevier, 1980.

Bowsky, William M. *A Medieval Italian Commune: Siena under the Nine, 1287–1355*. Berkeley and Los Angeles: University of California Press, 1981.

Branca, Vittorio, ed. *Storia della civiltà veneziana*. 3 vols. Florence: Sansoni, 1979.

Braswell, Michael C., et al., eds. *Prison Violence in America*. 2nd ed. Cincinnati: Anderson, 1994.

Braunfels, Wolfgang. *Urban Design in Western Europe: Regime and Architecture, 900–1900*. Trans. Kenneth J. Northcott. Chicago: University of Chicago Press, 1988.

Brown, Peter. "Vers la naissance du purgatoire. Amnistie et pénitence dans le christianisme occidental de l'Antiquité tardive au Haut Moyen Age." *Annales ESC* 6 (1997): 1247–61.

Buckner, Edward. *The Animal Factory*. New York: Viking Press, 1977.

Burckhardt, Jacob. *The Civilization of the Renaissance in Italy*. Trans. S.G.C. Middlemore. New York: Phaidon, 1860.

Cameron, Averil. *Christianity and the Rhetoric of Empire*. Berkeley and Los Angeles: University of California Press, 1991.

Canning, Joseph, et al., eds. *Power, Violence, and Mass Death in Pre-modern and Modern Times*. Aldershot: Ashgate, 2004.

Carniello, Brian R. "The Rise of an Administrative Elite in Medieval Bologna: Notaries and Popular Government, 1282–1292." *Journal of Medieval History* 28 (2002): 319–47.

Cassidy-Welch, Megan. "Testimonies from a Fourteenth-Century Prison: Rumor, Evidence and Truth in the Midi." *French History* 16 (2002): 3–27.

Cervi, Maurizio Corradi. "Evoluzione topografica della Piazza Grande di Parma dall'epoca romana alla fine del secolo XIII." *Archivio storico per le provincie parmenesi*, 4th ser., 14 (1962): 31–52.

I ceti dirigenti dell'eta comunale nei secoli XII e XIII: Atti del II Convegno, Firenze, 14–15 dicembre 1979. Pisa: Pacini, 1979.

I ceti dirigenti nella Toscana tardo comunale: Atti del III Convegno, Firenze, 5–7 dicembre 1980. Florence: F. Papafava, 1983.

Chevalier, Bernard. "La paysage urbain à la fin du Moyen Age." In *Le paysage urbain au Moyen Age*, pp. 7–21. Lyon: Presses Universitaires de Lyons, 1981.

Chiffoleau, Jacques. *Les justices du Pape: Délinquance et criminalité dans la région d'Avignon au quatorzième siècle*. Paris: Publications de la Sorbonne, 1984.

Chojnacki, Stanley. "Crime, Punishment and the Trecento Venetian State." In *Violence and Civil Disorder in Italian Cities, 1200–1500*, ed. Lauro Martines, pp. 184–228. Berkeley and Los Angeles: University of California Press, 1972.

———. "In Search of the Venetian Patriciate: Families and Factions in the Fourteenth Century." In *Renaissance Venice*, ed. J. R. Hale, pp. 47–90. London: Faber and Faber, 1973.

Ciacco, Lisetta. *Il cardinal legato Bartrando del Poggetto in Bologna (1327–1334)*. Bologna: N. Zanichelli, 1906.

Clay, Rotha Mary. *The Mediæval Hospitals of England*. London: Methuen, 1909.

Clemmer, Donald, *The Prison Community*. Boston: Christopher Publishing House, 1940. Reprint, New York: Holt, Rinehart and Winston, 1958.

Cohen, Albert K., et al., eds. *Prison Violence*. Lexington, MA: Lexington Books, 1976.

Cohen, Esther. *The Crossroads of Justice: Law and Culture in Late Medieval France*. Leiden: E. J. Brill, 1993.

Cohen, Jay. "The History of Imprisonment for Debt and Its Relation to the Development of Discharge in Bankruptcy." *Journal of Legal History* 3 (1982): 153–71.

Cohen, Sherrill. *The Evolution of Women's Asylums since 1500: From Refuges for Ex-Prostitutes to Shelters for Women*. Oxford: Oxford University Press, 1992.

Cohn, Norman. *Europe's Inner Demons*. Rev. ed. London: Pimlico, 1993.

———. *The Pursuit of the Millennium*. 3rd ed. New York: Oxford University Press, 1970.

Cohn, Jr., Samuel K. *Lust for Liberty: The Politics of Social Revolt in Medieval Europe, 1200–1425*. Cambridge: Harvard University Press, 2006.

Colli, Vincenzo. "Le opere di Baldo. Dal codice d'autore all'edizione a stampa." In *VI centenario della morte di Baldo degli Ubaldi, 1400–2000*, ed. C. Frova et al., pp. 25–85. Perugia: Università degli Studi di Perugia, 2005.

Coopland, G. W. "Crime and Punishment in Paris, September 6, 1389 to May 18, 1390." In *Medieval and Middle Eastern Studies in Honor of Aziz Suryal Atiya*, ed. Sami A. Hanna, pp. 64–85. Leiden: E. J. Brill, 1972.

Constable, Olivia Remie. *Housing the Stranger in the Mediterranean World: Lodging, Trade, and Travel in Late Antiquity and the Middle Ages*. Cambridge: Cambridge University Press, 2003.

Cordilia, Ann. *The Making of an Inmate: Prison as a Way of Life*. Cambridge, MA: Schenkman, 1983.

Cracco, Giorgio. *Un "altro mondo": Venezia nel Medioevo. Dal secolo XI al secolo XIV*. Turin: UTET, 1986.

———. "La cultura giuridico-politica nella Venezia della 'Serrata'." In *Storia della cultura veneta*, vol. 2: *Il Trecento*, pp. 238–71. Vicenza: Neri Pozza Editore, 1976.

Crescimbeni, Giovan Mario. *L'istoria della poesia volgare*. 2nd ed. 6 vols. Venice: L. Basegio, 1730.

Crouzet-Pavan, Elisabeth. "Police des mœurs, société et politique à Venise à la fin du Moyen Age." *Revue historique* 536 (1980): 241–88.

———. "Recherches sur la nuit vénetienne à la fin du moyen âge." *Journal of Medieval History* 7 (1981): 339–56.

Cunningham, Colin. "For the Honour and Beauty of the City: The Design of Town Halls." In *Siena, Florence, and Padua: Art, Society, and Religion, 1280–1400*, ed. Diana Norman, 1:29–53. New Haven: Yale University Press, 1995.

Curtius, Ernst Robert. *European Literature and the Latin Middle Ages*. Trans. Willard R. Trask. New York: Pantheon, 1953.

Dahm, Georg. *Das Strafrecht Italiens im ausgehenden Mittelalter*. Berlin: Walter de Gruyter, 1931.

Danto, Bruce L., ed. *Jail House Blues: Studies of Suicidal Behavior in Jail and Prison*. Orchard Lake, MI: Epic Publications, 1973.

Davey, Richard. *The Tower of London*. London: Methuen, 1910.

Davidsohn, Robert. *Forschungen zur Geschichte von Florenz*. 4 vols. Berlin: E. S. Mittler und Sohn, 1896–1908.

———. *Storia di Firenze*. Trans. Eugenio Dupré Theseider. 8 vols. Florence: Sansoni, 1956–68.

Davis, Mike. *City of Quartz: Excavating the Future of Los Angeles*. New York: Vintage, 1992.

Davis, Wendy, and Paul Fouracre, eds. *The Settlement of Disputes in Early Medieval Europe*. Cambridge: Cambridge University Press, 1986.

de Jong, Mayke. "Power and Humility in Carolingian Society: The Public Penance of Louis the Pious." *Early Medieval Europe* 1 (1992): 29–52.

———. "Monastic Prisoners or Opting Out? Political Coercion and Honour in the Frankish Kingdoms." In *Topographies of Power in the Early Middle Ages*, ed. Mayke de Jong and Frans Theuws with Carine van Rhijn, pp. 291–328. Leiden: E. J. Brill, 2001.

de Rossi, Giovanni Battista. "Scoperta d'una cripta storica nel Cimiterio di Massimo Ad sanctam Felicitatem sulla via Salaria Nuova." *Bullettino di archaeologia cristiana*, 4th ser., 3 (1884–85): 149-84.

de Vogüé, Adalbert. *Histoire littéraire du mouvement monastique dans l'antiquité*. 9 vols. Paris: Éditions du Cerf, 1991–2005.

Dean, Trevor. "Marriage and Mutilation: Vendetta in Late Medieval Italy." *Past & Present* 157 (1997): 3–36.

———. *Crime in Medieval Europe, 1200–1550*. Harlow, England: Longman, 2001.

Delogu, Paolo, et al. *Longobardi e Bizantini*. Turin: UTET, 1980.

Desmaze, Charles. *Le Châtelet de Paris, son organisation, ses privilèges*. 2nd ed. Paris: Didier, 1870.

Devereux, George, and Malcolm C. Moos. "The Social Structure of Prisons, and the Organic Tensions." *Journal of Criminal Psychopathology* 4 (1942): 306–24.

Dix, Gregory. *The Shape of the Liturgy*. 2nd ed. Westminster: Dacre Press, 1960.

Donati, Fortunato. "Il Palazzo del Comune di Siena." *Bullettino senese di storia patria* 11 (1904): 311–54.

Dondarini, Rolando. *Bologna medievale nella storia delle città*. Bologna: Pàtron, 2000.

Dossat, Yves. *Les crises de l'Inquisition toulousaine au XIIIe siècle, 1233–1273*. Bordeaux: Bière, 1959.

Drees, Clayton J. "Sainthood and Suicide: The Motives of the Martyrs of Córdoba, A.D. 850–859." *Journal of Medieval and Renaissance Studies* 20 (1990): 59–89.

Dupré Theseider, Eugenio. "L'eresia a Bologna nei tempi di Dante." In *Mondo cittadino e movimenti ereticali nel medio evo (saggi)*, pp. 261–315. Bologna: Pàtron, 1978.

Dyer, Christopher. *Standards of Living in the Later Middle Ages: Social Change in England c. 1200–1500*. Cambridge: Cambridge University Press, 1989.

Edgar, Kimmett, et al. *Prison Violence: The Dynamics of Conflict, Fear and Power*. Cullompton, Devon: Willan, 2003.

Elias, Norbert. *The Civilizing Process: Sociogenic and Psychogenic Investigations*. Rev. ed. by Eric Dunning et al. Trans. Edmund Jephcott. Malden, MA: Blackwell, 2000.

Ellis, Desmond, et al. "Violence in Prisons: A Sociological Analysis." *American Journal of Sociology* 80 (1974): 16–43.

Elukin, Jonathan. *Living Together, Living Apart: Rethinking Jewish-Christian Relations in the Middle Ages*. Princeton: Princeton University Press, 2007.

Erikson, Kai T. *Wayward Puritans: A Study in the Sociology of Deviance*. New York: Macmillan, 1966.

Fabbri, Giuseppe. *Le fortificazioni del Medio Evo a Bologna. Studio critico, pagine di storia e documenti*. Bologna: Arti Grafiche Tamari, 1955.

Fadalti, Luigi, et al. *Gli artigli del leone. Giustizia e carcere a Venezia dal XII al XVIII secolo*. Treviso: Antilla, 2004.

Falletti-Fossati, Carlo. *Costumi senesi nella seconda metà del secolo XIV*. Siena: G. Bargellini, 1881.

Fanelli, Giovanni. *Firenze architettura e città*. Florence: Vallecchi, 1973.

Fanti, Mario. "La Confraternita di Santa Maria della Morte e la Conforteria dei condannati in Bologna nei secoli XIV e XV." In *Confraternite e città a Bologna nel Medioevo e nell'Età Moderna*, pp. 63–173. Rome: Herder, 2001.

———. "Intorno alle mura e alle torri di Bologna. Note storico-critiche a proposito di una recente pubblicazione." *Strenna Storica Bologense* 7 (1957): 161–70.

———, ed. *Gli schizzi topografici originali di Giuseppe Giudicini per le Cose notabili della Città di Bologna*. Bologna: A. Forni, 2000.

Fasoli, Gina. "Bologna nell'età medievale (1115–1506)." In *Storia di Bologna*, ed. Antonio Ferri and Giancarlo Roversi, pp. 127–96. Bologna: Alfa, 1984.

———. "La coscienza civica nelle 'Laudes civitatum.'" In *La coscienza cittadina nei comuni italiani del Duecento*, pp. 9–44. Todi: Accademia Tedertina, 1972.

Ferrante, Joan M. "Images of the Cloister—Haven or Prison." *Mediaevalia* 12 (1989 for 1986): 57–66.

Fine, Bob. "The Birth of Bourgeois Punishment." *Crime and Social Justice* 13 (1980): 19–26.

Finelli, Angelo. *Bologna ai tempi che vi soggiornò Dante*. Bologna: Stabilimento Poligrafici Riuniti, 1929.

Finzch, Norbert, and Robert Jütte, eds. *Institutions of Confinement: Hospitals, Asylums, and Prisons in Western Europe and North America, 1500–1950*. Cambridge: Cambridge University Press, 1996.

Fishman, Joseph F. *Sex in Prison: Revealing Sex Conditions in American Prisons*. London: John Lane, 1935.

Fitzgerald, Mike. "The Telephone Rings: Long-Term Imprisonment." In *Long-Term Imprisonment*, ed. Anthony E. Bottoms and Roy Light, pp. 142–57. Aldershot: Gower, 1987.

Flanagan, Timothy J., ed. *Long-Term Imprisonment: Policy, Science and Correctional Practice*. Thousand Oaks, CA: Sage, 1995.

Fortunato, Bruno. "La raccolta dei testamenti bassomedievali dell'Archivio di Stato di Bologna. Alcune osservazioni." *Atti e memeorie della Deputazione di Storia Patria per le Provincie di Romagna*, n.s. 53 (2003): 183–222.

Foschi, Paola. "Da magazzini di governo a centro amministrativo." In *Il Palazzo Comunale di Bologna. Storia, architettura e restauri*, ed. Camilla Bottino, pp. 47–63. Bologna: Editrice Compositori, 1999.

———. "I palazzi del Comune di Bologna nel Duecento." In *Bologna, Re Enzo e il suo mito: atti della Giornata di studio, 11 giugno 2000*, ed. Antonio Ivan Pini and Anna Laura Trombetti Budriesi, pp. 65–102. Bologna: Deputazione di Storia Patria per le Provincie di Romagna, 2001.

———. "I Palazzi del Podestà, di Re Enzo e del Capitano del Popolo: Problemi e proposte di interpretazione." *Il Carrobbio. Tradizioni, problemi, immagini dell'Emilia Romagna* 24 (1998): 13–42.

Foucault, Michel. *Discipline and Punish: The Birth of the Prison*. Trans. Alan Sheridan. New York: Vintage, 1979.

———. *Madness and Civilization: A History of Insanity in the Age of Reason*. Trans. Richard Howard. London: Tavistock, 1967.

———. *Naissance de la clinique*. Paris: Presses Universitaires de France, 1988.

Franzoi, Umberto. *Le prigioni della Repubblica di Venezia*. Venice: Stamperia di Venezia Editrice, 1966.

Fraticelli, P. I. *Delle antiche carceri di Firenze denominate Le Stinche, ora demolite e degli edifizi in quel luogo eretti l'anno 1834. Illustrazione storica*. Florence: G. Formigli, 1834.

Frend, W.H.C. *Martyrdom and Persecution in the Early Church: A Study of a Conflict from the Maccabees to Donatus*. Oxford: Basil Blackwell, 1965.

Gallo, Ermanno, and Vicenzo Ruggiero. *Il carcere in Europa*. Verona: Bertani, 1983.

Galtung, Johan. "The Social Functions of a Prison." *Social Problems* 6 (1958): 127–40.

Garabedian, Peter C. "Social Roles and Processes of Socialization in the Prison Community." *Social Problems* 11 (1963): 139–52.

Garcia, Venessa. "History of Prisons." In *The Encyclopedia of Prisons and Correctional Facilities*, ed. Mary Bosworth, pp. 414–20. Thousand Oaks, CA: Sage, 2005.

Garfinkel, Harold. "Conditions of Successful Degradation Ceremonies." *American Journal of Sociology* 61 (1956): 420–24.

Garnsey, Peter. *Social Status and Legal Privilege in the Roman Empire*. Oxford: Clarendon Press, 1970.

Gatier, P.-L. "Nouvelles inscriptions de Gerasa." *Syria* 62 (1985): 297–305.

Gauvard, Claude. *Violence et ordre public au Moyen Age*. Paris: Picard, 2005.

Gauvard, Claude, et al. "Le Châtelet de Paris au début du XVe siècle d'après les fragments d'un registre d'écrous de 1412." *Bibliothèque de l'École des Chartes* 157 (1999): 565–606.

Geltner, G. "*Detrusio*: Penal Cloistering in the Middle Ages." *Revue Bénédictine* 118 (2008), forthcoming.

———. "Medieval Prisons: Marginality at the City Center, 1250–1400." PhD diss., Princeton University, 2006.

Geremek, Bronisław. "La lutte contre vagabondage à Paris aux XIVe et XVe siècles." In *Ricerche storiche ed economiche in memoria di Corrado Basbagallo*, ed. Luigi de Rosa, pp. 211–36. Naples: Edizioni Scientifiche Italiane, 1970.

———. *The Margins of Society in Late Medieval Paris*. Trans. Jean Birrell. Cambridge: Cambridge University Press, 1987.

———. *La pietà e la forca. Storia della miseria e della carità in Europa*. Trans. Anna Marx Vannini. Rome: Laterza, 2003.

Giallombardo, Rose. *Society of Women: A Study of a Women's Prison*. New York: John Wiley and Sons, 1966.

Gibbs, John J. "The First Cut Is the Deepest: Psychological Breakdown and Survival in the Detention Setting." In *The Pains of Imprisonment*, ed. Robert Johnson and Hans Toch, pp. 97–114. Beverly Hills: Sage, 1982.

Giudicini, Giuseppe, ed. *Cose notabili della Città di Bologna*. 5 vols. Bologna: Tipografia Militare, 1868–73.

Goffman, Erving. *Asylums: Essays on the Social Situation of Mental Patients and Other Inmates*. Garden City, NY: Anchor, 1961.

Goldwaithe, Richard, and Giulio Mandich. *Studi sulla moneta fiorentina (Secoli XIII–XVI)*. Florence: Leo S. Olschki, 1994.

Gonthier, Nicole. *La châtiment du crime au Moyen Âge, XIIe–XVIe siècles*. Rennes: Presses Universitaires de Rennes, 1998.

Grand, Roger. "Justice criminelle: procédure et peines dans les villes aux XIIIe et XIVe siècles." *Bibliothéque de l'École des Chartes* 102 (1941): 51–108.

———. "La prison et la notion d'emprisonnement dans l'ancien droit." *Revue historique de droit français et étranger*, 4th ser., 19–20 (1940–41): 58–87.

Graus, František. "Die Gewalt bei den Anfängen des Feudalismus und die 'Gefangenenbefreiungen' der merowingischen Hagiographie." *Jahrbuch für Wirtschaftsgeschichte* 1 (1961): 61–156.

———. *Volk, Herrscher und Heiliger im Reich der Merowinger. Studien zur Hagiographie der Merowingerzeit*. Prague: Nakladatelsví Ceskoslovenské akademie ved, 1965.

Green, V.H.H. *Medieval Civilization in Western Europe*. London: Edward Arnold, 1971.

Grob, Gerald N. *Mental Institutions in America: Social Policy to 1875*. New York: Free Press, 1973.

Guzzetti, Linda. "Le donne a Venezia nel XIV secolo: Uno studio sulla loro presenza nella società e nella famiglia." *Studi Veneziani*, n.s. 35 (1998): 15–88.

Hanawalt, Barbara A. *Crime and Conflict in English Communities, 1300–1348*. Cambridge: Harvard University Press, 1979.

Hastings, Margaret. *The Court of Common Pleas in Fifteenth Century England*. Ithaca, NY: Cornell University Press, 1947.

Haverkamp, Alfred. "The Jewish Quarters in German Towns during the Late Middle Ages." In *In and Out of the Ghetto: Jewish-Gentile Relations in Late Medieval and Early Modern Germany*, ed. R. Po-chia Hsia and Hartmut Lehman, pp. 13–28. Cambridge: Cambridge University Press, 1995.

Hayner, Norman S., and Ellis Ash. "The Prison as a Community." *American Sociological Review* 5 (1940): 577–83.

Heers, Jacques. *Le clan familial au Moyen Age. Étude sur les structures politiques et sociales des milieux urbains*. Paris: Presses Universitaires de France, 1974.

———. *La ville au Moyen Âge en Occident: Paysages, pouvoirs et conflits*. Paris: Hachette, 1990.

Hefferman, Esther. *Making It in Prison: The Square, the Cool, and the Life*. New York: Wiley Interscience, 1972.

Heffernan, Thomas J., and James E. Shelton. "*Paradisus in carcere*: The Vocabulary of Imprisonment and the Theology of Martyrdom in the *Passio*

Sanctarum Perpetuae et Felicitatis." *Journal of Early Christian Studies* 14 (2006): 217–23.

Henderson, John. *Piety and Charity in Late Medieval Florence.* Oxford: Clarendon Press, 1994.

———. *The Renaissance Hospital: Healing the Body and Healing the Soul.* New Haven: Yale University Press, 2006.

Herlihy, David. "Some Psychological and Social Roots of Violence in the Tuscan Cities." In *Violence and Civil Disorder in Italian Cities, 1200–1500,* ed. Lauro Martines, pp. 129–54. Berkeley and Los Angeles: University of California Press, 1972.

Herzman, Ronald, and Weston Kennison. "Jacopone Da Todi: The Aesthetics of Imprisonment." *Franziskanische Studien* 72 (1990): 248–56.

Hessel, Alfred. *Geschichte der Stadt Bologna von 1116 bis 1280.* Berlin: E. Ebering, 1910.

Hohenberg, Paul M., and Lynn Hollen Lees. *The Making of Urban Europe, 1000–1950.* Cambridge: Harvard University Press, 1985.

Home Office. *New Directions in Prison Design: Report of a Home Office Study of New Generation Prisons in the U.S.A.* London: HMSO, 1985.

[Horn, Andrew]. *The Mirror of Justices.* Ed. William Joseph Whittaker. Selden Society Publications 7. London: Bernard Quaritch, 1895.

Howard, John. *The State of the Prisons in England and Wales.* 3rd ed. Warrington: William Eyres, 1784.

Howell, Martha C. "The Spaces of Late Medieval Urbanity." In *Shaping Urban Identity in Late Medieval Europe,* ed. Marc Boone and Peter Stabel, pp. 3–23. Leuven-Apeldoorn: Garant, 2000.

Hubert, Hans W. *Der Palazzo Comunale von Bologna. Von Palazzo della Biada zum Palatium Apostolicum.* Cologne: Böhlau, 1993.

Human Rights Watch. *Prison Conditions in the United States.* New York: Human Rights Watch, 1991.

Huxley, Aldous. "Variations on *The Prisons.*" In *Themes and Variations,* pp. 192–208. London: Chatto and Windus, 1950.

Hyde, J. K. "Medieval Descriptions of Cities." *Bulletin of the John Rylands Library* 48 (1966): 308–40.

Ignatieff, Michael. *A Just Measure of Pain: The Penitentiary in the Industrial Revolution, 1750–1850.* New York: Pantheon, 1978.

———. "State, Civil Society, and Total Institutions: A Critique of Recent Social Histories of Punishment." *Crime and Justice* 3 (1981): 153–92.

Ireland, Richard W. "Theory and Practice within the Medieval English Prison." *American Journal of Legal History* 31 (1987): 56–67.

Irwin, John. *The Jail.* Berkeley and Los Angeles: University of California Press, 1985.

Iser, Wolfgang. *The Implied Reader: Patterns of Communication in Prose Fiction from Bunyan to Beckett.* Baltimore: Johns Hopkins University Press, 1974.

Ives, George. *A History of Penal Methods: Criminals, Witches, Lunatics.* London: Stanley Paul, 1914.

Jacobs, James B. "Stratification and Conflict among Prison Inmates." *Journal of Criminal Law and Criminology* 66 (1976): 476–82.

James, Edward. "'Beati pacifici': Bishops and the Law." In *Disputes and Settlements: Law and Human Relations in the West*, ed. John Bossy, pp. 25–46. Cambridge: Cambridge University Press, 1983.

Jamieson, Ruth, and Adrian Grounds. "Release and Adjustment: Perspectives from Studies of Wrongly Convicted and Politically Motivated Prisoners." In *The Effects of Imprisonment*, ed. Alison Liebling and Shadd Maruna, pp. 33–65. Portland, OR: Willan, 2005

Jarry, Daniel. "Diététique et hygiène au XIIIe et XIVe siècle." *Languedoc Medical* 41 (1958): 5–24.

Jauss, Hans Robert. *Toward an Aesthetic of Reception*. Trans. Timothy Bahti. Brighton: Harvester Press, 1982.

Johnson, Robert. *Hard Time: Understanding and Reforming the Prison*. Belmont, CA: Wadsworth, 1996.

Johnson, Robert, and Hans Toch, eds. *The Pains of Imprisonment*. Beverly Hills: Sage, 1982.

Johnston, Norman. *Forms of Constraint: A History of Prison Architecture*. Urbana: University of Illinois Press, 2000.

Jones, Philip. *The Italian City-State: From Commune to Signoria*. Oxford: Clarendon Press, 1997.

Kaminski, Marek M. *Games Prisoners Play: The Tragicomic Worlds of Polish Prison*. Princeton: Princeton University Press, 2004.

Kantorowicz, Hermann U. *Albertus Gandinus und das Strafrecht der Scholastik*. Berlin: J. Guttentag, 1907.

Karras, Ruth Mazo. "The Regulation of Brothels in Later Medieval England." *Signs* 14 (1989): 399–433.

Katz, Michael B. "Origins of the Institutional State." *Marxist Perspectives* 1 (1978): 6–22.

Keene, D. J. "Rubbish in Medieval Towns." In *Environmental Archaeology in the Urban Context*, ed. A. R. Hall and H. K. Kenward, pp. 26–30. London: Council for British Archaeology, 1982.

King, Roy D., and Kathleen McDermott. "'My Geranium Is Subversive': Some Notes on the Management of Trouble in Prisons." *British Journal of Sociology* 41 (1990): 445–71.

Koenig, John. "Prisoner Offerings, Patron Saints and State Cults at Siena and Other Italian Cities from 1250 to 1550." *Bullettino senese di storia patria* 108 (2001): 222–96.

Koscheski, Mary, et al. "Consensual Sexual Behavior." In *Prison Sex: Practice and Policy*, ed. Christopher Hensely, pp. 111–31. Boulder, CO: Lynne Riener, 2002.

Kotkin, Steven. *Magnetic Mountain: Stalinism as a Civilization*. Berkeley and Los Angeles: University of California Press, 1995.

Krause, Jens-Uwe. *Gefängnisse im Romischen Reich*. Stuttgart: F. Steiner Verlag, 1996.

Krauss, F.A.K. *Im Kerker vor und nach Christus. Schatten und Licht aus dem profanen und kirchlichen Cultur und Rechtsleben vergangener Zeiten*. Freiburg: Mohr, 1895.

Lane, Frederic C. "L'ampliamento del Maggior Consiglio di Venezia." *Ricerche Venete* 1 (1989): 21–58.

————. *Venice: A Maritime Republic*. Baltimore: Johns Hopkins University Press, 1973.

Lane, Frederic C., and Rheinhold C. Mueller. *Money and Banking in Medieval and Renaissance Venice*. Vol. 1: *Coins and Moneys of Account*. Baltimore: Johns Hopkins University Press, 1985.

Langbein, John H. "The Historical Origins of the Sanction of Imprisonment for a Serious Crime." *Journal of Legal Studies* 5 (1976): 35–60.

Lansing, Carol. *Power and Purity: Cathar Heresy in Medieval Italy*. New York: Oxford University Press, 1998.

Larner, John. *The Lords of Romagna: Romagnol Society and the Origins of the Signorie*. London: Macmillan, 1965.

Laschi, Rodolfo. "Pene e carceri nella storia di Verona." *Atti del Reale Istituto Veneto di Scienze, lettere ed arti* 64 (1904–5): 13–93.

Lazzarini, Vittorio. "L'avvocato dei carcerati poveri a Venezia." In *Proprietà e feudi, offizi, garzoni, carcerati in antiche leggi veneziane*, pp. 89–113. Rome: Edizioni di Storia e Letteratura, 1960.

Lea, H. C. *A History of the Inquisition of the Middle Ages*. 3 vols. New York: Harper and Brothers, 1888.

Le Goff, Jacques. *The Birth of Purgatory*. Trans. Arthur Goldhammer. Chicago: University of Chicago Press, 1984.

Le Roy Ladurie, Emmanuel. *Monataillou: The Promised Land of Error*. Trans. Barbara Bray. New York: George Braziller, 1978.

Leclercq, Jean. "Le cloître est-il une prison?" *Revue d'ascétique et de mystique* 47 (1971): 407–20.

LeDieu, Alcius. "Restitutions de prisonniers à Abbeville au XIIIe et au XIVe siècle." *Bulletin historique et philologique* 3–4 (1904): 608–19.

Leicht, Pier Silvio. "Lo stato veneziano e il diritto comune." In *Miscellanea in onore di Roberto Cessi*, pp. 203–11. Rome: Edizioni di Storia e Letteratura, 1958.

Lembo, Joseph James. "The Relationship of Institutional Disciplinary Infractions and the Inmate's Personal Contact with the Outside Community." *Criminologica* 50 (1969–70): 50–54.

Lerner, Jimmy A. *You Got Nothing Coming: Notes from a Prison Fish*. New York: Broadway Books, 2002.

Lester, Anne E. "Gender and Social Networks in Medieval France: The Convents of the County of Champagne." PhD diss., Princeton University, 2003.

Lévi-Strauss, Claude. *Tristes Tropiques*. Trans. John Weightman and Doreen Weightman. London: Cape, 1973.

Liebling, Alison. *Suicides in Prison*. London: Routledge, 1992.

Liebling, Alison, and Shadd Maruna, eds. *The Effects of Imprisonment*. Portland, OR: Willan, 2005.

Lindner, Robert M. *Stone Walls and Men*. New York: Odyssey Press, 1946.

Lochhead, Sheila R. *Outside In: A Study of Prison Visiting*. York: William Sessions, 1993.

Lopez, Robert S. "The Crossroads within the Wall." In *The Historian and the City*, ed. Oscar Handlin and John Burchard, pp. 27–43. Boston: MIT Press and Harvard University Press, 1963.

MacEvitt, Christopher Hatch. *The Crusades and the Christian World of the East: Rough Tolerance*. Philadelphia: University of Pennsylvania Press, 2007.

Magherini, Graziella, and Vittorio Biotti. *L'isola delle Stinche e i percorsi della follia a Firenze nei secoli XIV–XVIII*. Florence: Ponte Alle Grazie, 1992.

Maire Vigueur, Jean-Claude, ed. *I Podestà dell'Italia comunale*. Rome: Istituto storico italiano per il Medio Evo/École française de Rome, 2000.

Malone, E. E. *The Monk and the Martyr*. Washington, DC: Catholic University of America Press, 1950.

Manca, Pietro. "Istituti di pena." In *Enciclopedia del diritto*, 23:1–14. Milan: A. Giuffrè, 1973.

Manikowska, Halina. "Polizia e servizi d'ordine a Firenze nella seconda metà del XIV secolo." *Ricerche Storiche* 26 (1986): 17–38.

———. "The Florentine Communal Prison—*Le Stinche*—in the Fourteenth Century." *Acta Poloniae Historica* 71 (1995): 133–60.

Mathiesen, Thomas. *The Defences of the Weak: A Sociological Study of a Norwegian Correctional Institution*. London: Tavistock, 1965.

Mathieu, Isabelle. "Prisons et prisonniers en Anjou au bas Moyen Âge." *Annales de Bretagne et des Pays de l'Ouest* 112 (2005): 147–69.

Matthews, Jill. *Forgotten Victims: How Prison Affects the Family*. London: NACRO, 1983.

Matthews, Roger. *Doing Time: An Introduction to the Sociology of Imprisonment*. Houndmills, Basingstoke: Macmillan, 1999.

Mayhew, Henry, and John Binny. *The Criminal Prisons of London and Scenes of Prison Life*. London: Griffin, Bohn, 1862.

McAvoy, Liz Herbert, and Mari Hughes-Edwards, eds. *Anchorites, Wombs, and Tombs: Intersections of Gender and Enclosure in the Middle Ages*. Cardiff: University of Wales Press, 2005.

McCorckle, Lloyd W., and Richard Corn. "Resocialization within Walls." *Annals of the American Academy of Political and Social Sciences* 293 (1954): 88–98.

Melossi, Dario, and Massimo Pavarini. *The Prison and the Factory: Origins of the Penitentiary System*. Trans. Glynis Cousin. Totowa, NJ: Barnes and Noble Books, 1981.

Menage, René. "Deux poètes en prison: Maître Jean Régnier e *le prisonnier desconforté* de Loches." In *Exclus et systemes d'exclusion dans la litterature et la civilisation médiévales*, pp. 239–49. Aix-en-Provence: CUERMA, 1978.

Meneghetti, Maria Luisa. "Scrivere in carcere nel medioevo." In *Studi di filologia e letteratura italiani in onore di Maria Picchio Simonelli*, ed. Pietro Frassica, pp. 185–99. Alessandria: Edizioni dell'Orso, 1993.

Mentgen, Gerd. "'Die Juden waren stets eine Randgruppe': Über eine fragwürdige Prämisse der aktuellen Judenforschung." In *Liber Amicorum necnon et Amicarum für Alfred Heit: Beiträge zur mittelalterichen Geschichte und geschichtlichen Landeskunde*, ed. Friedhelm Burgard et al., pp. 393–411. Trier: Verlag Trier Historische Forschungen, 1996.

Millar, Fergus. "Condemnation to Hard Labour in the Roman Empire, from the Julio-Claudians to Constantine." *Papers of the British School at Rome* 52 (1984): 128–47.

Mollat, Michel. *Histoire des hôpitaux en France*. Toulouse: Privat, 1982.

———. *Les pauvres au Moyen Âge: Étude social*. Paris: Hachette, 1978.

Molmenti, Pompeo. *La storia di Venezia nella vita privata dalle origini alla caduta della Repubblica*. 7th ed. 3 vols. Bergamo: Istituto italiano d'arti grafiche, 1927–29.

Moore, R. I. *The Formation of a Persecuting Society: Power and Deviance in Western Europe, 950–1250*. Oxford: Basil Blackwell, 1987.

Moranvillé, H. "Note sur les prisons à la fin du XIVe siècle." *Bulletin de la société d'histoire de Paris* 21 (1894): 73–76.

Morris, Pauline. *Prisoners and Their Families*. London: George Allen and Unwin, 1965.

Muir, Edward. *Civic Ritual in Renaissance Venice*. Princeton: Princeton University Press, 1981.

———. "Idee, riti, simboli di potere." In *L'Età del Comune*, ed. Giorgio Cracco and Gherardo Ortalli, pp. 739–60. Rome: Istituto della Enciclopedia Italiana, 1995.

Muir, Edward, and Guido Ruggiero, eds. *History from Crime*. Baltimore: Johns Hopkins University Press, 1994.

Murray, Alexander. *Suicide in the Middle Ages*. 3 vols. Oxford: Oxford University Press, 1998–.

Mutinelli, Fabio. *Annali urbani di Venezia dall'anno 810 al 12 maggio 1797*. Venice: Tipografia di G. B. Merlo, 1841.

———. *Delle antiche prigioni della repubblica di Venezia chiamate i Piombi e i Pozzi. Commentario*. Venice, 1833. [= Biblioteca Marciana, Venezia MS It. VII 2205 (9580)]

Nacci, Peter L., and Thomas R. Kane. "The Incidence of Sex and Sexual Aggression in Federal Prisons." *Federal Probation* 47 (1983): 31–36.

Nagel, William G. *The New Red Barn: A Critical Look at the Modern American Prison*. New York: Walker, 1973.

Nelson, Victor F. *Prison Days and Nights*. Boston: Little, Brown & Co., 1933.

Newcomb, Rexford. "The Evolution of the Prison Plan." *American Architect* 110 (1916): 243–47, 274–78, 281–82, 391–95.

Niccolini di Camugliano, Ginevra. *The Chronicles of a Florentine Family, 1200–1470*. London: J. Cape, 1933.

Nicholas, David M. "Crime and Punishment in Fourteenth-Century Ghent." *Revue belge de philologie et d'histoire* 48 (1970): 289–334, 1141–76.

———. *The Growth of the Medieval City: From Late Antiquity to the Early Fourteenth Century*. London: Longman, 1997.

———. *The Later Medieval City, 1300–1500*. London: Longman, 1997.

Nirenberg, David. *Communities of Violence: Persecution of Minorities in the Middle Ages*. Princeton: Princeton University Press, 1996.

O'Brien, Patricia. "Crime and Punishment as a Historical Problem." *Journal of Social History* 4 (1978): 508–19.

Origo, Iris. *The Merchant of Prato: Francesco di Marco Datini, 1335–1410*. London: J. Cape, 1957. Reprint, Boston: Nonpareil, 1986.

Orme, Nicholas, and Margaret Webster. *The English Hospital, 1070–1570*. New Haven: Yale University Press, 1995.

Ortalli, Gherardo, ed. *Gioco e giustizia nell'Italia di Comune*. Treviso: Fondazione Benetton, 1993.

Otis, Leah L. *Prostitution in Medieval Society: The History of an Urban Institution in Languedoc*. Chicago: University of Chicago Press, 1985.

Padovani, Andrea. "La politica del diritto." In *L'Età del Comune*, ed. Giorgio Cracco and Gherardo Ortalli, pp. 303–29. Rome: Istituto della Enciclopedia Italiana, 1995.

Pansolli, Lamberto. *La gerarchia delle fonti di diritto nella legislazione medievale veneziana*. Milan: A. Giuffrè, 1970.

Pazzaglini, Peter R. "Comments on the Comparable Practices of Medieval Imprisonment." *Studi Senesi* 86 (1974): 154–67.

Pegg, Mark Gregory. *The Corruption of Angels: The Great Inquisition of 1245–1246*. Princeton: Princeton University Press, 2001.

Penco, G. "Monasterium-Carcer." *Studia Monastica* 8 (1966): 133–43.

Peters, Edward M. *Inquisition*. Berkeley and Los Angeles: University of California Press, 1989.

———. "Prison before the Prison: The Ancient and Medieval Worlds." In *The Oxford History of the Prison: The Practice of Punishment in Western Society*, ed. N. Morris and D. J. Rothman, pp. 3–43. Oxford: Oxford University Press, 1995.

———. *Torture*. Oxford: Basil Blackwell, 1985.

Petersilia, Joan. *When Prisoners Come Home: Parole and Prisoner Reentry*. Oxford: Oxford University Press, 2003.

Piccinni, Gabriella. "Modelli di organizzazione dello spazio urbano dei ceti dominanti nel Tre e Quattrocento. Considerazioni sul caso senese." In *I ceti dirigenti nella Toscana tardo comunale*, pp. 221–36.

Pini, Antonio Ivan. "La 'burocrazia' comunale nella Toscana del Trecento." In *La Toscana nel secolo XIV. Caratteri di una civiltà regionale*, ed. Sergio Gensini, pp. 215–40. Ospedaletto (Pisa): Pacini, 1988.

———. *Città, comuni e corporazioni nel medioevo italiano*. Bologna: CLUEB, 1986.

———. "Problemi di demografia bolognese del Duecento." *Atti e memeorie della Deputazione di Storia Patria per le Provincie di Romagna*, n.s. 17–19 (1965–68): 147–222.

Pollock, Frederick, and Frederic W. Maitland. *The History of English Law before the Time of Edward I*. 2nd ed. 2 vols. Cambridge: The University Press, 1898.

Porteau-Bitker, Annik. "L'emprisonnement dans le droit laïque du moyen âge." *Revue historique de droit français et étranger* 46 (1968): 211–45, 389–428.

Pound, Roscoe. "Law in Books and Law in Action." *American Law Review* 44 (1910): 12–36.

Pugh, Ralph B. "The King's Prisons before 1250." *Transactions of the Royal Historical Society*, 5th ser., 5 (1955): 1–22.

Pullan, Brian. *La politica sociale della Repubblica di Venezia, 1500–1620*. Trans. Paola Pavanini. 2nd ed. 2 vols. Rome: Il Veltro, 2002.

———. "The Relief of Prisoners in Sixteenth-Century Venice." *Studi Veneziani* 10 (1968): 221–29.

———. "Support and Redeem: Charity and Poor Relief in Italian Cities from the Fourteenth to the Seventeenth Century." *Continuity and Change* 3 (1988): 177–208.

Rawcliffe, Carole. *Leprosy in Medieval England*. London: Boydell, 2006.

Redi, Fabio. "Dalla torre al palazzo: Forme abitative signorili e organizzazione dello spazio urbano a Pisa dall'IX al XV secolo." In *Ceti dirigenti nella Toscana tardo medievale*, pp. 271–96.

———. *Pisa com'era: Archeologia, urbanistica e strutture materiali (secoli V–XIV)*. Naples: Liguori Editore, 1991.

Reverchon, Alexander, and Guido Schneider. "Die Metzer Rotlichtbezirke. Zur Geschichte der Prostitution in späteren Mittlerlater (13.–15. Jahrhundert)." In *Liber Amicorum necnon et Amicarum für Alfred Heit: Beiträge zur mittelalterichen Geschichte und geschichtlichen Landeskunde*, ed. Hans Hubert Anton et al., pp. 203–31. Trier: Verlag Trier Historische Forschungen, 1996.

Richmond, Katy. "Fear of Homosexuality and Modes of Rationalisation in Male Prisons." *Australian and New Zealand Journal of Sociology* 14 (1978): 51–57.

Roach, Andrew P. "Penance and the Making of the Inquisition in Languedoc." *Journal of Ecclesiastical History* 52 (2001): 409–33.

Roberti, Melchiorre. *Le magistrature giudiziarie veneziane e i loro capitolari fino al 1300*. 3 vols. Padua: Tipografia Editrice del Seminario, 1906–11.

Rocke, Michael. *Forbidden Friendships: Homosexuality and Male Culture in Renaissance Florence*. Oxford: Oxford University Press, 1996.

Rodolico, Niccolò. *Dal comune alla signoria. Saggio sul governo di Taddeo Pepoli in Bologna*. Bologna: N. Zanichelli, 1898.

Rodriguez, Jarbel. *Captives and Their Saviors in the Medieval Crown of Aragon*. Washington, DC: Catholic University Press, 2007.

Romano, Dennis. *Patricians and Popolani: The Social Foundations of the Venetian Renaissance State*. Baltimore: Johns Hopkins University Press, 1987.

———. "Quod sibi fiat gratia: Adjustment of Penalties and the Exercise of Influence in Early Renaissance Venice." *Journal of Medieval and Renaissance Studies* 13 (1983): 251–68.

Rösch, Gerhard. "Serrata of the Great Council and Venetian Society, 1286–1328." In *Venice Reconsidered: The History and Civilization of an Italian City-State, 1297–1797*, ed. John Martin and Dennis Romano, pp. 67–88. Baltimore: Johns Hopkins University Press, 2000.

Rosenthal, Joel T. *The Purchase of Paradise: Gift Giving and the Aristocracy, 1307–1485*. London: Routledge and Kegan Paul, 1972.

Rossiaud, Jacques. *Medieval Prostitution*. Trans. Lydia G. Cochrane. Oxford: Basil Blackwell, 1988.

Roth, Robert. "La prison et ses histoires." *Déviance et Société* 2 (1978): 309–24.

Rothman, David, J. *The Discovery of the Asylum: Social Order and Disorder in the New Republic*. Boston: Little, Brown, 1971.

Rubiés, Joan Pau. "Travel Writing as a Genre: Facts, Fiction and the Invention of a Scientific Discourse in Early Modern Europe." *Journeys* 1 (2000): 5–35.

Rubini, Edoardo. *Giustizia veneta. Lo spirito veneto nelle leggi criminali della Repubblica*. Venice: Filippi Editore, 2003.

Ruggiero, Guido. *Violence in Early Renaissance Venice*. New Brunswick, NJ: Rutgers University Press, 1980.

Rusche, Georg, and Otto Kirchenheimer. *Punishment and Social Structure*. New York: Columbia University Press, 1939.

Sagredo, Agostino. *Il patronato dei carcerati in Venezia sotto il governo della Serenissima Repubblica*. Venice: G. Antonelli, 1865.

Saleebey, George. *The Non-Prison: A New Approach to Treating Youthful Offenders*. Milwaukee: Bruce, 1970.

Salvioni, Giovanni Battista. *Il valore della lira bolognese dalla sua origine all fine del secolo xv*. Bologna: N. Zanichelli, 1902.

Sargent, Steven. D. "Religion and Society in Late Medieval Bavaria: The Cult of Saint Leonard, 1258–1500." PhD diss., University of Pennsylvania, 1982.

———. "Religious Responses to Social Violence in Eleventh-Century Aquitaine." *Historical Reflections / Réflexions Historiques* 12 (1985): 228–40.

Sarti, Nicoletta. "Appunti su carcere-custodia e carcere-pena nella dottrina civilistica dei secoli XII–XVI." *Rivista di Storia del Diritto Italiano* 53–54 (1980–81): 67–110.

Satchell, Max. "The Emergence of Leper-Houses in Medieval England, 1100–1250." DPhil thesis, Oxford University, 1988.

Saunders, A. D. "Lydford Castle, Devon." *Medieval Archaeology* 24 (1980): 123–86.

Scarabello, Giovanni. *Carcerati e carceri a Venezia nell'età moderna*. Rome: Instituto della Enciclopedia Italiana, 1979.

———. "Per una storia della prostituzione a Venezia tra il XIII e il XVIII sec." *Studi Veneziani*, n.s. 47 (2004): 15–101.

Schiaparelli, Attilio. *La casa fiorentina e i suoi arredi nei secoli XIV e XV*. Rev. ed. by Maria Sframeli and Laura Pagnotta. 2 vols. Florence: Le Lettere, 1983.

Schiera, Pierangelo. "Legitimacy, Discipline, and Institutions: Three Necessary Conditions for the Birth of the Modern State." In *The Origins of the State in Italy, 1300–1600*, ed. Julius Kirshner, pp. 11–33. Chicago: University of Chicago Press, 1995.

Schmidt, Eberhard. *Einführung in die Geschichte der deutschen Strafrechtspflege*. Göttingen: Vandenhoeck & Ruprecht, 1947.

———. "Gotthold Bohne, Die Freiheitsstrafe in den Italienischen Stadtrechten des 12. bis 16. Jahrhunderts. Teil I: das Aufkommen der Freiheitsstrafe." *Zeitschrift für die gesamte Strafrechtswissenschaft* 24 (1925): 309–21.

Schnapper, Bernard. *Les peines arbitraires du XIIIe au XIVe siècle. Doctrines savantes et usages français*. Paris: R. Pichon et R. Durand-Auzia, 1974.

Schrag, Clarence. "Leadership among Prison Inmates." *American Sociological Review* 19 (1954): 37–42.

Sensi, Mario. "Incarcerate e penitenti a Foligno nella prima metà del Trecento." In *I frati penitenti di san Francesco nella società del Due e Trecento. Atti del 2° Convegno di Studi Francescani (Roma, 12–14 ottobre 1976)*, ed. Mariano D'Alatri, pp. 291–308. Rome: Istituto Storico dei Cappuccini, 1977.

Shahar, Shulamit. *Childhood in the Middle Ages*. London: Routledge, 1990.

———. *The Fourth Estate: A History of Women in the Middle Ages*. London: Methuen, 1983.

———. *Growing Old in the Middle Ages: "Winter Clothes Us in Shadow and Pain."* London: Routledge, 1997.

Shaw, Roger. *Children of Imprisoned Fathers*. London: Hodder and Stoughton, 1987.

————, ed. *Prisoners' Children: What Are the Issues?* London: Routledge, 1993.

Sjoberg, Gideon. *The Preindustrial City: Past and Present.* Glencoe, IL: Free Press, 1960.

Skinner, Patricia. "Material Life." In *Italy in the Central Middle Ages, 1000–1300,* ed. David Abulafia, pp. 147–60. Oxford: Oxford University Press, 2004.

Smail, Daniel Lord. "Common Violence: Vengeance and Inquisition in Fourteenth-Century Marseilles." *Past & Present* 151 (1996): 28–59.

————. *The Consumption of Justice.* Ithaca, NY: Cornell University Press, 2003.

Smith, Jonathan Z. "The Bare Facts of Ritual." *History of Religions* 20 (1980): 112–27.

Sofsky, Wolfgang. *Saggio sulla violenza.* Trans. Barbara Trapani and Luca Lamberti. Turin: Einaudi, 1998.

Soman, Alfred. "Deviance and Criminal Justice in Western Europe: 1300–1800: An Essay in Structure." *Criminal Justice History* 1 (1980): 3–28.

Sparks, Richard, et al. *Prisons and the Problem of Order.* Oxford: Clarendon Press, 1996.

Spilner, Paula Lois. "'Ut civitas amplietur.' Studies in Florentine Urban Development, 1282–1400." PhD diss., Columbia University, 1987.

Spufford, Peter. *Handbook of Medieval Exchange.* London: Royal Historical Society Publications, 1986.

Stacey, Robert C. "The Conversion of Jews to Christianity in Thirteenth-Century England." *Speculum* 67 (1992): 264–66.

Stancliffe, Clare. "Red, White and Blue Martyrdom." In *Ireland in Early Medieval Europe: Studies in Memory of Kathleen Hughes,* ed. Rosamond McKitterick et al., pp. 21–46. Cambridge: Cambridge University Press, 1983.

Stonequist, Everett V. *The Marginal Man: A Study in Personality and Culture Conflict.* New York: Russell and Russell, 1961.

Storia di Venezia. 8 vols. Rome: Istituto della Enciclopedia Italiana, 1995–2002.

Stow, Kenneth R. *Alienated Minority: The Jews of Medieval Latin Europe.* Cambridge: Harvard University Press, 1992.

Strayer, Joseph R. *On the Medieval Origins of the Modern State.* Princeton: Princeton University Press, 1970.

Sujinah. *In a Jakarta Prison: Life Stories of Women Inmates.* Trans. Irfan Kortschak. Jakarta: Lontar Foundation, 2000.

Swanson, Robert N. *Religion and Devotion in Europe, c. 1215– c. 1515.* Cambridge: Cambridge University Press, 1995.

Sweetinburgh, Sheila. *The Role of the Hospital in Medieval England: Gift-Giving and the Spiritual Economy.* Portland, OR: Four Courts Press, 2004.

Sykes, Greshan M. "Men, Merchants and Toughs." *Social Problems* 4 (1956): 130–38.

————. *The Society of Captives: A Study of a Maximum Security Prison.* Princeton: Princeton University Press, 1958.

Sznura, Franek. "Le città toscane nel XIV secolo. Aspetti edilizi e urbanistici." In *Toscana nel secolo XIV. Caratteri di una civiltà regionale,* ed. Sergio Gensini, pp. 385–402. Ospedaletto (Pisa): Pacini, 1988.

Tarra, P. *Prigioni di stato; la Bastiglia, la Fortezza di Pietro e Paolo, i Piombi di Venezia, la Torre di Londra.* Milan: Edizioni Athena, 1928.

Tassini, Giuseppe. *Curiosità veneziane, ovvero Origini delle denominazioni stradali di Venezia*. Rev. ed. Venice: Filippi Editrice, 1990.

Taylor, Ian, et al. *The New Criminology: For a Social Theory of Deviance*. London: Routledge and Kegan Paul, 1973.

Tega, Walter, ed. *Storia illustrata di Bologna*. 8 vols. San Marino: AIEP, 1987–91.

Thomas, Piri. *Down These Mean Streets*. New York: New American Library, 1967.

Thompson, Augustine. *Cities of God: The Religion of the Italian Communes, 1125–1325*. University Park: Pennsylvania State University Press, 2005.

Thorndike, Lynn. "Sanitation, Baths, and Street-Cleaning in the Middle Ages and Renaissance." *Speculum* 3 (1928): 192–203.

Toaff, Ariel. *Vino e la carne*. Bologna: Il Mulino, 1989.

Toch, Hans. *Living in Prison: The Ecology of Survival*. New York: Free Press, 1977.

———. *Men in Crisis: Human Breakdowns in Prison*. Chicago: Aldine, 1975.

Tommaseo, N. *Della bellezza educatrice*. Venice: Tipi del Gondeliere, 1838.

Touati, François-Olivier. *Maladie et société au Moyen Âge. Le lèpre, les lépreux et léproseries dans la province ecclésiastique de Sens jusqu'au milieu du XIVe siècle*. Paris: De Boeck & Larcier, 1998.

Trachtenberg, Marvin. *Dominion of the Eye: Urbanism, Art, and Power in Early Modern Florence*. Cambridge: Cambridge University Press, 1997.

Trexler, Richard C. "La prositution florentine au XVe siècle: Patronage et clientèles." *Annales ESC* 36 (1981): 983–1015.

———. *Public Life in Renaissance Florence*. Ithaca, NY: Cornell University Press, 1980.

Turner, Victor W. *The Ritual Process: Structure and Anti-Structure*. Chicago: Aldine, 1969.

———. "Variations on a Theme of Liminality." In *Secular Ritual*, ed. Sally F. Moore and Barbara G. Meyerhoff, pp. 36–52. Amsterdam: Van Gorcum, 1977.

Uccelli, Giovan Battista. *Il Palazzo del Potestà. Illustrazione storica*. Florence: Tipografia delle Murate, 1865.

Van der Slice, Austin. "Elizabethan Houses of Correction." *Journal of Criminal Law and Criminology* 45 (1936–37): 45–67.

van Gennep, Arnold. *The Rites of Passage*. Trans. Monika B. Vizedom and Gabrielle L. Caffee. Chicago: University of Chicago Press, 1960.

Varanini, Gian Maria, and Giuseppina De Sandre Gasparini. "Gli ospedali dei 'malsani' nella società veneta del XII–XIII secolo. Tra assistenza e disciplinamento urbano. I. L'iniziativa pubblica e privata." In *Città e servizi sociali nell'Italia dei secoli XII–XV*, pp. 141–65. Pistoia: Centro Italiano Studi di Storia e d'Arte, 1990.

Ventura, Angelo. "Politica del diritto e amministrazione della giustizia nella Repubblica veneta." *Rivista Storica Italiana* 94 (1982): 589–608.

Vigarello, Georges. *Concepts of Cleanliness: Changing Attitudes in France since the Middle Ages*. Trans. Jean Birrell. Cambridge: Cambridge University Press, 1988.

Vincent-Cassy, Mirielle. "Prison et châtiments à la fin du Moyen Âge." In *Les marginaux et les exclus dans l'histoire*, pp. 262–74. Paris: Inédit, 1979.

Vitale, Vito. *Il dominio della parte guelfa in Bologna (1286–1326)*. Bologna: N. Zanichelli, 1901.

von Hippel, Robert. *Strafrechtsreform und Strafzwecke*. Göttingen: W. Fr. Kästner, 1907.

Wacquant, Löic J. D., *Punishing the Poor: The New Government of Social Insecurity*. Durham, NC: Duke University Press, 2008.

Wakefield, Walter L. "Friar Ferrier, Inquisition at Caunes, and Escapes from Prison at Carcassone." *Catholic History Review* 58 (1972): 220–37.

Waley, Daniel. *Siena and the Sienese in the Thirteenth Century*. Cambridge: Cambridge University Press, 1991.

Watson, Sethina C. "*Fundatio, Ordinatio* and *Statuta*: The Statutes and Constitutional Documents of English Hospitals to 1300." DPhil thesis, Oxford University, 2004.

Weber, Max. *Theory of Social and Economic Organization*. Ed. Talcott Parsons. Trans. A. M. Henderson and Talcott Parsons. New York: Free Press, 1947.

Wheeler, Stanton. "Socialization in Correctional Communities." *American Sociological Review* 26 (1961): 697–712.

Wickham, Chris. "*Fama* and the Law in Twelfth-Century Tuscany." In *Fama: The Politics of Talk and Reputation in Medieval Europe*, ed. Thelma Festner and Daniel Lord Smail, pp. 15–26. Ithaca, NY: Cornell University Press, 2003.

Wiesheu, Annette. "Bischof und Gefängnis. Zur Interpretation der Kerkerbefreiungswunder in der merowingischen Hagiographie." *Historisches Zeitschrift* 121 (2001): 1–23.

Wolfgang, Martin E. "A Florentine Prison: Le Carceri delle Stinche." *Studies in the Renaissance* 7 (1960): 148–66.

Wooden, Wayne S., and Jay Parker. *Men behind Bars: Sexual Exploitation in Prison*. New York: Plenum Press, 1982.

Wray, Shona Kelly. *Communities and Crisis: Bologna during the Black Death*. Leiden: Brill, forthcoming.

Zamble, Edward, and Frank J. Porporino. *Coping, Behavior, and Adaptation in Prison Inmates*. New York: Springer-Verlag, 1988.

Zanotto, Francesco. *Il Palazzo Ducale di Venezia*. 2nd ed. 4 vols. Venice: G. Antonelli, 1853–61.

Zdekauer, Ludovico. "Il gioco in Italia nei secoli XIII e XIV e specialmente in Firenze." *Archivio Storico Italiano*, ser. 4, 18 (1886): 20–74; 19 (1887): 3–22.

Zola, Irving Kenneth. "Observations on Gambling in a Lower-Class Setting." *Social Problems* 10 (1962): 353–61.

Zordan, Giorgio. *L'ordinamento giuridico veneziano. Lezioni di storia del diritto veneziano con una nota bibliografia*. Padua: CLUEP, 1980.

Zorzi, Andrea. "La cultura della vendetta nel conflitto politico in età comunale." In *Le storie e la memoria. In onore di Arnold Esch*, pp. 135–70. Florence: Reti Medievali / Firenze University Press, 2002.

———. "I rettori di Firenze. Reclutamento, flussi, scambi (1193–1313)." In *I podestà dell'Italia comunale; Parte I: Reclutamento e circolazione degli ufficiali forestieri (fine XII sec.–metà XIV sec.)*, ed. Jean-Claude Maire Vigueur, pp. 453–594. Rome: Istituto Palazzo Berromini, 2000.

———. "Politica e giustizia a Firenze al tempo degli Ordinamenti antimagnatizi." In *Ordinamenti di giustizia fiorentina. Studi in occasione del VII centenario*, ed. Vanna Arrighi, pp. 105–47. Florence: Archivio di Stato di Firenze, 1995.

Zucchini, Guido. *Il Palazzo del Podestà di Bologna. Nuovi documenti e note*. Bologna: Beltrami, 1912.

Zug Tucci, Hannelore. "Venezia e i prigionieri di guerra nel Medioevo." *Studi Veneziani*, n.s. 14 (1987): 15–89.